The Life & Teachings of Christ

Volume I

The Early Years

by Gordon Lindsay

Published by
CHRIST FOR THE NATIONS INC.
P.O. Box 769000
Dallas, TX 75376-9000
Twelfth Printing 1999

CONTENTS

Chapter 1

Is Jesus the Son of God?

In attempting to write the story of the Man of Nazareth, one feels keenly his inadequacy to do the subject even minimum justice. So far beyond the human ken lies the full measure of the greatness of the God-man, that even the most gifted pen must fall far short in accomplishing its purpose. Indeed, were one to have the talents of an archangel, he could hardly hope to portray in human words the full majesty of His unique character, the dignity and grace of His matchless person, and the exquisite beauty and perfection of His words. Truly Christ stands far above and in the starkest contrast to the most noble of our race. For this person is none other than He "whose goings forth have been from of old, from everlasting"(Micah 5:2).

Everlasting is a word that the human mind can only vaguely grasp. "From everlasting," means Christ has existed from the eternity that is behind us. But who can understand even partially the meaning of eternity? The thought staggers the imagination and baffles the profoundest intellect.

As the inhabitant of eternity, Christ holds the position of Lord of the universe in His own right. First, because He is the Creator. "All things were made by him: and without him was not anything made that was made" (John 1:3). But He is Lord of all for another equally cogent reason. When sin entered the universe and bid to despoil God's fair creation, until as Paul says, "The whole creation groaneth and travaileth in pain together" (Rom. 8:22), only one Person, and He at infinite cost, could repair the damage.

In this present century scientific discovery has enlarged the scope of the known universe by a million-fold. Powerful telescopes have probed the distant galaxies, glimpsing some which lie in the most remote regions of the universe as "mere fuzzy points of light." Yet each galaxy is composed of millions of flaming suns, many perhaps attended by unknown planets, and each of them millions and in some cases billions of light years distant.

To the rationalist the universe has become too big for God to have created it! The atheist thus reduces his philosophy to the absurdity that dead matter created itself! Instead of beginning with God and working down, he begins with dirt and tries to work up. But the honest believer as he considers the majesty of the heavens and the boundless extent of the universe, can only in bowed reverence exclaim, "O God, how great Thou art!"

The Incarnation is another mystery quite beyond the capacity of the natural man to understand. It was and is a miracle. But is not the universe altogether a miracle? How did it come into existence out of nothing? Yet the universe is here, and we must accept it. The condescension of Deity in the miracle of the Incarnation links God to man by blood. By this Christ became our elder brother. The humility of Him who emptied Himself of His pre-incarnation attributes and became very man is not less awe-inspiring than His infinite exaltation.

God became man that He might save man. Nothing is more obvious than the fact that humanity to survive must have a Saviour. The wise men of this world, the philosophers, the intellectuals, are preoccupied in devising ways and means for man to save himself. The utter failure of man's best efforts to become his own Saviour is reflected in today's appalling breakdown and disintegration of the very foundations of society. Today we see law and order and even the basic principles of common decency rapidly giving way to lawlessness, anarchy, crime, immorality, perversion, and wickedness of so revolting a nature as to shock the sensibilities of all but the most depraved. This corruption of society proceeds at an ever-accelerating pace, although never before in history have the masses enjoyed such affluence, or such educational opportunities. Notwithstanding, the proliferation of psychiatrists and psychologists and physicians of the mind, all appear helpless to stem the tide of social disintegration. The number of emotionally disturbed persons in proportion to the population continues to increase at an alarming rate. Man has indeed proven beyond all shadow of doubt that he cannot save himself. Vainly he tries to lift himself to heaven by his bootheels.

The only answer to the world's ills is Christ. In Him alone is the secret of redemption; in Him alone is the power to regenerate fallen human nature and to heal and restore the sinsick soul.

6

Christ's words are both majestically simple and infinitely profound. They go with startling directness straight to the conscience of the human heart. Colonel Charles W. Larned in his introduction to *Teachings of Jesus in Subjects* expresses this thought beautifully in the following words:

> "In nothing else have I seen or realized so fully the sublime conciseness of this delivery of truth to man—the holy grandeur of its reticence and completeness. The great silences are no less imposing and overwhelming than the terrible directness and simplicity of its rhetoric. In both, the soul of man stands naked before its maker, abashed and conscience-stricken as in the first day of sin, but to receive instead of a curse the absolution; instead of rejection reconciliation; instead of forfeiture, the promise."

While the finite cannot hope to comprehend fully the infinite, God did not intend the purpose of the Lord's mission to the world to remain a mystery. The beauty of Christ's words is in their simplicity, as well as their profoundness. While His salvation may be hid to "the wise and prudent," its great truths are fully open to the devout and humble. This Jesus clearly brought out in his words in Matthew 11:25-30.

> "At that time Jesus answered and said, I thank thee, O Father, Lord of heaven and earth, because thou hast hid these things from the wise and prudent, and hast revealed them unto babes. Even so, Father: for so it seemed good in thy sight. All things are delivered unto me of my Father: and no man knoweth the Son, but the Father; neither knoweth any man the Father, save the Son, and he to whomsoever the Son will reveal him. Come unto me, all ye that labour and are heavy laden, and I will give you rest. Take my yoke upon you, and learn of me; for I am meek and lowly in heart; and ye shall find rest upon your souls. For my yoke is easy, and my burden is light."

One thing is essential to the understanding of the mission and teachings of Christ. The hearer must first settle in his heart the all-important question of whether Jesus is actually divine or only human, whether He is the Son of God, uniquely the only begotten of the Father, or merely a human. Jesus said, "I am the Son of God" (John 10:36), but the proud Pharisees could not accept the revelation. On the other hand, He made His Messianic mission known to the Samaritan outcast, and she believed it.

7

Are Christ's claims true? Was He what He represented Himself, or was He a pretender? This question must be answered before the study of His life can be of real value.

Proof 1—Jesus declared Himself to be the Son of God

> "Say ye of him, Whom the Father hath sanctified, and sent into the world, Thou blasphemest; because I said, I am the Son of God?" (John 10:36).

Through this Scripture we find that Christ Himself claimed He was the Son of God. There are some who say that Jesus was a good man, but that He was not divine. Yet if Jesus lied when He said He was the Son of God, He was not actually a good man but either an usurper or a man greatly deluded.

Notice what Jesus claimed. He said that He lived before Abraham, the father of the Hebrew and Arab nations. "Verily, verily, I say unto you, Before Abraham was, I am" (John 8:58).

He was in heaven with God before He came into the world. "What and if ye shall see the Son of man ascend up where he was before?" (John 6:62).

God had given His Son power to give men eternal life with God. Just before Christ was put upon a cross to die, He was praying.

> "These words spake Jesus, and lifted up his eyes to heaven, and said, Father, the hour is come; glorify thy Son, that thy Son also may glorify thee: As thou hast given him power over all flesh, that he should give eternal life to as many as thou hast given him" (John 17:1-2).

Proof 2—Christ's rise out of obscurity

There is nothing in all history or in the processes of nature to account for this man Jesus who emerged out of total obscurity—this one who is incomparably the most perfect figure of all time—one so immeasurably superior to all other humans that no comparison is possible.

During the nearly thirty years Jesus was growing up in Nazareth, Israel, there was no striking evidence that an extraordinary person was living there. The remarks of the people who lived in that village and knew Him revealed their amazement at the power displayed in His ministry in the following words:

> "From whence hath this man these things? and what wisdom is this which is given to him, that even such mighty works are wrought by his hands? Is not this the carpenter, the son of Mary, the brother of James, and Joses, and of Juda, and Simon? and are not his sisters with us? And they were offended at him" (Mark 6:2, 3).

9

In other words, although his brothers and sisters had lived in the same house with Jesus a good part of thirty years, they seemingly had seen nothing unusually remarkable about Him. To them and their neighbors He was probably above average, but that was all. Jesus occupied a position as a humble carpenter of the village who attracted little notice. His customers were acquaintances and peasants from neighboring areas. He earned a small wage, enough to supply the simple needs of the family and nothing more.

And yet in three years' time, the impact of His ministry made Him the hope of this life and the life to come for millions of men who have accepted Him into their lives. His words were carefully collected and written down to be treasured as the words of more than a man. Though hated by His enemies, He so captivated the hearts of multitudes down through the centuries that many have considered it a supreme honor to die for Him.

Proof 3—He spoke with authority as "no man spoke"

The first thing that impressed people about Christ when they heard Him was the authority with which He spoke. Although there was a remarkable tenderness in His voice, at the same time there was a strange directness about His words that pierced the very hearts and consciences of men. When people heard His famous sermon which he preached on the mountain, they were not only struck by the majestic simplicity of His words, but with the authority with which He spoke. "And it came to pass, when Jesus had ended these sayings, the people were astonished at his doctrine: For he taught them as one having authority, and not as the scribes" (Matt. 7:28-29). Following this sermon on the mountain when Jesus came to Capernaum and spoke on the Sabbath day, the record says, "And they were amazed at His teaching, for His word was with authority . . ." (Luke 4:32) Amplified

Soldiers, though hardened by their occupation, were affected as much as any by His presence. When the religious leaders and chief priests heard about the stir that His ministry was making, they sent officers to take Him. The officers returned without Him saying, "Never man spake like this man (John 7:46). When the soldiers came to arrest Jesus after Judas had betrayed Him with a kiss, He said to the officers, "I am he." They went backward, and fell to the ground" (John 18:6). When the army officer charged with oversight of the crucifixion witnessed the death of that noble figure hanging on the cross, he could only exclaim, "Truly this was the Son of God" (Matt. 27:54).

Proof 4—Christ knew the innermost thoughts of the sinner and bestowed forgiveness on him

"But Jesus did not commit himself unto them, because he knew all men, And needed not that any should testify of man: for he knew what was in man" (John 2:24-25).

Sinners loved to be near Christ, not because they felt at ease in their sins, for indeed His presence made them painfully aware of their sinfulness. But somehow in Him they saw a cure for their maladies. They saw in Him their deliverance. The book of John speaks of a woman who met Christ while she was drawing water from a well. When she realized that there was something unusual about Christ, she began to ask Him questions. Christ had only to say a few words before the woman felt her soul laid bare. Christ knew all about her even though she had never seen Him before. Christ told her, "Thou hast had five husbands; and he whom thou now hast is not thy husband: in that saidst thou truly" (John 4:18). Yet the purity of Christ in contrast to her own sinfulness did not cause her to despair. So kind and compassionate was His voice that she saw hope and forgiveness in the very One who had called attention to her sinful past. Her testimony to her neighbors carried such conviction that they also came and believed "that this is indeed the Christ, the Saviour of the world" (John 4:42).

Every evil deed and thought of man is open to the omnipotent God. As the Scripture says, "Neither is there any creature that is not manifest in his sight: but all things are naked and opened unto the eyes of him with whom we have to do" (Heb. 4:13). Some day men must stand before Him and give an account of their deeds and "they were judged every man according to their works" (Rev. 20:13). But if our sins are confessed, they will be remembered against us no more (I John 1:9; Jer. 31:34). Christ paid the penalty for sin with His spilled blood upon the cross. Today He is our Saviour; but if we do not accept Him, tomorrow He will be our judge.

Proof 5—Christ was the only sinless man

Beyond the impact of His miracles Christ impressed men with His sinlessness. The only thing His enemies could charge Him with was His eating with sinners or doing good on the Sabbath day. Because of their jealousy of his ability to perform miracles and to cause people to love and follow him, they wished to accuse Him of some wrong doing. But all they could accuse him of was doing good deeds on their day of rest— the Sabbath—or eating with sinners. Christ replied, "They that be whole need not a physician, but they that are sick" (Matt. 9:12). Christ had come to help even the worst of men.

Christ's sinlessness is an amazing thing, for ours is a fallen race. The best of us, without Christ's redemption power, find evil tendencies seeking ascendancy within us.

The great saint Paul, whom God used to write much of the New Testament and who was one of the first to spread the good news of Christ said,

> "For I fail to practice the good deeds I desire to do, but the evil deeds that I do not desire to do are what I am (ever) doing. Now if I do what I do not desire to do, it is no longer I doing it—it is not myself that acts—but the sin (principle) which dwells within me (fixed and operating in my soul)" (Romans 7:19-21) Amplified

As a race we have all disobeyed and, therefore, sinned. Then to find a man who is perfect and without sin is to find one whose root is not in the human race.

Proof 6—Christ performed miracles never before performed by man

> "Since the world began was it not heard that any man opened the eyes of one that was born blind. If this man were not of God, he could do nothing" (John 9:32-33).

The man who was healed had been born blind. The enemies of Christ tried to belittle the miracle by saying that He was a sinner. The man responded with unanswerable logic saying, "Whether he be a sinner or no, I know not: one thing I know, that, whereas I was blind, now I see" (John 9:25). Christ proved that He was unique by His power to perform miracles, even to giving sight to the blind. By creating sight He identified Himself as the Creator of the eye.

The miracle is the universal language understood by all peoples. When genuine miracles take place, most people (although not all) will believe. As Jesus said, "But if I do, though ye believe not me, believe the works: that ye may know, and believe, that the Father is in me, and I in him" (John 10:38).

Some years ago a minister was standing before a great audience. The people of this audience had been taught that Jesus was only a man, that He was dead in the tomb. The evangelist stood before the crowd and said, "You have been told that Jesus Christ is dead, that He was only a man. But if Christ were to come in spirit and heal the sick, would you believe that He is alive?" The audience made it known that it was a fair test. The minister then began to pray for the sick. One person after another was healed. The blind saw, and the lame walked. When the people witnessed these things, they began to cry out, "Jesus is alive! Jesus is alive! He is healing our sick."

So it is; the great miracles that are taking place today through the power of Jesus' name are proof that He is indeed alive today— that He is the Son of God at the right hand of God the Father in heaven.

Proof 7—Jesus predicted the fall of three cities: Capernaum, Chorazin, and Bethsaida

> "Woe unto thee, Chorazin! woe unto thee, Bethsaida! for if the mighty works, which were done in you, had been done in Tyre and Sidon, they would have repented long ago in sack-cloth and ashes. But I say unto you, It shall be more tolerable for Tyre and Sidon at the day of judgment, than for you. And thou, Capernaum, which are exalted unto heaven, shalt be brought down to hell: for if the mighty works, which have been done in thee, had been done in Sodom, it would have remained until this day. But I say unto you, That it shall be more tolerable for the land of Sodom in the day of judgment, than for thee" (Matt. 11:21-24).

At the beginning of the ministry of Jesus, He made the city of Capernaum, Israel, his home. Capernaum, with Bethsaida and Chorazin, enjoyed privileges that few other cities ever had. The Son of God from heaven dwelt in their midst. For a season the people heard His words, saw His miracles, and rejoiced (Luke 8:40). But these cities situated in northern Galilee were at the crossroads of the great trade routes of the world. Many of the inhabitants were absorbed in sharing in the booming prosperity, and their attention was diverted to accumulating material wealth. So it was that no deep work of repentance took place in their lives. This was the case despite the fact that they had witnessed miracles of a nature that would have converted Sodom and Gomorrah, two cities which were destroyed because of their evil. Jesus in sorrow warned them of their impending fate. Still they gave no heed.

What happened to Capernaum, Bethsaida, and Chorazin? At the time of the Jewish rebellion in 65 A.D., the Fifth and Tenth Legions of the Roman army were brought in by the emperor Titus. The Romans began a systematic devastation of the country. One by one the cities of Galilee fell, including those cities that Jesus had denounced—Capernaum, Bethsaida, and Chorazin. Many of the inhabitants were killed in battle, and those who survived were sold into slavery. No doubt some of the people who lived in the days when Christ preached on the shores of Galilee would still be alive and could remember His words. They could recall His miracles. His invitation to repentance and His words of warning to those who would not repent could be remembered too. Alas! Capernaum's prosperity and pride of life which had been her downfall were swept away forever. Ironically an earthquake later shook the area and levelled all that was left standing.

Today only one city, Tiberias, still stands on the Sea of Galilee, and it is not one of the three mentioned above. Capernaum, Bethsaida, and Chorazin have been no more for many centuries. Jesus said, "Heaven and earth shall pass away: but my words shall not pass away" (Luke 21:33). His words were fulfilled to the exact letter.

Proof 8—Jesus predicted the fall of Jerusalem to take place within one generation

Jesus stood on the Mt. of Olives overlooking the city of Jerusalem, Israel. The people had rejected Him as their Lord. He knew what it meant, and He wept over Jerusalem because they knew not the time of their visitation" (Luke 19:41-44).

> "And when he was come near, he beheld the city, and wept over it, Saying, If thou hadst known, even thou, at least in thy day, the things which belong unto thy peace! but now they are hid from thine eyes. For the days shall come upon thee, that thine enemies shall cast a trench about thee, and compass thee round, and keep thee in on every side, And shall lay thee even with the ground, and thy children within thee; and they shall not leave in thee one stone upon another; because thou knewest not the time of thy visitation."

Jesus foresaw that ere that generation would pass away (Luke 21:32), an enemy would come and throw up fortifications against the city and destroy it.

What happened? The Jews, unmindful of the warning, carried on a steady persecution of the followers of Christ, killing many and imprisoning others. Then in the year 65 A.D., the fateful drama began to unfold. Becoming bolder, the more radical elements thought to throw off the yoke of their Roman masters. The spirit of rebellion flared throughout the country. The Jews had some preliminary successes and were encouraged to believe that they could win against the might of Rome.

Then came the seasoned legions of Titus who broke through the walls of Jerusalem and destroyed the city after a long siege. This event took place exactly forty years after Christ had made the prediction of its destruction, just one generation later.

Proof 9—Christ foretold the dispersion of the Jews

After foretelling the siege of Jerusalem and the great catastrophe that was to overtake the city, Jesus then warned what would happen to the Jews because they had rejected Christ. His followers were now to go to the whole world to acquaint all peoples with Christ. (Later Christ would come back to the Jews after the other peoples, or Gentiles, had had an opportunity to accept Christ.)

> "And they shall fall by the edge of the sword, and shall be led away captive into all nations: and Jerusalem shall be trodden down of the Gentiles, until the times of the Gentiles be fulfilled" (Luke 21:24).

That is exactly what happened. The Jews by their rejection of their Lord had forfeited the divine protection that God intended them to have. After the fall of Jerusalem, the survivors were herded together like animals and marched to the slave markets. The marts became so glutted that their captors had to sell them at unbelievably low prices. Many died on the way because of the inhuman treatment they received.

From the slave markets, the Jews were dispersed throughout the nations of the world. And thus it has been during what is called the Gentile Age. Jerusalem was demolished by the Gentiles, or non-Jewish people. That the Jew at long last has returned to his home land is startling proof that it is close to the time for Christ to return to earth again. The Holy Scriptures said that one of the signs of Christ's soon coming would be that the Jewish people would return to their country.

> "Thus says the Lord God: In the day that I cleanse you from all your iniquities I will also cause (Israel's) cities to be inhabited, and the waste places shall be rebuilt. And the desolate land shall be tilled, that which had laid desolate in the sight of all who passed by, And they shall say, This land that was desolate has become like the garden of Eden, and the waste and desolate and ruined cities are fortified and inhabited" (Ezekiel 36:33-35) **Amplified**

15

1948 Israel a nation again.

Proof 10—Christ gave His own life to establish His kingdom

The pages of history are marked by illustrious men whose genius was dedicated to the building of great empires. Alexander the Great and his armies moved across the world in a conquering fury. In a series of battles in which he demonstrated his remarkable generalship, he created an empire from Macedonia to the Indus River. Just before his death Alexander is said to have wept because there were no more worlds to conquer.

Caesar conquered Gaul and became the father of the Roman Empire, and in a series of lightning maneuvers subdued all of Europe to the Rhine River. Crossing the Rubicon against orders, he entered Rome and became its master.

All these sought to build their empires by shedding the blood of others. Christ, too, came to establish a kingdom—one that is universal and eternal—not with the blood of others but by giving His own life. Christ's kingdom is not of this present age, except as it is in the hearts of His people. Before He was crucified Christ told Pilate the governor, "My kingdom is not of this world: if my kingdom were of this world, then would my servants fight, that I should not be delivered to the Jews: but now is my kingdom not from hence" (John 18:36). And when His disciple Peter sought to prevent the officers from arresting him, Jesus said, "Put up again thy sword into his place: for all they that take the sword shall perish with the sword" (Matt. 26:52).

Christ is unique in that He inaugurated His kingdom not by shedding the blood of others but by giving His own blood.

Proof 11—The Bible predicted all the main events that accompanied Christ's trial, death, and resurrection

The Old Testament was written by God through prophets who lived 500 to 1500 years before Christ was born. They prophesied of His coming to earth and of many events in His life, even though Christ was not to be born for many more centuries.

The New Testament, inspired also of God, and written by devout followers of Christ, points again and again to how Christ's life fulfilled these prophesies.

Compare these Old Testament prophesies with the New Testament recordings of their fulfillment.

    1. The Messiah was to be rejected (Isa. 53:3; John 1:11).

2. He was to be betrayed by one of His close followers and friends (Psa. 41:9; Mark 14:10).

3. He was to be sold for 30 pieces of silver (Zech. 11:12; Matt. 26:15).

4. He was to be silent before His accusers (Isa. 53:7; Matt. 26:62-63).

5. He was to be smitten and spat upon (Isa. 50:6; Mark 14:65).

6. He was to bring healing to the people (Isa. 53:4-5; Matt. 8:14-17).

7. He was to be mocked and taunted (Psa. 22: 6-8; Matt. 27:39-40).

8. He was to suffer with transgressors and pray for His enemies (Isa. 53:12; Matt. 27:38; Luke 23:34).

9. His hands and feet were to be pierced (Psa. 22:16; John 20:27).

10. He was to be given gall and vinegar (Psa. 69:21; John 19:29).

11. His side was to be pierced (Zech. 12:10; John 19:34).

12. They were to cast lots for His garments (Psa. 22:18; Mark 15:24).

13. He was to be buried with the rich (Isa. 53:9; Matt. 27:57-60).

14. He was to be a sacrifice for sin (Isa. 53:5, 8, 10, 12; John 1:29).

15. He was to be raised from the dead (Psa. 16:10; Matt. 28:9).

16. He was to ascend to the right hand of God (Psa. 68: 18; Luke 24:50-51).

17. He was to come again (Dan. 7:13-14; Matt. 24:30).

Who can see all these detailed prophesies and their amazing fulfillments and not be compelled to say as the centurion of old, "Truly this was the Son of God" (Matt. 27:54).

Proof 12—He proved He was the Christ by His power over death

Many great men have lived and made their mark on the world; but they all died, and their bones still lie in their graves. Go to the Invalides of Paris, and you may gaze at the sealed tomb of Napoleon. His body is still there. In Westminster Abbey in London, one can see the Mausoleum that holds the bodies of many of Britain's greatest statesmen and kings. Their bones are all there

17

moldering in the dust. At Mount Vernon is the last resting place of George Washington, called "Father of the United States." His body still lies sleeping in the tomb. One by one the world's great, as well as its small, have been laid away in their resting places. Only in one place in the world is there an empty tomb. That is in Jerusalem, at the foot of Calvary where they once laid the Lord Jesus. It was there three days later that the angel appeared to some of his followers who had come to the tomb to weep. The angel said, "Why seek ye the living among the dead? He is not here, but is risen" (Luke 24:5-6).

Jesus said that one sign should be given to that generation: "There shall no sign be given unto it, but the sign of the prophet Jonas" (Matt. 16:4). "For as Jonas was three days and three nights in the whale's belly; so shall the Son of man be three days and three nights in the heart of the earth" (Matt. 12:40).

It was this sign that gave faith and inspiration to the Early Church. Jesus had overcome for all time the age-old problem of death. It was upon this incontestable victory over death that the apostles with great power gave "witness of the resurrection of the Lord Jesus: and great grace was upon them all" (Acts 4:33).

Proof 13—Christ had a new body

> "And after eight days again his disciples were within, and Thomas was with them: then came Jesus, the doors being shut, and stood in their midst, and said, Peace be unto you. Then saith he to Thomas, Reach hither thy finger, and behold my hands; and reach hither thy hand, and thrust it into my side: and be not faithless, but believing" (John 20:26-27).

Christ was the first man who lived on earth and received a resurrected body. The risen Christ was more than a spirit; He had a real body. In appearance it was much the same body that He had had before. It bore the marks of nails and the spear. The voice was recognizable. When Jesus said, "Mary," to one of His followers she knew that the speaker was her Lord. Except when Jesus wished to conceal His identity, He was instantly recognizable as the "same Jesus." He could eat food as He did when in His physical body. He could walk at the same natural pace as others did. Yet when He desired, He could travel instantaneously to distant places or go through locked doors.

At the resurrection, Christ's body underwent a fundamental change—a glorification. It was able to accommodate itself to two

18

worlds. In other words, the Lord could adapt Himself to physical laws, but He was not bound by them.

The revelation we have of Christ's resurrection is relevant to the Christian. One day when Christ returns to earth, we shall receive a body like His, for it is written, "We shall be like him." It will be a distinctively different body from the one we have now. It will not be subject to disease, aging, or physical limitations. And like Christ, we shall never die.

Proof 14—The very city where Christ was to be born was named 500 years earlier

The only person in the world to have the city where He was to be born identified centuries before the event took place was Jesus Christ. Micah, the Jewish prophet, writing 500 years before Christ's birth tells of One "whose goings forth have been from of old, from everlasting" (Micah 5:2). This is clearly a reference to Christ who as the Son of God had existence previous to His earthly birth. He was the God-man who was to be born in the little town of Bethlehem, Israel.

> "But thou, Bethlehem Ephratah, though thou be little among the thousands of Judah, yet out of thee shall he come forth unto me that is to be ruler in Israel: whose goings forth have been from of old, from everlasting" (Micah 5:2).

Only a few weeks before His birth, Jesus' mother, Mary, great with child, was in the city of Nazareth. She had no plans to travel the many miles south to Bethlehem.

However, the Roman Emperor Augustus made a decree that all the world should be taxed. Mary, to obey the law, was forced even in the advanced stages of pregnancy to make the long trip south with her husband Joseph in order to register in the city of their lineage. Reaching Bethlehem after a tiring journey, Mary found that she was about to give birth to her firstborn. Her husband, Joseph, looked about desperately for some kind of shelter. To his dismay every room in the inn had been taken, and no other lodging was available. He finally found a manger among the animals which was appropriated to serve the purpose. In these crude surroundings the greatest event of history occurred—the birth of the Christ-child. The inhabitants of Bethlehem, except some humble shepherds to whom angels appeared (Luke 2:8), were quite unaware of the stupendous event that had taken place in their little city. Yes, the child Jesus was born in the city of Bethlehem where the prophet Micah five centuries earlier said He would be born.

Proof 15—The prophet Isaiah predicted 800 years before Christ's birth that He was to be born of a virgin

Some eight centuries before Jesus was born, the prophet Isaiah predicted that a virgin should be with child, and his name would be called Immanuel.

> "Therefore the Lord himself shall give you a sign; Behold, a virgin shall conceive, and bear a son, and shall call his name Immanuel" (Isa. 7:14).

And that is exactly what took place. The angel Gabriel appeared to the Virgin Mary and told her that she would be with child by the Holy Ghost (Luke 1:26:38). Her espoused husband Joseph became aware of her condition and at first sadly thought to put her away. But the angel appeared in a dream to him saying, "Joseph, thou son of David, fear not to take unto thee Mary thy wife: for that which is conceived in her is of the Holy Ghost" (Matt. 1:20).

Christ was the only person in the world who was born of the Holy Spirit rather than the will of man. Indeed the fact is that if Christ were the Son of God, He had to be born of the Holy Spirit. He could not have partaken of man's fallen state and still be our Savior. Christ was truly more than a man; He was the only begotten of the Father (God) (John 3:16). We shall speak further on this important subject of the virgin birth in another chapter.

Proof 16—The time of Christ's birth was prophesied nearly 500 years before He was born

The most amazing fact about Christ's birth was that prophecy predicted the very time He was to be born! From "the going forth of the commandment to restore and to build Jerusalem" there should be 69 weeks of years.

> "Know therefore and understand that from the going forth of the commandment to restore and to build Jerusalem until (the coming of) the anointed one, a prince, shall be seven weeks (of years), and sixty-two weeks (of years); it shall be built again with city square and moat, but in troublous times. And after the sixty-two weeks (of years) shall the anointed one be cut off or killed, and shall have nothing (and no one belonging) to (and defending) him. And the people of the other prince who shall come will destroy the city and

20

the sanctuary. Its end shall come with a flood, and even to the end there shall be war, and desolations are decreed" (Dan-9:25-26) **Amplified.**

Daniel, a prophet living five centuries before Christ was born, prophesied under the inspiration of God as to what the future held.

He said that Jerusalem which lay in ruins would be rebuilt. Another prophet, Isaiah, had even foretold who would give the command to rebuild Jerusalem—King Cyrus.

"Who says of Cyrus, He is My shepherd, and he shall perform all My pleasure, and fulfill all My purpose; even saying of Jerusalem, She shall again be built, and of the temple, Your foundation shall again be laid" (Isa. 44:28) **Amplified.**

History records the time of the giving of the command for the restoration of the city of Jerusalem to be during the reign of Cyrus.

Therefore, the question is, when does history say that the going forth of the commandment of Cyrus to restore and to rebuild Jerusalem was actually given? The commonly accepted chronologies which differ slightly among themselves show the event to be just before the 5th century B.C. Bible chronology sets the time in the 5th century. One thing is certain: the edict to rebuild Jerusalem took place shortly before, or shortly after, the beginning of the 5th century B.C. There is no question about this.

This being so, then according to the prophet Daniel, "69 weeks" of years later, after the edict to restore Jerusalem was given, the Messiah was to come. The question we ask then is, did the Messiah appear to Israel at this time?

Before we answer this question, we must define what is meant by "69 weeks." Plainly, they could not be weeks of 24 hour days, since 69 weeks of days is 483 days, or only a little over a year. In Bible times, a period of seven years instead of seven days is often spoken of as a "week" of years. This is shown in the book of Genesis, where Laban bargains with Jacob to work another "week" or "seven other years" for his younger daughter Rachel.

"Finish the week (seven years), then we will give you (Rachel) also, and you shall work for me yet seven more years in return" (Gen. 29:27) **Amplified.**

A "week" of years being seven years, then 69 weeks would be 483 years. So the prophet Daniel is saying, 483 years after the commandment went forth to rebuild Jerusalem, the Messiah would appear. Now when did these 483 years run out? Did the Messiah, the Son of God, appear about 5 centuries later? The only Messiah the world knows anything about did appear at about that time—and that was Jesus Christ! Although the secular calendar may be a little uncertain so that the date is not exactly determined, nevertheless, it definitely indicates the years as running out at the era of Christ!

Could we want a more irrefutable proof that Jesus is the Messiah? Could a fraud possibly have been perpetrated? How could it? Daniel's prophecy was given many centuries earlier. Either the Messiah had to appear at that time, or else Daniel's prophecy was false. The fact is that Jesus came at that time, and His life had such an impact upon the world that the peoples of many nations have accepted Him as the Christ!

Proof 17—Christ's death as the Messiah was predicted 900 years before His birth

There is another very remarkable thing about the prophecy of Daniel 9:24. The children of Israel supposed that when the Lord, whom the Jewish people called the Messiah, came He would set up His kingdom on earth. Even the apostles of Christ assumed that He would at once sit on His throne (Acts 1:6-7). But the prophecy says instead that the Messiah was to be "cut off, or killed" (Dan. 9:26). Rather than setting up a visible kingdom at His first coming, prophecy declared that He was going to die! There is only one person in history that could possibly have fulfilled that prophecy at that time, and He was Jesus Christ.

Even the kind of death the Messiah was to die was foretold. His hands and feet were to be pierced—that is by crucifixion. So said the Psalmist David 900 years before it happened:

> "For (like a pack of) dogs they have encompassed me; a company of evildoers has encircled me; they pierced my hands and my feet" (Psa. 22:16) **Amplified.**

So not only the manner of His birth was predicted but also the kind of death—many centuries in advance. Only the One that created this world could make these prophecies come to pass in this fashion.

Proof 18—Christ gives a personal experience today

Beyond all else the religion of Christ satisfies, because the believer possesses Christ Himself. He promised He would come into our life, change it so that we become a new creature, take away our burden of sin, and bring peace into our hearts. Some may argue against Christianity, but they cannot argue against the experience Christ gives. Christ is able to do what no other religion can— live and dwell within the human heart, and so it has been that through the ages, millions have accepted Christ and found Him their all in all.

Again and again the apostle Paul referred to his own experience that time he met Christ on the Damascus Road (Acts, Chapter 9). It was the high point of his preaching. He told and retold the story wherever he went. The Christian's personal experience with Christ is the greatest proof of His reality. It is as the poet wrote:

> He lives, He lives, Christ Jesus lives today
> He walks with me and talks with me.
> Along life's narrow way.
> He lives, He lives, salvation to impart.
> You ask me how I know He lives.
> He lives within my heart.

Chapter 2

The Miracle
of the Virgin Birth

In the first chapter we considered 18 proofs that Jesus Christ is the Son of God. The central pillar of the whole matter of His peculiar origin and destiny is His virgin birth—a circumstance which is uniquely different from the birth of any other human being. While Christ received His human nature through His mother Mary, His God identity came by reason of His supernatural conception by the Holy Spirit. The whole structure of Christianity must rest upon this fact. For while the Scriptures teach that Christ took upon Himself human nature through His mother Mary, nevertheless, if He Himself had been of the seed of the first man Adam, He would have been a fallen human being as are all human beings, and utterly unable to redeem humanity. Thus, the first foretelling of Christ's birth was written 1500 years before by Moses referring to Christ as "the seed" of the woman rather than the seed of Adam, or man (Gen. 3:15).

So important is this fundamental and basic truth of the gospel that we present in brief the seven great proofs of the virgin birth of Christ.

1. Christ's name in prophecy was called Immanuel, "God with us." The words of Isaiah straightly declared that this Immanuel should be born of a virgin:

> "Therefore, the Lord himself shall give you a sign; Behold, a virgin shall conceive, and bear a son, and shall call his name Immanuel" (Isaiah 7:14).

2. Matthew 1:23 declares that the birth of Jesus of the virgin Mary was a fulfillment of prophecy.

3. Joseph, the betrothed husband of Mary, discovered before they were married that she was with child. While pondering over what he should do about the matter, the angel of the Lord appeared to him and informed him that which had been conceived in Mary was not of man but by the Holy Ghost (Matt. 1:18-20).

24

4. Luke 1:26-38 tells of the angel's visit to Mary during which she was acquainted with the fact that she would be with child by the Holy Ghost, and this child would be called the Son of God.

"Then said Mary unto the angel, How shall this be, seeing I know not a man? And the angel answered and said unto her, The Holy Ghost shall come upon thee, and the power of the Highest shall overshadow thee: therefore also that holy thing which shall be born of thee shall be called the Son of God" (Luke 1:34-35).

5. It was prophesied that the Messiah would come from the line of David, the greatest king to have ever ruled the Hebrew nation, after the flesh (II Sam. 7:12-19; Psa. 89:3, 4, 34-37; 132:11; Acts 2:30; 13:22-23). These prophecies were fulfilled in Jesus as the son of Mary, who came of the line of David. Joseph, Mary's espoused husband, also of the royal line, was the legal father but not the real father. That Jesus, the King of Israel, could not be the son of Joseph after the flesh is confirmed by a very significant circumstance. Joseph was a descendant of Jeconiah, a particularly wicked king. Because of the extreme flagrance of his evil reign, God said that none of the seed of Jeconiah (also called Coniah) would sit upon the throne of David forever.

"O land, land, land, hear the word of the Lord! Thus says the Lord, Write this man (Coniah) down as childless, a man who shall not prosper in his days; for no man of his offspring shall succeed in sitting upon the throne of David, and ruling any more in Judah" (Jer. 22:29-30) Amplified

If, therefore, Jesus had actually been the son of Joseph after the flesh, He would not have been eligible to the throne of David. Thus Christ was the son of David through the maternal line (Mary).

Through His mother Jesus became eligible to the throne of David. Thus we see the amazing preciseness of the fulfillment of the Scriptures. Here is a fact casually mentioned in the Scriptures but of such significance as to give pause to anyone who would doubt the virgin birth of Christ.

6. That Jesus was not the son of David on His paternal side is further proved by the words of Jesus Himself. He asked the Pharisees whose son they thought Christ was. They answered, "The son of David," thinking of him as a direct seed of David through a human father. Jesus then asked them a question as to why David speaking in the inspiration of the Spirit called Him Lord.

"He saith unto them, How then doth David in spirit call him Lord, saying, The Lord said unto my Lord, Sit thou on my right hand, till I make thine enemies thy footstool? If David then call him Lord, how is he his son?" (Matt. 22: 43-45).

This the Pharisees could not answer. It certainly seemed inappropriate for David in the Spirit to call a descendant of his, after the flesh, his Lord.

It is also evident from these words that Jesus knew of His own virgin birth and that He was not the son of Joseph.

7. Finally the Early Church fathers believed in the virgin birth. The belief is found in the Apostles' Creed, which was written in the early part of the second century.

Great historians such as Ignatius believed in the virgin birth and defended it against the heresies of his time. Origen, in his treatise against Celsus and Tertullian, believed it and defended the virgin birth.

We need not lengthen the list of names since the Early Church fathers consistently put themselves on record as believing in the virgin birth. Moreover, they vigorously defended it against all heresies.

The virgin birth is the clue as to why Christ is uniquely different from all other men. He was a man through His mother Mary; but He was also God by being conceived not of the will of the flesh, but by the Holy Spirit.

The Boy Jesus

Joseph, the husband of Mary, was a righteous man according to the Scriptures, but he was probably considered by the upper classes as a peasant. He worked in his carpenter shop as an honest son of toil, supporting his large family to the best of his ability. As Jesus and His brothers grew older, they joined Joseph in the shop, contributing to the support of the family.

At the age of eight Jesus was sent to the synagogue where He was taught to read and to write from the rolls of the Scriptures. It appears from Luke 4:16 that the reading ability of Jesus was considered superior enough that He was given the regular task each Sabbath of reading from the sacred scrolls.

Jesus as a youth made no deep impression upon the community. At a later date when His ministry made its first impact upon the nation, the local inhabitants of Nazareth spoke to each other in amazement saying, "From whence hath this man these things? and what wisdom is this which is given unto him that even such mighty works are wrought by his hands?" Indeed it appears from John 7:3-5 that His own brethren in the flesh were not convinced of His divine mission. Later on, however, they did believe (Acts 1:14).

The silent years were not idle years by any means. During the day He was busy in the carpenter shop. In the evening His mother would find Him studying and storing away in His mind the Holy Scriptures. Obviously His thoughts were much occupied in pondering those portions of the inspired writings of the Old Testament, which related to His future work.

And so the years one by one slipped away as Jesus came to full manhood. At length there came the day when Jesus laid down His tools and left the carpenter shop forever. For Him it was the hour of decision. Bidding goodbye to His family, He went his way to the river Jordan where an itinerant evangelist, oddly dressed in a girdle of camel's hair, was preaching a fiery message of repentance. It was John the Baptist. Against the Baptist's protest Jesus was baptized in water by him in the River Jordan. Then He disappeared from the haunts of men, and for six weeks gave Himself over to fasting and to meditation in the solitude of the wilderness.

Then reappearing once more, He began a ministry which in three short years would rock the nation from center to circumference and eventually, the whole world.

Jesus did not begin His ministry in His hometown, Nazareth. As He said, "A prophet is not without honour, but in his own country" (Mark 6:4). Moreover, the village was hidden away off the main road. The Lord needed a center from which His ministry could radiate out into all parts of the nation. So it was that He chose as His headquarters the flourishing city of Capernaum, located on the Sea of Galilee.

There among the teeming population of the cities that lay along the Galilean shore, Christianity was cradled. There Jesus began the proclamation of the good news of the gospel. At times He preached from a small ship standing off from the shore. On other occasions He ministered upon the neighboring hills that overlooked the sea. There in Galilee the multitudes came to hear Him teach and to be healed of their diseases. The good news of His work soon spread far and wide. It was a ministry which in a few months' time resulted in thousands of followers.

Chapter 3

The Mission of Christ

After Christ appeared it became possible to compare the actual events of His life with the passages in the ancient writings, thus confirming our faith that the One who came was indeed the Christ, the Son of the living God.

There was another purpose served in Christ's being born at the time He was. The world by this time had been given an opportunity to make full proof of its capabilities and dispositions. Many notable results were achieved in the development of the varied civilizations. It was proved that man could rise to higher levels in the arts and refinements of life, in literature, in painting, and in architecture; but in the religious realm it became a matter of fact that man could not rise unaided to God. While man had made great progress in other fields of knowledge—improving his intellect, refining his tastes, and correcting his manners—he could not purify his heart. The sad story of the moral decline of mankind is drawn by the inspired writer in Romans 1:21-23.

> "Because that when they knew God, they glorified him not as God, neither were thankful; but became vain in their imaginations, and their foolish heart was darkened. Professing themselves to be wise, they became fools, And changed the glory of the uncorruptible God into an image made like to corruptible man, and to birds, and four-footed beasts, and creeping things."

Man must have a Saviour; he is not complete in himself. Contrary to the speculations of blind philosophers who contend that there is an upward urge in nature, the sad fact is that apart from Christ the inherent tendency in the moral life of mankind is downward.

So although Christ performed many marvelous miracles, it was not His purpose merely to heal the afflicted and infirm who might become sick again or to raise the dead that they might die again. Nor did He come to satisfy the physical appetite of men, only to have them hunger again. He came into the world to give men the

28

bread of life—bread for the soul, so that they might never hunger nor thirst spiritually. He came to preach a gospel of repentance to save men from their sins, that they should never perish. When people told Him of the governor Pilate who had slain certain persons or of the tower of Siloam that had fallen on eighteen others causing their death, He said,

> "Suppose ye that these Galileans were sinners above all the Galileans, because they suffered such things? I tell you nay: but except ye repent, ye shall all likewise perish" (Luke 13:2-3).

Not all accepted Christ's call to repentance. There in north Galilee where the great trade routes crossed, the temptation was strong for men to become deeply engaged in the pursuit of riches and the material things of life. Although the inhabitants seemed deeply impressed with Christ's miracles and His teachings, the urge to get their part of the prosperity outweighed, for most of them, Christ's call to "forsake all and follow me."

Some who were drawn by Christ's appeal followed Him for a time; but they had not fully counted the cost. A rich young ruler came to Him and asked, "Good Master, what good thing shall I do, that I may have eternal life" (Matt. 19:16). Looking with deep emotion at the earnest young man, Jesus told him to leave his riches and follow Him. Christ said this because He knew the young man loved his money more than God. Sadly the youth turned away; the price was too great for him to pay. He wanted to give God second place in his life.

> "Then Jesus beholding him loved him, and said unto him, One thing thou lackest: go thy way, sell whatsoever thou hast, and give to the poor, and thou shalt have treasure in heaven: and come, take up the cross and follow me. And he was sad at that saying, and went away grieved: for he had great possessions" (Mark 10:21-22).

But whether men accept or reject Him, Christ is the stone by which the destinies of men are forever settled. He spoke to the religious leaders saying, "Whosoever shall fall on this stone shall be broken: but on whomsoever it shall fall, it will grind him to powder (Matt. 21:44). In other words, he who accepts Christ will be broken, but only that his life might be reshaped anew. But he who rejects Christ will be ground to powder and that without remedy.

The teachings of Christ are beautifully illustrated in His conversations with people who came to Him with their questions.

Always He went straight to the heart of the person's need or problem.

Peter under deep conviction said to Him, "Depart from me; for I am a sinful man, O Lord" (Luke 5:8). Jesus replied saying, "Fear not; from henceforth thou shalt catch men." Why did Jesus give Peter this answer instead of reproaching him for his sinful past? Because Peter was already convicted of his sins; he knew that without Christ he was a lost man. Actually, the last thing he desired was for the Lord to depart from him. What Peter really wanted was to follow Jesus. The Lord told him that he would still be a fisherman, but from then on he would be fishing for men.

Nicodemus, a religious leader, came to Christ at night to talk about the miracles and Christ's standing as a prophet. But the Lord ignored this and turned the conversation around to the spiritual need of Nicodemus saying, "Except a man be born again, he cannot see the kingdom of God" (John 3:3). At this statement Nicodemus registered deep surprise, and his patronizing manner abruptly changed. "How can a man be born when he is old? can he enter the second time into his mother's womb, and be born?" Nicodemus asked. Christ continued to hold the initiative in the conversation. He drove home the point that although Nicodemus was a ruler in a high religious court called the Sanhedrin, this could not give him entrance into the Kingdom of God. No one can enter the Kingdom of God unless he is born of the spirit. This rebirth takes place when a person accepts Christ into his soul and life as Saviour and Lord. "Marvel not that I said unto thee, Ye must be born again" (John 3:7), Jesus said. All must have a radical change in their nature. The startled Nicodemus was altogether overwhelmed by these words which seemed to him so revolutionary. Three years later, however, Nicodemus dared to risk his position in the Sanhedrin court when He and Joseph of Arimathea went to Pilate and claimed the body of Christ for burial (John 19:38-40).

At another time they brought to Jesus a woman who had been taken in adultery. As she cringed before her accusers, they craftily asked Jesus whether or not she should be stoned according to the Law of Moses. The Lord looked upon her with pity and compassion. Turning to the self-righteous religious leaders who were using the miserable woman as a means to entrap Him, He said, "He that is without sin among you, let him first cast a stone at her. And again he stooped down, and wrote on the ground" (John 8:7-8). According to tradition, Jesus was writing in the sand the sins of each of the Pharisees, religious leaders, beginning with the eldest and ending with the youngest. Smitten with conviction, her accusers had nothing further to say and shamefacedly made a hurried departure. Jesus said to the woman, "Neither do I condemn thee: go, and sin no more" (John 8:11).

To a man who came and asked Jesus to speak to his brother to divide the inheritance, He gave a sharp rebuke saying, "Take heed, and beware of covetousness: for a man's life consisteth not in the abundance of the things which he possesseth" (Luke 12:15). He then described the fate of a rich fool who thought to pull down his barns and build greater so that he might have more room to store his goods. The rich man said to his soul, "Thou hast much goods laid up for many years; take thine ease, eat, drink, and be merry." Jesus told how on that very night "God said unto him, Thou fool, this night thy soul shall be required of thee: then whose shall those things be, which thou hast provided?" (Luke 12:19-20).

When Jesus heard that his close friend Lazarus was dead, and He saw the people mourning and weeping, He Himself wept (John 11:35), obviously not for those who in a brief moment would witness His power over death because He raised Lazarus from the dead. But rather He wept for the sorrows of a whole forelorn world suffering from the consequences of sin that had cursed the race.

Again on the way to the cross, Jesus saw the women weeping because of Him, and He said, "Daughters of Jerusalem, weep not for me, but weep for yourselves, and for your children" (Luke 23:28). Always He was thinking of others rather than Himself.

On the cross as the soldiers, sadly ignorant of whom they had crucified, went about casting lots for His raiment. Jesus prayed, "Father, forgive them; for they know not what they do" (Luke 23:34).

On either side of Him were crucified two thieves. At first both of the malefactors reviled Him (Matt. 27:44). One of them said, "If thou be Christ, save thyself and us" (Luke 23:39). But the other, soon convinced that Jesus was the Son of God, rebuked his companion and sought the Lord for mercy. Jesus, forgetting His own suffering, spoke words of peace telling him, "To day shalt thou be with me in paradise" (Luke 23:40-43).

The fateful afternoon waned; darkness descended upon the earth. Death had overtaken the Prince of Life. Men took His body down from the cross and wrapped it in a linen garment preparatory to putting it in the tomb. Pilate, the governor, stationed soldiers around the sepulcher to make certain there was no molestation of the body. For three days and nights they guarded the tomb. But early in the morning of the third day something happened that shook the earth, as well as the spirit world. The powers of Satan were broken; death loosed its grip; and Christ arose from the grave! When grief-stricken followers of Jesus came to the tomb to perform what they thought was the last service for the dead, two men in bright shining clothes stood by them. Full of fear, the women bowed down to the ground, as the men said to them: "Why seek ye the living among the dead? He is not here, but is risen: remember how he spake unto you when he was yet in Galilee, Saying, The Son of man must be delivered into the hands of sinful men, and be crucified, and the third day rise again" (Luke 24:5-7).

Christ was indeed raised from death and was alive forevermore. The risen Saviour then appeared before the disciples and gave them the Great Commission by which they were to preach the gospel to all the world.

> "And he said unto them, Go ye into all the world, and preach the gospel to every creature. He that believeth and is baptized shall be saved; but he that believeth not shall be damned. And these signs shall follow them that believe; In my name shall they cast out devils; they shall speak with new tongues; They shall take up serpents; and if they drink any deadly thing, it shall not hurt them; they shall lay hands on the sick, and they shall recover. So then after the Lord had spoken to them, he was received up into heaven, and sat on the right hand of God. And they went forth and preached everywhere, the Lord working with them, and confirming the word with signs following Amen" (Mark 16:15-20).

Chapter 4

Why We Must Accept Christ

There is only one true God. God, Creator of the Universe, existed before the beginning of the world. God is a good God, a God of love. He created man to be a companion and friend of God.

But since Satan deceived man and caused him to rebel and sin against God, sinful man is separated from God which is a most terrible punishment.

Because God is holy and perfect He cannot associate with anyone who has sin in his life. Thus our sins will cause us to be eternally separated from God. In order to bring man back into communion with Himself, He allowed His only Son, Christ, to pay the penalty of death for our sins. If we accept His Son, God will forgive our sins, and we will be as though we have never sinned. As redeemed men, we can now commune with God while we live on this earth, and when our life on earth is finished, we will go to live with Him forever.

What Does Christ's Death On The Cross Mean To You Personally?

Let us think back upon the day when Christ was crucified. There He hung between earth and heaven—a spectacle to men and angels with the tortures becoming more unendurable every moment. Death by crucifixion includes the sum total of all the suffering a body can experience: thirst, fever, open shame, long continual torment.

It was now the noon hour, ordinarily the brightest hour of the day. But instead, a darkness began to descend upon the earth. Nature itself, unable to bear the scene, withdrew its light, and the heavens became black. This darkness had an immediate effect upon the onlookers. There were no more jeers and taunts. People began to slip away silently to leave Jesus alone to drink to the deepest depths the dregs of suffering and humiliation. Yet a greater horror was yet to come. Instead of a joyful communion with God, there

33

was a cry of distress. Jesus found himself utterly deserted by both man and God. His cry even today brings a shudder of terror. It was . . .

"My God, my God, why hast thou forsaken me?"

There was apparently one thing that God had held back from his son Christ, lest even He should be unable to bear it. The terrible truth came to Him only in the last hours of darkness. As the sun withdrew its shining, so the presence of God was being withdrawn also. Though sometimes forsaken of men, He could always turn in confidence to His heavenly Father. But now even God had forsaken Him.

God indeed had forsaken Him, though only for a moment; and the reason is clear: at that moment the sin of the world with all its hideousness rested upon Jesus. He became sin; "For he hath made him to be sin for us, who knew no sin; that we might be made the righteousness of God in him" (II Cor. 5:21).

There we have the answer to what happened. Christ was made sin for us. He took upon Him the sin of the world, including yours and mine. Therefore, He had to receive the judgment that fell upon sin.

And now at last the end was drawing near. The loss of blood produces a thirst that is beyond description. Jesus cried, "I thirst." The One who hung on the cross thirsted. He is the same One who now satisfies our souls' thirst—"If any man thirst, let him come unto me, and drink" (John 7:37).

The final moment had come. Jesus bowed his head in death saying as He died, "It is finished!" Salvation had been completed. It was a salvation, not of works to be earned by fastings, by penances, by pilgrimages. Salvation is forever a finished work. We need not complete it by our own efforts. There is nothing more to do but to accept it. There is no need to struggle and to labor, but to take quietly what God has prepared at infinite sacrifice.

So did Christ die for our salvation. So was He raised again three days and nights later in glorious triumph to die no more. Therefore, He says, "BECAUSE I LIVE, YE SHALL LIVE ALSO" (John 14:19).

God has done all that is possible to bring you eternal life. He paid the full price of punishment for your sins. It is now your turn to accept Him. God sees your mind and soul. He knows all of your thoughts. If you sincerely want to accept Jesus Christ, the Son of God, into your life, you will be reborn. You will become a child of God, and God the Father will become your father.

Chapter 5

The Birth of John the Baptist

"There was in the days of Herod, the king of Judaea, a
certain priest named Zacharias, of the course of Abia: and his
wife was of the daughters of Aaron, and her name was Elisabeth. And they were both righteous before God, walking in
all the commandments and ordinances of the Lord blameless.
And they had no child, because that Elisabeth was barren,
and they both were now well stricken in years. And it came
to pass, that while he executed the priest's office before God
in the order of his course, According to the custom of the
priest's office, his lot was to burn incense when he went into
the temple of the Lord. And the whole multitude of the
people were praying without at the time of incense. And there
appeared unto him an angel of the Lord standing on the right
side of the altar of incense. And when Zacharias saw him, he
was troubled, and fear fell upon him. But the angel said unto
him, Fear not, Zacharias: for thy prayer is heard; and thy
wife Elisabeth shall bear thee a son, and thou shalt call his
name John" (Luke 1:5-13).

The angel's announcement of the coming of John the Baptist
broke the 400 years of silence of the spirit of prophecy. In all
ways John was unique. Compared with the other prophets, Jesus
said, "There were none greater born of women." His incorruptible
sincerity, his humility, his fearlessness and courage, together with
the tragic story of his death all combine to give him a distinctive
place in the Bible narrative. We are told that he came to Israel
in the power and the spirit of Elijah. He stood alone between the
Jewish dispensation and the Christian dispensation. But his greatest work and the ministry by which he will ever be remembered
was that he was the forerunner of the Messiah.

The book of Luke begins with relating events associated with
the birth of John the Baptist. High up in the hill country near
Jerusalem, there lived a certain priest by the name of Zacharias

with his wife, Elisabeth. They were a godly couple well advanced in age at the time of the events narrated. They had long desired a child, but this had been denied them. Nevertheless, they had prayed many times about the matter, but at last, their best years having passed, they ceased to indulge this hope. They reconciled themselves to the fact that they apparently would live and die childless (Luke 1:13).

Zacharias was a priest "of the course of Abia," and twice a year it was his duty to journey to Jerusalem to fulfill his office of a week of six days and two Sabbaths. At this time in history, according to Josephus, there were 20,000 priests settled in and about Judea. Many were no credit to the priesthood but were in fact "blind leaders of the blind." On the other hand, there were those priests who were deeply sincere and led devout lives. Of this latter class was Zacharias, as well as his wife Elisabeth. "And they were both righteous before God, walking in all the commandments and ordinances of the Lord blameless" (Luke 1:6).

As we have noted, the couple had long prayed for a son, but apparently their prayer had not been answered. Although they did not know it, their petition had been heard, but the answer had been withheld because the hour set by Providence had not yet come. Elisabeth was to bear a son who was to be the forerunner of the Messiah. The fulness of time when the Messiah was to appear, and therefore, also His forerunner, was settled in the divine plan prepared from the foundation of the world and could not be moved backward nor forward.

But at last the time came. So it was that on this memorable occasion when Zacharias left his home in the hills to fulfill his duty in the temple service, he little knew of the strange event which was to await him. Among the priestly duties was the offering of incense in the Holy Place at the time of prayer. The priest who offered the incense was determined by lot. And none in a lifetime offered it twice. But on this day, it so happened that the lot had been cast, and it fell to Zacharias.

It was a great honor indeed. Zacharias was chosen from out of all Israel to enter the Holy Place and minister at the altar and make intercession for the people. Since Zacharias had never before performed this solemn task, his mind was naturally in a state of awe and suppressed excitement. At the time of offering, Zacharias went into the Holy Place with his head covered and his shoes removed. Taking his censer full of incense in his hand, he poured it upon the perpetual fire of the altar. Then he made intercession for the people even as the whole multitude without, was also praying.

But suddenly Zacharias looked up and beheld an angel of the Lord standing at the right side of the altar of incense. The priest, already in a state of emotional suspense, when he saw the angel standing there "was troubled, and fear fell upon him" (Verse 12).

The angel was none other than Gabriel, who stands in the presence of God. The angel reassured Zacharias and told him to fear not, for his prayer had been heard. His wife, Elisabeth was to bear him a son, and he was to call his name John.

> "But the angel said unto him, Fear not, Zacharias: for thy prayer is heard; and thy wife Elisabeth shall bear thee a son, and thou shalt call his name John. And thou shalt have joy and gladness; and many shall rejoice at his birth. For he shall be great in the sight of the Lord, and shall drink neither wine nor strong drink; and he shall be filled with the Holy Ghost, even from his mother's womb. And many of the children of Israel shall he turn to the Lord their God. And he shall go before him in the spirit and power of Elias, to turn the hearts of the fathers to the children, and the disobedient to the wisdom of the just; to make ready a people prepared for the Lord" (Luke 1:13-17).

The event, the angel declared, would bring great joy to the household of Zacharias. He went on to give further instructions. The child was to be brought up a Nazarite and was not to drink wine nor strong drink of any kind. He would be filled with the Holy Ghost from the time of his birth. When the child grew up, he would become a great prophet who would turn many souls to the Lord. But most important, he was to be a forerunner of the Messiah, preparing a people for His coming. In the accomplishment of this great task, he would go forth in the power and the spirit of Elias.

As the angel continued speaking, the priest somewhat composed himself. Beginning to realize the astonishing significance of the angel's message, his human reasoning began to assert itself. True, he had prayed for a son, but had not the angel come too late, much too late? The time when Elisabeth could bear a son was past. How could these things possibly be? And so Zacharias, as many others since have done, tried to reason out how a miracle could take place. "Whereby shall I know this? for I am an old man, and my wife well stricken in years?" (Verse 18). Zacharias wanted a sign and he got it. The angel in rebuke told him he was to be stricken dumb until the event of the birth of the child took place.

"And the angel answering said unto him, I am Gabriel, that stand in the presence of God; and am sent to speak unto thee, and to shew thee these glad tidings. And, behold, thou shalt be dumb, and not able to speak, until the day that these things shall be performed, because thou believest not my words, which shall be fulfilled in their season. And the people waited for Zacharias, and marvelled that he tarried so long in the temple. And when he came out, he could not speak unto them: and they perceived that he had seen a vision in the temple: for he beckoned unto them, and remained speechless. And it came to pass, that, as soon as the days of his ministration were accomplished, he departed to his own house" (Luke 1:19-23).

The people marvelled that the priest stayed so long in the temple. When Zacharias finally came out, they saw he could not speak. He made signs to them, and finally they understood that he had seen a vision. Zacharias stayed in the temple until he had fulfilled the days of his ministration, then returned to his own house.

Since he could not speak when Elisabeth his wife saw him, she must have been quite dismayed. But after he had written out on paper the story of what happened and Elisabeth had read it, her alarm gave way to joyful anticipation. The couple decided, however, that all circumstances considered, it was best for the time being to say nothing to anyone. It would be an awkward thing to explain, and despite their happy anticipation of the coming event, they felt that any explanation at the moment would be misunderstood. For the next five or six months, they kept to themselves and said nothing of these things.

But at the end of six months, they had an unexpected visitor. She was certainly a welcome one. It was none other than Mary, the mother-to-be of the Christ Child! Whether the cousins had met before, we do not know for certain. Probably so, for Mary though she made the trip by herself, apparently knew the place where the elderly couple lived. As Mary stood at the door, two remarkable things happened. At the moment Mary spoke, the babe leaped in Elisabeth's womb. Then suddenly, the Spirit of God came upon the elderly woman, and a beautiful prophecy came forth acknowledging Mary as the mother of the Messiah.

It was a happy meeting, indeed, as the women exchanged all the little details and secrets of the wonderful events that had taken place. Two women with Zacharias were for the time being, in almost exclusive possession of the secret of the destiny of the world! Elisabeth and Mary no doubt talked about little else than the meaning of these strange things that had happened to them. Poor Zacharias sat mute, saying nothing, although no doubt he conveyed his thoughts to them from time to time in writing.

We may well assume the priest was not idle. He probably was busy studying from a scroll, the Psalms and the Prophets. Everything that he could find that related to the coming of the Messiah and his forerunner was searched out and then, of course, shared with the women. The prophecy that Zacharias gave, after John was born, makes it appear that his spirit had been enriched with the great Messianic truths of the Old Testament.

The time that Mary could remain with Elisabeth ran its course. Whether she stayed until after John was born cannot be said with certainty. If she did, she left immediately after, for travelling as the days of her pregnancy advanced would become increasingly difficult.

On the eighth day after Elisabeth gave birth to a son, the neighbors and cousins came to rejoice with the parents and to circumcise the child. They wanted to call him Zacharias after the father. The mother said that he should be called John. The relatives were not pleased with this, for they had a name already selected. But when they made signs to Zacharias, he wrote the words, "His name is John." In his answer all former hesitation was gone. He told them what his name was—not what it would be! And no sooner had he done this than his tongue was loosed and he gave forth a beautiful Messianic prophecy:

> "And his father Zacharias was filled with the Holy Ghost, and prophesied, saying, Blessed be the Lord God of Israel; for he hath visited and redeemed his people, And hath raised up an horn of salvation for us in the house of his servant David; As he spake by the mouth of his holy prophets, which have been since the world began: That we should be saved from our enemies, and from the hand of all that hate us; To perform the mercy promised to our fathers, and to remember his holy covenant; The oath which he sware to our father Abraham, That he would grant unto us, that we being delivered out of the hand of our enemies might serve him without fear, In holiness and righteousness before him, all the days of our life. And thou, child, shalt be called the prophet of the Highest: for thou shalt go before the face of the Lord to prepare his ways; To give knowledge of salvation unto his people by the remission of their sins, Through the tender mercy of our God; whereby the dayspring from on high

hath visited us, To give light to them that sit in darkness and in the shadow of death, to guide our feet into the way of peace" (Luke 1:67-79).

These events had a solemn effect upon the people who lived in that region. It was something they would not quickly forget. Thirty years later when John the Baptist began his preaching, many of those then living would be gone, including his mother and father. But some probably were still alive, and would remember.

We can believe that the boy growing up would find a home noted for its piety and devotion. His recollection in after-years would be of the constant perusal of the sacred books by his father and of his teaching them to him even as God had instructed by the hand of Moses:

> "And these words, which I command thee this day, shall be in thine heart: And thou shalt teach them diligently unto thy children, and shalt talk of them when thou sittest in thine house, and when thou walkest by the way, and when thou liest down, and when thou risest up" (Deut. 6:6-7).

Each day the aged priest would pray with fervent spirit that God would indeed use their son in the ministry of which the angel had spoken. And that the Messiah would come and bring salvation to Israel.

Zacharias probably knew he would never live to see it himself, but he was sure that it would come to pass. As for the lad, we are told that "the child grew, and waxed strong in spirit, and was in the deserts till the day of his shewing unto Israel" (Luke 1:80).

Chapter 6

The Voice Crying in the Wilderness

"In those days came John the Baptist, preaching in the wilderness of Judaea, And saying, Repent ye: for the kingdom of heaven is at hand. For this is he that was spoken of by the prophet Esaias, saying, The voice of one crying in the wilderness, Prepare ye the way of the Lord, make his paths straight. And the same John, had his raiment of camel's hair, and a leathern girdle about his loins; and his meat was locusts and wild honey. Then went out to him Jerusalem, and all Judaea, and all the region round about Jordan, And were baptized of him in Jordan confessing their sins" (Matt. 3:1-6).

As son of a priest and a direct descendant of Aaron through Elisabeth, John the Baptist would have been in line to become a priest of the temple. The temple life would have brought him honour and security, rich robes and jewels. But he turned his back on all this and renounced his right to the priesthood.

Apparently John was a silent, lonely boy. An old man's only child, he was without brothers or sisters, without playmates or companions. Learning from his parents the work that was before him, he wandered in solitude, brooding and thinking. Assuming that John the Baptist was bereaved early, it is probable that he made it his habit, even as a youth, to retire to the desert for long seasons of meditation and prayer. This does not necessarily mean that he entirely avoided village life. It is probable that he came out on occasions.

While in the wilderness, he learned to subsist on meager food, wild honey taken from trees, and flying locusts, which are cooked as food by the Bedouins of the desert. His appearance was uncouth, his raiment was of camel's hair, and a leather girdle was about his loins.

John was not alone in the great wilderness of Judea. There were the Essenes who had left civilization and lived a life of poverty and self-denial. Josephus the historian in his early life had come under the influence of the Essenes, and he gives us an accurate account concerning their beliefs and practices.

The Essenes were recruited from among people who were tired of the world and its vanities. They evolved an idea of communal life which later was followed for a while by the early church. Some of the Essenes were married, but others practiced celibacy. One of the features of their belief was their strong faith in the coming of the Messiah.

The recent discovery of the Dead Sea Scrolls throws much additional light on the habits of the Essenes. For it was the members of this sect who prepared these documents and hid them in the caves beside the Dead Sea, where they would be rediscovered by a wandering Bedouin in the year 1947. The total number of the Essenes according to Josephus, was about 4,000. While they had disciples in many cities in Palestine, their main community was En-eglaim located south of Jericho. The Essenes set a common table, had a commissary, and when anyone needed clothes, he was permitted to take such as he desired from the common storehouse.

Although the Essenes participated in temple worship, they also conducted their own sacrificial rites. Each day at sunrise, they had special prayers. Grace was said before and after each meal. Above all, the Essenes gave great importance to the studying and copying of the Scriptures.

While we do not have proof that John the Baptist was an Essene, his austere life corresponds to that of this sect. It is likely that he was influenced by them and probably when he began preaching, he drew many of his disciples from among their number.

Thus we see John the Baptist reaching manhood, a hermit of the wilderness, living far from the haunts of men—except for the Essenes—who themselves lived an isolated existence. We may assume that occasionally he would come into their community to study the Scriptures, copies of which they kept available. Then back again he would go into solitude, giving his time to fasting and penitence and to the seeking of self-mastery. All during this time he would meditate on these utterances of the prophets and how God in the old days had spoken to men. He would be especially impressed by their bold denunciation of sin and their clarion calls to repentance.

There was a central thought in the prophecies that must have especially attracted him—the coming of the Kingdom of God. How soon would its King, the Messiah, appear? Some of the old prophecies were hard for John to understand, but gradually certain truths began to stand out before him. Little by little the parts of the prophetic puzzle began to fit together, and he saw that his ministry was to be forerunner to that of the Messiah.

His father and mother, while alive, had surely told him about his mysterious birth, of the coming of the angel who had foretold that "he should go before Him in the spirit and power of Elijah." And then one day, while he waited before the Lord in the wilderness, God spoke directly to him telling him to read the book of Isaiah, for there he would find himself referred to as the "voice crying in the wilderness." (Among the Dead Sea Scrolls has been found a manuscript of the book of Isaiah, identical with what we have today.)

Providentially, at the same time that John was in the wilderness, there was an unusual spiritual awakening going on in Israel. Many people were becoming concerned about the coming Messiah. Indeed their first thought when John the Baptist began preaching was to ask whether he was Elijah, or Christ. "Who art thou? . . . Art thou Elias? . . . Art thou that prophet?" (John 1:19-22).

Then suddenly, as the prophetic clock struck the hour, John the Baptist felt impelled to leave the hills to begin preaching the message of the Kingdom of God. Perhaps on occasion he spoke in cities round about, but mostly his preaching was on the banks of the river Jordan. His stern voice rang out against sin, as he called the nation to repentance and to preparation for the Coming One. When people asked him who he was, he would say, "This is he that was spoken of by the prophet Esaias saying, the voice of one crying in the wilderness, Prepare ye the way of the Lord, make his paths straight" (Luke 3:4).

What kind of person did the people see when John spoke? They saw a fiery young man tanned by wind and sun. They saw a man consumed with a vision, preaching his heart out, calling men to repentance and righteousness, telling them to make crooked ways straight and to get ready for the Christ. "Repent ye," he repeated again and again, "for the kingdom of heaven is at hand."

It is significant that John began his message of repentance near the city of Jericho. During the reign of the wicked Herod, Jericho had gained a position of economic and political importance. Under his son Archelaus, its voluptuous life continued unabated. Its rich lands were farmed out by the Romans, while revenues from them were collected by the publicans. Josephus and others describe the beauty of its gardens and splendor of its palaces and places of entertainment. It was a city of wealth and luxury of an effete society. A hippodrome and amphitheater offered exciting pleasures. Jericho became a resort of the idle rich, a place where they gave themselves to amusement, revelry, and an abandonment to sensual delights.

Only John the Baptist was capable of raising an effective protest against this way of living. The Essenes sick at heart with the luxury and frivolity of the times, could do nothing but withdraw themselves from it. But John sparing none, struck at the heart of the evil. When his preaching created such excitement that the people came out of the cities en masse to hear him, he thundered at them words that made them shake with terror and conviction:

> "Then said he to the multitude that came forth to be baptized of him, O generation of vipers, who hath warned you to flee from the wrath to come? Bring forth therefore fruits worthy of repentance, and begin not to say within yourselves, We have Abraham to our father: for I say unto you, That God is able of these stones to raise up children unto Abraham. And now also the axe is laid unto the root of the tree: every tree therefore which bringeth not forth good fruit is hewn down, and cast into the fire" (Luke 3:7-9).

What words from a man preaching from the sand dunes of a river which flowed into the Dead Sea! Still a more appropriate place for such preaching could hardly be found than in this region associated in memory with the guilty cities of Sodom and Gomorrah. There John stood, a weird figure with flowing locks and piercing eye — clothed in a rough garment, presenting a vivid picture of wrath to come. But instead of frightening off the hearers, the multitudes, even from Jerusalem and the cities of Judea, continued to flock to him. There was greatness in John, a grandeur in his mission, an authority in his message which compelled people to listen.

The consternation caused by his strong words as he presented the issues of life and death, stripped of all pretense, was profound. Under the spell of his powerful preaching, the consciences of people were stung to the quick. What were they to do? John told them to repent. Not only were they to repent, but they were to bring forth fruits meet for repentance. After they had confessed their sins, they were to be baptized as a symbolic act showing that their past sins had been washed away and a new life begun.

John cut through hypocrisy and pretense without compromise.

The Pharisees and Sadducees also came to his baptizing. He was thoroughly familiar with their hyprocrisies, how they devoured "widows' houses and for a pretence make long prayer" (Matt. 23:14). To them he said, "O generation of vipers, who hath warned you to flee from the wrath to come?" John took the picture from the flame of the little fires on which the people cooked their food on the desert. When the fire caught the brushwood, the scorpions and lizards and serpents that had hidden in the shade rushed out.

He warned the self-righteous not to say that "we have Abraham to our father," for God was able to raise up children to Abraham of the very stones that lay by the river bank.

"What must we do?" said the people in the throng who stood listening, and he answered saying, "He that hath two coats, let him impart to him that hath none; and he that hath meat, let him do likewise" (Luke 3:11).

The tax collectors also said, "What shall we do?" And he said unto them, "Exact no more than that which is appointed you."

A company of soldiers approached him saying, "And what shall we do?" And he said unto them, "Do violence to no man, neither accuse any falsely; and be content with your wages."

In no instance did he advise the people to change their livelihood, but to go on in their present work and to be just and honest and to show mercy.

When a man repented and said that he wanted to live a new life, John took him by the hand and plunged him into the waters of the Jordan. This was a symbol of the washing away of sin, and a preparation for the new kingdom.

John brought his sermons to a close with words about the coming Messiah. He explained that he was only the forerunner, that while he baptized in the water, the One who would come after him would baptize in the Holy Ghost and with fire.

> "John answered, saying unto them all, I indeed baptize you with water but one mightier than I cometh, the latchet of whose shoes I am not worthy to unloose: he shall baptize you with the Holy Ghost and with fire: Whose fan is in his hand, and he will thoroughly purge his floor, and will gather the wheat into his garner; but the chaff he will burn with fire unquenchable" (Luke 3:16-17).

Not since the days of Amos and Isaiah and Jeremiah had such a prophet arisen! The fire of his message swept through the land!

Young men from every side flocked to him. Disciples multiplied with such speed that thirty years later they were found in far away places such as Asia Minor and Egypt (Acts 18:24-25; 19:3). Caiaphas and his father Annas became alarmed. It caused Herod the king in his terraced gardens to send messengers to find out what the excitement was all about.

But an event was about to take place in which though John would participate, would completely overshadow his ministry. News of the Baptist's teaching had gone abroad to a hundred villages and cities in Israel. One of these towns was Nazareth. There in that village, a workman in a carpenter shop heard the rumors. He knew what it was all about. He knew by heart the words that John quoted from Isaiah:

> "The voice of him that crieth in the wilderness, Prepare ye the way of the Lord, make straight in the desert a highway for our God. Every valley shall be exalted, and every mountain and hill shall be made low: and the crooked shall be made straight, and the rough places plain" (Isa. 40:3-4).

Jesus, the carpenter, realized that at last His time had come. The hour had struck. He was now to leave the shop in Nazareth forever.

For the last time Jesus gathered up His tools and put them in their place. Then turning to his brothers James, Jude, Joses, and Simeon, then grown men, he handed the workshop over to them. He said farewell to his sisters, and had a long talk with his mother. Then embracing her, he bid her goodbye, and began His journey down the hill that led toward the Plain of Esdraelon. After a while, He turned east, and going through the gap of Jezreel, He went down toward the river Jordan.

Chapter 7

John and Jesus

Did Jesus and John ever meet in their boyhood days? If Zacharias and Elisabeth were still alive and in good health when Joseph and Mary went on their annual visits, it is almost certain that they did. Mary who had been so close to Elisabeth would certainly desire to see her and exchange experiences. Both Mary and Elisabeth would have an intense interest in the welfare of each other's sons, who they knew were destined to fulfill preeminent roles in human destiny.

Since Zacharias and Elisabeth lived not far from Jerusalem, it is highly probable that nothing except the infirmities of old age would keep them away from the Passover. Still, it might be that in the providence of God, Jesus and John were to be kept apart in their youth. At all events, the two did grow up apart, each moving toward his own peculiar mission. Both would accomplish a great work, but one was to soar higher than the other. One would increase, and then decrease. But of the other, "of the increase of his government and peace there shall be no end" (Isa. 9:7).

Having travelled for several days since He left Nazareth, Jesus at last came to the banks of the Jordan. He then moved south along the path to the ford where crowds had gathered to hear John. Straightway he went up to John and asked to be baptized. Although both men were related in the flesh, there was no apparent human recognition on the part of John. Nevertheless, his unerring spiritual insight instantly knew who He was. Immediately the prophet sought to restrain Him saying, "I have need to be baptized of thee, and comest thou to me?" (Matt. 3:14).

Here was no penitent seeking a new and better way of life. The Baptist knew that He was no ordinary candidate. This was none other than the Messiah! As John surveyed the solemn majesty of the Sinless One who stood before him, he irresistably felt the need of the Stranger's work for himself. Moreover, since there were no sins to wash away, baptism for the visitor seemed inappropriate.

But Jesus had subjected himself to all forms of human jurisdiction. He was circumcised according to the Law. He was obedient to the Law. According to the Mosaic Law, those who came in contact with anyone ceremonially unclean were required to submit to the appointed ablution. Jesus had been in touch with men. He was willing to be baptized to fulfill all righteousness. He recognized John's baptism as a symbol of purification. But more than a purification, baptism was an attestation. It was a symbol of the soul's consecration to God's will forever. It was a dedication on Jesus' part to become the Lamb of God slain from the foundation of the world.

So when Jesus said, "Suffer it to be so now: for thus it becometh us to fulfill all righteousness," John baptized Him.

Baptism of the Spirit

As Jesus rose out of the water, a wonderful experience broke upon Him. It was the glorious coming of the Holy Spirit in all fullness.

"And Jesus, when he was baptized, went up straightway out of the water: and, lo, the heavens were opened unto him, and he saw the Spirit of God descending like a dove, and lighting upon him: And lo a voice from heaven, saying, This is my beloved Son, in whom I am well pleased" (Matt. 3:16-17).

Jesus was not the only one who saw the Spirit descending as a dove. John saw the same thing, and thus he knew for certain that Jesus was the One who was to come, the Son of God (John 1:32-34).

In this event at the river Jordan, the triunity of the Godhead was revealed. God the Son being baptized; God the Holy Spirit coming upon Him in the form of a dove; God the Father saying, "This is my beloved Son, in whom I am well pleased."

One other thing should be noted concerning a remark of John's. He said that God had sent him to baptize. Some have assumed that John on his own initiative had adopted baptism as an appropriate rite to symbolize his ministry This is untrue. John baptized because God had specifically called him to do it. It is true that the ancients in some of their rituals used water in a symbolic act of purification. But it never included repentance. John's baptism was a baptism of repentance. It was something altogether new.

Jesus Himself certified that the baptism of John was of heaven

48

when he reasoned with the Pharisees. They demanded to know by what authority He did the things that He was doing. Jesus answered by asking them a question, "The baptism of John, whence was it? from heaven, or of men? (Matt. 21:25).

This put the chief priest and the elders in a tough spot. The inference was that John's baptism was of heaven. But if they so agreed, then Jesus would ask, "Why did ye then not believe him?" On the other hand, if they said "of men," they would have trouble with the people, "for all hold John as a prophet." Therefore, they did not answer.

The Apostle John's Record of John the Baptist

The book of John was written a number of years after the other gospels and was intended to fill in some of the details not covered by the evangelists. The apostle also provides some additional information concerning the ministry of John the Baptist.

He begins with a statement that John was a man sent from God, that he was not the Light, but was sent to bear witness of that Light. The Baptist's knowledge evidently included the fact of the pre-existence of Christ when he said, "He that cometh after me is preferred before me: for he was before me" (John 1:15).

Apparently in the midst of John's ministry at the Jordan, the Jews sent a committee of priests and Levites from Jerusalem to make an investigation of what was happening. They asked John if he were Elijah. Or was he the prophet that Moses spoke of? To each of these questions, John answered in the negative. Then they questioned him further asking him that if he were neither Christ nor Elijah, why then did he baptize?

John's answer was to tell them that he was "a voice crying in the wilderness," warning the people to make straight the way of the Lord, that the Christ, Israel's Messiah, already was standing in their midst.

These events took place at Bethabara on the other side of Jordan. The very next day after John's interview with the Levites and priests, who should appear before him but Jesus Himself. Immediately John cried out and said, "Behold the lamb of God, which taketh away the sin of the world" (John 1:29).

The next day, Jesus appeared again and John said, "Behold the lamb of God" (John 1:36). This time two of John's disciples heard him say this, and they turned and followed Jesus. One was the apostle John and the other was Andrew, Simon's brother. The latter went and found his brother Peter and said to him, "We have found the Messias!" From that day they were no longer the disciples of John, but disciples of Jesus.

The Rise of Christ's Ministry and the Decline of John's

John continued carrying on his ministry the same as he had been doing. He chose a place "in Aenon near to Salim, because there was much water there: and they came, and were baptized" (John 3:23).

More and more of his disciples left him to join with Jesus. But some remained with him, feeling that duty required it, even if the One John had pointed out to them was the Messiah.

News reached them that Jesus (or rather His disciples) was baptizing more disciples than John (John 4:1-2). The followers of John, jealous for their leader's ministry, called this to his attention: "And they came unto John and said unto him, Rabbi, he that was with thee beyond Jordan, to whom thou barest witness, behold, the same baptizeth, and all men come to him" (John 3:26).

It is one of the most natural things in the world for the followers of a noted personality to be jealous of their leader's prestige. It hardly seemed fair to them that after John had labored and given himself without stint to the work of rousing the people of Israel to their need of repentance, and indeed was risking his very life for the cause, that another should come on the scene and reap the benefits. Not only had Jesus taken some of John's disciples, but in fact he had begun baptizing and making even more disciples than John. Despite the Baptist's magnanimous spirit, it did not look altogether right.

But John the Baptist, noble soul, rose fully to the occasion and in a sublime discourse, he not only fully justified what Christ was doing, but made the most definitive statement of the Lord's divinity and Messiahship that had yet been made:

> "John answered and said, A man can receive nothing, except it be given him from heaven. Ye yourselves bear me witness, that I said, I am not the Christ, but that I am sent before him. He that hath the bride is the bridegroom: but the friend of the bridegroom, which standeth and heareth him, rejoiceth greatly because of the bridegroom's voice: this my joy therefore is fulfilled. *He must increase, but I must decrease.* He that cometh from above is above all: he that is

of the earth is earthly, and speaketh of the earth: he that cometh from heaven is above all. And what he hath seen and heard, that he testifieth; and no man receiveth his testimony. He that hath received his testimony hath set to his seal that God is true. For he whom God hath sent speaketh the words of God: for God giveth not the Spirit by measure unto him. The Father loveth the Son, and hath given all things into his hand. He that believeth on the Son hath everlasting life: and he that believeth not the Son shall not see life; but the wrath of God abideth on him" (John 3:27-36).

A careful perusal of these words of John shows that he had a comprehensive understanding of the nature and ministry of Christ.

1. John understood that he was but the forerunner; therefore, he said "He must increase, but I must decrease" (Verse 30).

2. John resisted all efforts to make him take the pre-eminence, and he called his disciples' attention to the fact that all along he had said that, "I am not the Christ, but that I am sent before him" (Verse 28).

3. His office was that of a "friend of the bridegroom" and in that position he could say, "this my joy therefore is fulfilled" (Verse 29), and that in fulfilling that office his purpose in life had been attained.

4. John followed with a statement of Christ's divinity, saying that He was from above, that is, from heaven (Verse 31).

5. He stated that "God giveth not the Spirit by measure unto him."

6. Christ was beloved of the Father and He "hath given all things into his hand."

7. To have faith in Jesus was to have everlasting life; to reject Him was to have the wrath of God abiding on him:

"He that believeth on the Son hath everlasting life: and he that believeth not the Son shall not see life; but the wrath of God abideth on him" (John 3:36).

In this remarkable declaration of faith in the Messiah, John the Baptist rose above all the petty human jealousies and rivalries. He completely renounced personal ambition and reaffirmed his absolute faith in the One whom he had heralded and identified as the Messiah of Israel.

Just what the future course of his ministry held for him, John did not know. He saw it as his duty, however, to continue to carry on as before, until he had received instructions otherwise.

51

Chapter 8

John the Baptist and Herod

"For Herod feared John, knowing that he was a just man and an holy, and observed him; and when he heard him, he did many things, and heard him gladly" (Mark 6:20).

Now it had so happened that King Herod, the tetrarch, had for some time been watching with no little interest the ministry of John the Baptist. There were two contrasting sides to this man Herod, a better nature that responded to John's earnest preaching, and also an evil side which more often than not, controlled the man. When Herod first heard John, he was much impressed. It is likely that he surprised his own court by his favorable attitude toward John. They no doubt had misgivings as to how Herod would react to the straight preaching of the Baptist. Notwithstanding, it seemed that Herod was not offended, but rather took to the Baptist's preaching. We are told that "when he heard him, he did many things, and heard him gladly."

But Herod's religious impressions did not endure long. In the first place, his wife Herodias, whom he had taken from his brother Philip, had no interest whatever in John. If she thought of him at all, it was to consider him only as an uncouth fanatic. But when she learned that John had the temerity to denounce her marriage publicly, she was furious. Herodias demanded that Herod have the Baptist taken into custody at once and executed. He refused her demand. But when he perceived that she was determined to accomplish her evil purpose by one means or another, he forestalled her by having John put in prison.

Failing to achieve her objective immediately, she apparently played on Herod's fears by insinuating that the Baptist was a revolutionary bent on inciting a rebellion. Josephus seems to bear this out saying that Herod "feared lest the great influence John had over the people might put it in his power and inclination to raise a rebellion; for they seemed ready to do anything he should advise."

John's faithfulness in preaching the truth to King Herod shows him at his very highest moment. It is common for preachers to preach straight to ordinary people. But it is also true that some who have been most vehement in denouncing the sins of the lower classes, often change their tone when they come face to face with sinners in high places. Herod probably presumed that John the Baptist would follow this policy and would refrain from saying anything about him of a personal nature. But John was not made that way. All men were alike to him. He bluntly told Herod that it "is not lawful to have thy brother's wife."

The interviews that Herod had with John left him in an unhappy frame of mind. The uncompromising Baptist completely dominated the conversation. There was something about the prophet that stirred Herod's slumbering conscience so that "he did many things." But the evil genius of Herodias held him back. With all the spitefulness of a thoroughly bad woman who was angry because John had dared to denounce her adulterous marriage, she clamoured for his blood.

Torn between these forces, the one good and the other bad, Herod vacillated between two opinions. Nevertheless, he made the imprisonment as easy as possible on John by permitting his disciples free access to their master. In this way, the Baptist was kept in close touch with all that was taking place on the outside.

The black fortress of Machairus where John was imprisoned was not a scene to inspire a man used to freedom as the prophet was. It was located in an area surrounded by fields of black lava, which overlooked the desolate waters of the Dead Sea.

Above the valley, there rose at this point the sheer precipices of black volcanic rock. One of these was surrounded on three sides by deep chasms and on the summit, Herod the Great had reared Machairus Castle. Its vast cellars were stocked with grain and food capable of withstanding a long siege. Its armoury was crammed with swords, javelins, and shields for a great army. Surely with such an impregnable fortress, Herold could defy any who dared to challenge his authority.

Nevertheless, Herod was beset with many fears. Every day rumors came to him of the massing of the Arabs against him. In marrying Herodias, Herod had sent his former Arab bride back to her father Aretas. The proud Arab was furious at this insult to his daughter, and began working might and main to draw the Arab tribes together for a fight to the death against Herod.

Tiberius Caesar was also interested in what was happening. He had his spies out to keep an eye on his vassal-king to find out the reason for all the restlessness on the Arab frontier. Would Tiberius give Herod assistance, or would he, being displeased with his actions, decide to remove him from his throne?

These were the reasons why Herod was fearful. He dared not risk any disturbances in his kingdom, which might arise from John's preaching. And so Herod, stilling the voice of conscience, did nothing. John, therefore, continued to languish in prison. Accustomed as he had been to the freedom of the open spaces, the confinement of the prison must have been peculiarly galling. Still he had hope. Would not Jesus the Messiah soon take a hand in the matter? His prison days could not last much longer.

From time to time John's disciples would come to him to give him the latest word on what was happening on the outside. On each occasion, John would listen eagerly, but each time the report was the same; nothing exciting was happening. It seemed that Jesus was spending most of his time teaching. There was no indication that he was taking any steps to restore the kingdom to Israel, or to help John out of his present predicament.

Then, for the first time, a question arose in John's mind. The days were swiftly passing, and his hopes apparently were not being fulfilled. He had called the people to repentance assuring them that the Kingdom of God was at hand. While John did not ask for a prominent place in that kingdom, He had dared to hope that when the Messiah came, his day of imprisonment would be over, and he could enjoy an honored retirement. But now it seemed as if he were going to remain in prison indefinitely.

It was a dark hour for the great prophet. Shut up in prison, deprived of his liberty, it was hard for him to believe the sun was shining anywhere. At last he felt that he must have a definite word from Jesus on how matters stood. Was Jesus the Messiah after all? He sent two of his disciples to say to him, "Art thou he that should come? or look we for another?" (See Luke 7:19-23).

Christ's answer to John's messengers was an attestation to His own wisdom. He might have sent John a list of proofs of His divinity. He might have reminded the prophet of the supernatural signs that took place at the river Jordan attesting to His Messiahship. He might have called John's attention to the revelations that God had given to John himself concerning Him. But He did no such thing. Instead he asked the messengers to observe His ministry that day, and then to go back and report to John what they had seen. The prophet could judge whether or not it had the marks and qualifications of Messiahship. Let them tell John that the blind receive their sight, the lepers are cleansed, the dead are raised, and the poor have the gospel preached to them. In other words, the needs of humanity were being met, the wounds of the suffering were being bound up, the sorrows of the broken-hearted were being comforted, and the sick and diseased were being made whole.

Here is a lesson for the church today. It is a curious thing to see sects and denominations in labored attempts trying to prove that they and they only represent the true church. One group claims that they have inherited the mantle of Christ through apostolic succession and they alone are God's elect, and all others are usurpers.

Christ showed that the proper way to prove that His ministry was of God was by His works. His credentials were, "Believe me that I am in the Father, and the Father in me: or else believe me for the very works' sake" (John 14:11). Men need to cease arguing over which church is the true church and instead begin to let the world see the signs following their ministry. The disciples of John went back and told him all things that they had seen and heard. We are certain that John was reassured by His answer and was thus strengthened for the final tragic scene in his life, though not a little ashamed that he had questioned.

The martyrdom of John was now at hand. The weak Herod was about to climax his evil career with a crime that must forever blacken his name and relegate him to the lowest hall of infamy. Like his father, Herod the Great, he could be cruel and crafty, but unlike his father, he was weak and vacillating. He was a man in whom many of the worst features of fallen human nature were compounded. Although Herod was not all bad, and there were times when he thought to do better, whatever there was in him for good was destroyed by his marriage to the execrable Herodias. It has been well said that what Jezebel was to Elijah in the Old Testament, Herodias was to the Elijah of the New Testament. But whereas Elijah escaped the deadly hatred of Jezebel, John the Baptist was to be the victim of the murderous Herodias.

Herodias had sound reasons for hating John If Herod followed John's instructions for putting her away, where would she go? She would be a disgraced and ruined woman. Her hatred, therefore, was implacable, and she bided her time in one consuming purpose: to vent her fury upon the hapless head of the faithful prophet.

Chapter 9

The Death of the Prophet

"And when a convenient day was come, that Herod on his birthday made a supper to his lords, high captains, and chief estates of Galilee; And when the daughter of the said Herodias came in, and danced and pleased Herod and them that sat with him, the king said unto the damsel, Ask of me whatsoever thou wilt, and I will give it thee. And he sware unto her, Whatsoever thou shalt ask of me, I will give it thee, unto the half of my kingdom. And she went forth, and said unto her mother, What shall I ask? And she said, The head of John the Baptist. And she came in straightway with haste unto the king, and asked, saying, I will that thou give me by and by in a charger, the head of John the Baptist. And the king was exceeding sorry; yet for his oath's sake, and for their sakes which sat with him, he would not reject her. And immediately the king sent an executioner, and commanded his head to be brought: and he went and beheaded him in the prison. And brought his head in a charger, and gave it to the damsel; and the damsel gave it to her mother. And when his disciples heard of it, they came and took up his corpse, and laid it in a tomb" (Mark 6:21-29).

The birthday of Herod had come and to celebrate the occasion, he invited as guests a number of the lords and captains of his kingdom to his princely castle at Machairus, where John was imprisoned.

Herodias was there with him at the castle, and still smarting under the stinging rebuke of John concerning her marriage, she had laid plans which she hoped would bring to a speedy end the career of the prophet.

While Herod and his nobles and officers were in the midst of their banqueting, Herodias introduced an unexpected diversion. She had a daughter by the name of Salome by her former husband whom she had so shamelessly abandoned. The young princess was sent by her mother to the banquet hall to perform before the wine-inflamed eyes of the revellers a lascivious dance. This lewd performance evoked an enthusiastic applause from the audience. The gratified Herod summoned the girl before him, and oblivious of the fact that he was only a vassal-king and had no right to transfer anything of the kingdom without the Emperor Tiberius' sanction, vowed in the manner of oriental munificence that he would grant her anything she might ask, even to the half of his kingdom.

Salome then went to her mother and sought her advice as to what she should request, and the wicked woman exulting in the success of her stratagem asked for the head of John the Baptist. It might be wondered that a young girl would not shrink from so gruesome a request as this. However, the mother no doubt persuaded her daughter that John the Baptist endangered their own security, that if his advice were followed by Herod, they would be left out in the cold, banished and exiled.

Herod the king was deeply distressed by this unexpected request, and would gladly have withdrawn his promise, were it not for those that were present. With the greatest of reluctance, he made good his ill-considered promise. Soon a soldier appeared at the cell of John the Baptist. Made aware that the vengeance of Herodias had at last succeeded, the great prophet committed Himself into the hands of God and prepared for his fate. Moments later the deed was done; and the head of the prophet was presented to Salome who carried the ghastly trophy to Herodias where she might gloat over it in triumph.

John the Baptist was as Moses, who led the children of Israel into the Promised Land which he himself could only see afar off, or like King David who prepared the materials for the temple which he himself could not build. He had begun a great work which, however, it would not be his to finish. As forerunner of Christ, he accurately described his place in the unfolding order of events when he said, "He must increase, but I must decrease."

The dastardly crime had been committed. The disciples of John at the risk of their own lives, came to the prison and after securing the body of the prophet, sorrowfully buried it. But Herod was far from happy with himself. His conscience now rose up to taunt and punish him. Before long, news came to him of the works of Jesus. When Herod's servants talked to him about it, he said, "This is John the Baptist; he is risen from the dead; and therefore mighty works do show forth themselves in him" (Matt.

14:2). The unhappy king had not many more years to enjoy the position of power that he held, of which he had proved himself so unworthy.

Retribution, ironically enough, was to come from Herodias' brother, Agrippa. Herod had treated the young man as a pauper relative and he had departed, vowing that Herod would pay dearly for his insults. When by a stroke of fortune the adventurer was made king of Palestine by the erratic Emperor Caligula, Herodias filled with envy, gave her husband no rest until they went to Rome to also ask the emperor for a larger kingdom. It was their undoing. Due to Agrippa's treachery, Caligula was made to believe that Herod planned a rebellion. Forthwith Herod and Herodias were banished into exile, there to begin to reap the harvest of evil they had sown. How unhappy the miserable Herodias must have been knowing that their misfortune had been caused by her scapegrace brother and her own insatiable ambition.

Herodias had followed a pattern of evil throughout her life. It was a retribution fully earned that she and her husband spent their last days in poverty and misery.

Chapter 10

Josephus' Record of
John the Baptist and Herod

"For Herod feared John, knowing that he was a just man
and an holy, and observed him; and when he heard him, he
did many things, and heard him gladly" (Mark 6:20).

There is only one other source of knowledge of John the
Baptist apart from the gospels, and that is Josephus. Since on the
whole his records are considered in the most part accurate, we,
therefore, shall include his story of Herod and John the Baptist.

Why the Samaritans Were Excluded from the Temple

"As the Jews were celebrating the Feast of Unleavened
Bread, which we call the Passover, it was customary for the
priests to open the temple gates just after midnight. When,
therefore, those gates were first opened, some of the Samaritans came privately into Jerusalem, and threw about dead
men's bodies in the cloisters; on which account the Jews
afterwards excluded them out of the temple, which they had
not used to do at such festivals; and on other accounts also
they watched the temple more carefully than they had formerly done."

Herod Builds Tiberias

"And now Herod the tetrarch, who was in great favour
with Tiberius, built a city of the same name with him, and
called it Tiberias. He built it in the best part of Galilee, at
the lake of Gennesaret. There are warm baths at a little
distance from it, in a village named Emmaus. Strangers came
and inhabited this city; a great number of the inhabitants
were Galileans also; and many were necessitated by Herod
to come thither out of the country belonging to him, and
were by force compelled to be its inhabitants; some of them
were persons of condition. He also admitted poor people,
such as those that were collected from all parts, to dwell in it.
Nay, some of them were not quite freemen, and these he was
a benefactor to, and made them free in great numbers; but

obliged them not to forsake the city, by building them very good houses at his own expense, and by giving them land also; for he was sensible, that to make this place a habitation was to transgress the ancient Jewish laws, because many sepulchres were to be here taken away in order to make room for the city Tiberias: whereas our law pronounces that such inhabitants are unclean for seven days." (Nu. 19:11)

Josephus' Record of Christ

"Now, there was about this time, Jesus, a wise man, if it be lawful to call him a man, for he was a doer of wonderful works—a teacher of such men as receive the truth with pleasure. He drew over to him both many of the Jews, and many of the Gentiles. He was (the) Christ; and when Pilate at the suggestion of the principal men amongst us, had condemned him to the cross, those that loved him at the first did not forsake him, for he appeared to them alive the third day as the Divine prophets had foretold these and ten thousand other wonderful things concerning him; and the tribe of Christians so named from him, are not extinct at this day."

How Herod Married the Adulterous Herodias

"About this time Aretas (the king of Arabia Petrea) and Herod had a quarrel, on the account following; Herod the tetrarch had married the daughter of Aretas, and had lived with her a great while; but when he was once at Rome, he lodged with Herod, who was his brother indeed, but not by the same mother; for this Herod was the son of the High Priest Simon's daughter. However, he fell in love with Herodias, this last Herod's wife who was the daughter of Aristobulus, their brother and the sister of Agrippa the Great. This man ventured to talk to her about a marriage between them; which address when she admitted, an agreement was made for her to change her habitation, and come to him as soon as he should return from Rome: one article of this marriage also was this, that he should divorce Areta's daughter. So Antipas, when he made this agreement, sailed to Rome; but when he had done there the business he went about, and was returned again, his wife having discovered the agreement he had made with Herodias, and having learned it before he had notice of her knowledge of the whole design, she desired him to send her to Macherus, which is a place on the borders of the dominions of Aretas and Herod, without informing him of any of her intentions. Accordingly, Herod sent her thither, as thinking his wife had not perceived anything. Now she had sent a good while before to Macherus, which was subject to her father, and so all things necessary for her journey were made ready for her by the general of Areta's army, and by that means she soon came to Arabia, under the conduct of the several generals who carried her from one to another successively; and she soon came to her father, and told him of Herod's intentions. So Aretas made this the first occasion of his enmity between him and Herod, who had also some quarrel with him about their limits at the country of Gamalitis. So they raised armies on both sides, and prepared for war, and sent their generals to fight instead of themselves and, when they had joined battle, all Herod's army was destroyed by the treachery of some fugitives, though they were of the tetrarchy of Philip, joined with Areta's army."

The Ministry of John the Baptist

"Now, some of the Jews thought that the destruction of Herod's army came from God, and that very justly, as a punishment of what he did against John, that was called the Baptist; for Herod slew him, who was a good man and commanded the Jews to exercise virtue, both as to righteousness toward one another, and piety towards God, and so to come to baptism; for that the washing (with water) would be acceptable to Him, if they made use of it, not in order to the putting away (or the remission) of some sins (only) but for the purification of the body: supposing still that the soul was thoroughly purified beforehand by righteousness. Now, when (many) others came to crowd about him, for they were greatly moved (or pleased) by hearing his words, Herod, who feared lest the great influence John had over the people might put it into his power and inclination to raise a rebellion (for they seemed ready to do anything he should advise), thought it best by putting him to death, to prevent any mischief he might cause, and not bring himself into difficulties, by sparing a man who might make him repent of it when it should be too late. Accordingly, he was sent a prisoner, out of Herod's suspicious temper, to Macherus, the castle I before mentioned, and was there put to death. Now the Jews had an opinion that the destruction of this army was sent as a punishment upon Herod, and a mark of God's displeasure against him."

Herod's Treatment of Herod Agrippa

"For these reasons he went away from Rome, and sailed to Judea, but in evil circumstances, being dejected with the

61

loss of that money which he once had, and because he had not wherewithal to pay his creditors, who were many in number, and such as gave no room for escaping them. Whereupon, he knew not what to do; so for shame of his present condition, he retired to a certain tower at Malatha, in Idumea, and had thoughts of killing himself: but his wife Cypros perceived his intentions, and tried all sorts of methods to divert him from his taking such a course: so she sent a letter to his sister Herodias, who was now the wife of Herod the tetrarch, and let her know Agrippa's present design, and what necessity it was which drove him thereto, and desired her as a kinswoman of his, to give him her help, and to engage her husband to do the same, since she saw how she alleviated these her husband's troubles all she could, although she had not the like wealth to do it withal. So they sent for him and allotted him Tiberias for his habitation, and appointed him some income of money for his maintenance, and made him a magistrate of that city, by way of honour to him. Yet did not Herod long continue in that resolution of supporting him, though even that support was not sufficient for him; for, as once they were at a feast at Tyre, and in their cups, and reproaches were cast upon one another, Agrippa thought that was not to be borne, while Herod hit him in his teeth with his poverty, and with his owing his necessary food to him. So he went to Flaccus, one that had been consul, and had been a very great friend to him at Rome formerly, and was now president of Syria."

Herod Agrippa Made King of Tiberius

"However, there did not many days pass, ere he sent for him to his house, and had him shaved, and made him change his raiment; after which he put a diadem upon his head, and appointed him to be king of the tetrarchy of Phillip. He also gave him the tetrarchy of Lysanias, and changed his iron chain for a golden one of equal weight. He also sent Marullus to be procurator of Judea.

"Now in the second year of the reign of Caius Caesar, Agrippa desired leave to be given him to sail home, and settle the affairs of his government; and he promised to return again when he had put the rest in order, as it ought to be put. So, upon the emperor's permission, he came into his own country and appeared to them all unexpectedly as a king, and thereby demonstrated to the men that saw him, the power of fortune, when they compared his former poverty with his present happy affluence; so some called him a happy man; and others could not well believe that things were so much changed with him for the better."

How Herodias' Envy Led to Herod's Ruin

"But Herodias, Agrippa's sister, who now lived as wife to that Herod who was tetrarch of Galilee and Perea, took this authority of her brother in an envious manner, particularly when she saw that he had a greater dignity bestowed on him than her husband had; since, when he ran away, he was not able to pay his debts; and now he was come back, it was because he was in a way of dignity and of great fortune. She was therefore grieved and much displeased at so great a mutation of his affairs; and chiefly when she saw him marching among the multitude with the usual ensigns of royal authority, she was not able to conceal how miserable she was, by reason of the envy she had towards him; but she excited her husband, and desired him that he would sail to Rome, to court honours equal to his; for she said that she could not bear to live any longer, while Agrippa, the son of that Aristobulus, who was condemned to die by his father, one that came to her husband in such extreme poverty, that the necessaries of life were forced to be entirely supplied him day by day; and when he fled away from his creditors by sea, he now returned a king.

"But let us go to Rome, and let us spare no pains nor expenses, either of silver or gold, since they cannot be kept for any better use than for the obtaining of a kingdom.

"But for Herod, he opposed her request at this time, out of the love of ease, and having a suspicion of the trouble he should have at Rome; so he tried to instruct her better. But the more she saw him draw back, the more she pressed him to it, and desired him to leave no stone unturned in order to be king: and at last she left not off till she engaged him, whether he would or not, to be of her sentiments, because he could not otherwise avoid her importunity. So he got all things ready, after as sumptuous a manner as he was able, and spared for nothing, and went up to Rome, and took Herodias along with him. But Agrippa, when he was made sensible of their intentions and preparations, he also prepared to go thither; and as soon as he heard they set sail, he sent Fortunatus, one of his freedmen, to Rome, to carry presents to the emperor, and letters against Herod, and to give Caius a particular account of those matters, if he should have any opportunity. This man followed Herod so quick, and had so prosperous a voyage and came so little after Herod, that while Herod was with Caius, he came himself, and delivered his letters; . . . wherein he accused him, that he had been in confederacy with Sejanus, against Tiberius's government, and that he was now confederate with Artabanus, the king of

63

Parthia, in opposition to the government of Caius; as a demonstration of which he alleged that he had armour sufficient for seventy thousand men ready in his armoury. Caius was moved at this information and asked Herod whether what was said about the armour was true; and when he confessed there was such armour there, for he could not deny the same, the truth of it being too notorious, Caius took that to be a sufficient proof of the accusation, that he intended to revolt. So he took away from him his tetrarchy, and gave it by way of addition to Agrippa's kingdom; he also gave Herod's money to Agrippa, and, by way of punishment, awarded him a perpetual banishment, and appointed Lyons, a city of Gaul, to be his place of habitation.

"But when he was informed that Herodias was Agrippa's sister, he made her a present of what money was her own and told her that it was her brother who prevented her being put under the same calamity with her husband, but she made this reply:—'Thou indeed O emperor! actest after a magnificent manner, and as becomest thyself, in what thou offerest me; but the kindness which I have for my husband, hinders me from partaking of the favour of thy gift; for it is not just that I, who have been made a partner in his prosperity, should forsake him in his misfortunes.' Hereupon, Caius was angry at her, and sent her with Herod into banishment, and gave her estate to Agrippa. And thus did God punish Herodias for her envy at her brother, and Herod also for giving ear to the vain discourses of a woman."

Thus the curtain was rung down on the lives of two of the most execrable characters found in the entire Bible.

Chapter 11

The World When Jesus Was Born

There was a remarkable woman in the city of Jerusalem by the name of Anna who lived in the days just before the coming of Christ (Luke 2:36-38). She stayed in the temple, and there she prayed night and day for her people. She had married in the year 91 B.C., but her husband had died seven years later. She with a few others like her had interceded to God continually with fastings for the Messiah to come. During her lifetime she had witnessed the world passing through great political convulsions. Rome was shaken again and again by bloody civil wars. Kingdoms rose and fell in her march to world power.

In 63 B.C. Pompey invaded Palestine and besieged Jerusalem. Anna could well remember the awful day when the Roman army broke down the wall with battering rams. The battle had been fought on the Sabbath when many of the Jews refused to fight. The slaughter that had followed had been terrible. After breaking into the temple, Pompey went into the holy place where only the priest was supposed to go. Eleven years later another general by the name of Crassus entered the temple and plundered it again.

Then came Julius Caesar. Caesar crossed the Rubicon and made himself master of Italy. Pompey, who had profaned the temple, fought desperately; but his army was crushed in the battle of Tapsus. Three years later it was Caesar's turn to meet his fate. He was assassinated in Rome on the Ides of March. More civil war followed, and Mark Antony came to power; but he and his paramour, the ambitious and unscrupulous Cleopatra, lost the battle at Actium. Augustus Caesar was the victor. All these things took place in Anna's life time, but she prayed on. In time her prayers and those of others like her were to change the world more than all the armies of the Caesars.

During Augustus Caesar's reign, a man by the name of Herod had watched these events warily, and he was always careful to throw his lot on the winning side. As a reward for his services, Augustus made him king of Palestine. Ambitious and ruthless, he beautified Jerusalem and authorized the building of a new and magnificent temple. Anna could remember when the great edifice was far enough along that they could worship in it. From that time on, day and night, she was in the temple fasting and praying that the Messiah might come. Then one day she was prompted to go to that part of the temple where the priests were making ready the offerings for the people. The Spirit had witnessed to her that a certain child who was being presented in the temple was none other than the One who would bring redemption to Jerusalem. She went in and gave thanks to God and told the people that it was He who would save Israel. At about the same time a man called Simeon had also received a similar revelation. After seeing the Babe and taking Him in his arms, he blessed God and said, "Lord now lettest thy servant depart in peace, according to thy word; for mine eyes have seen thy salvation" (Luke 2:29-30).

The State of the Nation Israel

With the appearance of the Messiah, an altogether new force came into the world. If we are to understand the impact of this epochal event, we must know something of the state of Israel at that time. Let us, therefore, take a brief view of those conditions existing in the nation within whose borders the life of the Messiah was to be passed.

As one reads through the Bible and passes from the Old Testament to the New, he may think that the people of Israel in Jesus' day were much the same as they were in the earlier period. But during the four centuries that elapsed after the days of Malachi, as great a change took place in Israel as ever occurred in the history of any nation. Even the language of the people had changed, as well as many of its customs and institutions.

Politically, Israel had passed through evil times. In the days of Ezra and Nehemiah the nation had been organized as a sort of theocratic state. One conqueror after another had passed through the land, gradually but surely changing everything. The brave Maccabees had raised the battle cry of freedom, and for a certain period they had thrown off the yoke of the oppressor. However, within a century after the Maccabees the Jewish state had fallen completely under the sway of Rome.

The Herod dynasty which came to power a few years before Christ's birth held the nation under subjection. But shortly after

Jesus was born, the country was divided into three parts. Galilee and Peraea were reigned over by vassal kings. Judea, after suffering the misrule of Archelaus, was ruled by a governor. The iron heel of Rome was now felt everywhere. Roman soldiers were stationed throughout the country. Roman standards waved over the nation's fortresses. Roman tax gatherers were in every town of any size.

The Sanhedrin, which was the supreme religious body of the nation, retained only a shadow of power, they being mere puppets of Rome and subject to the caprice of the imperial rulers. Notwithstanding, religious and national patriotism burned with as fierce a passion as at any time in Israel's history.

Religiously, the people were more orthodox than in any previous period. Prior to the Babylonian captivity, the nation had been cursed with idolatry. But the captivity had cured them of that. The priestly orders had since been reorganized, and the temple services and the annual feasts were regularly observed.

Although Herod the Great had built a new temple in Jerusalem that rivaled that of Solomon, a new institution had sprung up which almost put the temple into the background—the synagogue. There were synagogues wherever the Jews worshipped in Israel, as well as throughout the civilized world. People filled the synagogues on Sabbath days. There they prayed, heard the Scriptures read, and listened to an exhortation of a rabbi. Schools of theology had sprung up in which rabbis were trained and the sacred books interpreted.

With all this activity true religion in Israel, nevertheless, greatly declined. Even during periods of apostasy in ancient Israel, there had arisen great prophets who spoke to the conscience of the nation and maintained a contact with heaven. But for four hundred years no prophet had appeared in Israel.

During this period, there had arisen several new religious sects, one of which was the Pharisees, who became champions of Jewish racial superiority. Characterized by an extreme narrowness and sectarianism, they were committed to legalism and externals. They despised and hated other races and came to look upon themselves as the special favorites of heaven, simply because they were descendants of Abraham.

There were the scribes who were associated with the Pharisees and who devoted their lives to copying the Scriptures. They professed great reverence for the Scriptures, counting every word and letter in them. However, their interpretation of the Old Testament was entirely legalistic, and much that was spiritual and noble in it they passed by.

The rabbis added their mass of opinions to the Scriptures, and in the course of time the scribes came to regard these traditions as being as authoritative as the Holy Writings themselves. The multiplication of interpretations finally reached such proportions as to regulate every detail of human life—personal, domestic, and social. The learning of a scribe consisted of memorizing a vast number of these opinions. It was these traditions that the scribes taught the people in the synagogues which became such a burden that the people were unable to bear it. The spiritual and moral issues were forgotten as rituals and ceremonies multiplied and proliferated.

The Sadducees were the "modernists" of their day. They rejected the authority of tradition, but their protest was merely negative. They had nothing to offer in the place of the traditions. They were a worldly group of men, many of whom were wealthy. They ridiculed the exclusiveness of the Pharisees, but at the same time they had lost all faith in that which had once been the hope of the nation. They did not believe in miracles or angels. The Sadducees were entirely materialistic in their thinking and even denied the resurrection. They can best be described as a worldly sophisticated group with a superficial veneer of religion who reflected Greek culture and enjoyed foreign amusements. They worshipped wealth and worldly position. One special section of the Sadducees flattered Herod; they sought his favor and were for that reason called Herodians.

Outside the pale of these religious parties were the masses of the lower social scale—the publicans, harlots, and sinners—the flotsam and jetsam of humanity for whose souls no man cared. These were the people that God had once called the children of Abraham. These were the people to whom the Messiah had been promised. There were still some among them who cherished the hope of the consolation of Israel. There were those such as Anna and Simeon who prayed night and day with fastings and tears that the Lord might come and redeem His people from their sins.

Chapter 12

Mary, the Mother of Jesus

As the mother of Jesus, Mary stands apart from all other women. No other in history has ever been so honored. Both the angel Gabriel and Mary's cousin Elizabeth said to her, "Blessed art thou among women" (Luke 1:28, 42). To get the true picture of Mary, we must escape the legend and fancy of centuries and confine our attention to what the Scriptures actually say about her.

Mary had a humble beginning. She was an obscure peasant girl living in the village of Nazareth of a poor family, although of the royal Davidic line. She seemed to be of a retiring nature, reticent, and shrinking from public view.

When we first see Mary, she is a young girl having scarcely crossed the threshhold of womanhood. Marriage was early in the East; and a Jewish maiden just betrothed could hardly have been out of her teens. To this young woman, born in a peasant's home, accustomed to the little round of domestic duties and completely ignorant of the world and its ways, came a startling and overwhelming revelation.

> "And in the sixth month the angel Gabriel was sent from God unto a city of Galilee, named Nazareth. To a virgin espoused to a man whose name was Joseph, of the house of David; and the virgin's name was Mary. And the angel came in unto her, and said, Hail, thou that art highly favoured, the Lord is with thee: blessed art thou among women. And when she saw him, she was troubled at his saying, and cast in her mind what manner of salutation this should be" (Luke 1:26-29).

The first thoughts of Mary could only have been those of bewilderment and dismay. First the appearance of the archangel which in itself would have startled anyone—and then his message of expectant virgin motherhood must have astonished her beyond measure. But she managed to recover her composure and bowing in submission to the angel listened to what he had to say:

"And the angel said unto her, Fear not, Mary: for thou hast found favour with God. And, behold, thou shalt conceive in thy womb, and bring forth a son, and shalt call his name Jesus. He shall be great, and shall be called the Son of the Highest: And he shall reign over the house of Jacob for ever; and of his kingdom there shall be no end. Then said Mary unto the angel, How shall this be, seeing I know not a man? And the angel answered and said unto her, The Holy Ghost shall come upon thee, and the power of the Highest shall overshadow thee: therefore also that holy thing which shall be born of thee shall be called the Son of God. And, behold, thy cousin Elisabeth, she hath also conceived a son in her old age: and this is the sixth month with her, who was called barren. For with God nothing shall be impossible. And Mary said, behold the handmaid of the Lord; be it unto me according to thy word. And the angel departed from her" (Luke 1:30-38).

It is the artists rather than the theologians who have tried to convey to us the feeling of the Nazarene maiden at the time of the annunciation. Rosselli shows Mary shrinking from the angel, almost cowering at his feet, but not because she is dazzled by coming into the presence of so great a personage, for she keeps her eyes upon him in a steadfast gaze. The dark eyes have in them the terror of the hunted deer. It is his overwhelming message, not Gabriel, that smites her with alarm.

Mary recovered herself, and in humble self-possession answered the angel with simple dignity. She did not say as Zacharias did, "Whereby shall I know this?", but rather, "How shall this be?" The first statement was one of unbelief, but Mary took the words of the angel for granted. She only inquired how the event would come about.

The angel informed Mary that the conception would occur by the power of the Holy Ghost who would overshadow her, and that the child that was to be born would be called the Son of God. In humble submission the young maiden said, "Behold the handmaid of the Lord; be it unto me according to thy word" (Luke 1:38).

We are then told that "Mary arose in those days, and went into the hill country with haste, unto a city of Juda" (Luke 1:39). What was the reason for this haste in departure? Was her mother a person that she could not confide in? Or was Mary already an orphan? Since the Scriptures are silent on this point, we cannot be sure. But the fact that Mary left "in haste" is significant. It was important to

70

her that she should have time to ponder the meaning of her strange experience and adjust herself to it. It would seem that there was no one in Nazareth in whom she could fully confide. Moreover, women have a way of quickly discovering when another woman is with child. Although betrothed to Joseph, she did not feel that the subject was one that she could tell him about at that particular time.

The angel Gabriel had mentioned that her cousin Elisabeth had "conceived a son in her old age." Mary apparently felt that a visit to Elisabeth's home at that time would provide her with wisdom and counsel for the events that were to come. She made the trip southward to the home which was located in the hill country not far from Jerusalem.

The warm welcome she received at the household of Elisabeth and Zacharias was reassuring. Even as Mary entered the house and gave her salutation, her cousin was filled with the Holy Ghost. Elisabeth began to prophesy, speaking of Mary as the "mother of my Lord."

> "And she spake out with a loud voice, and said, Blessed art thou among women, and blessed is the fruit of thy womb. And whence is this to me that the mother of my Lord should come to me? For lo, as soon as the voice of thy salutation sounded in mine ears, the babe leaped in my womb for joy. And blessed is she that believed; for there shall be a performance of those things which were told her from the Lord" (Luke 1:42-45).

The words of Elisabeth spoken under the Holy Spirit were just the encouragement that Mary needed at the time. Following Elisabeth's prophecy, Mary spoke in the Spirit the beautiful Magnificat:

> "And Mary said, My soul doth magnify the Lord. And my Spirit hath rejoiced in God my Saviour. For he hath regarded the low estate of his handmaiden: for, behold, from henceforth all generations shall call me blessed. For he that is mighty hath done to me great things; and holy is his name. And his mercy is on them that fear him from generation to generation. He hath shewed strength with his arm; he hath scattered the proud in the imagination of their hearts. He hath put down the mighty from their seats, and exalted them of low degree. He hath filled the hungry with good things; and the rich he hath sent empty away. He hath holpen his servant Israel, in remembrance of his mercy; As he spake to our fathers, to Abraham, and to his seed for ever" (Luke 1:46-55).

These Scriptures are Mary's hymn of praise to God, and they showed that apart from being the mother of the Lord, Mary was a prophetess in her own right. This jubilant song pouring from her lips revealed Mary's wonderful breadth of spiritual experience. Her words remind us of the song of Hannah, but as the mother of the Lord her song reaches even more sublime heights.

Mary found in Elisabeth a true mother in Israel. They spent many a holy hour together, discussing the tremendous significance of the events that had come into their lives. Zacharias sat near them with sealed lips, mute evidence of the goodness and severity of God. (Luke 1:18-23). From time to time he would send them a note from his writing table, informing them of things he had discovered from the prophecies and the Messianic psalms.

The three happy months spent in Elisabeth's home came to an end all too soon. Perhaps Mary remained until Elisabeth's child was born, for the three months added to the six would have completed Elisabeth's time. If so, Mary left immediately after that event and returned to Nazareth.

Mary, although a pure virgin, was soon to face the problem that a young unmarried girl does when she becomes pregnant. She could not keep the news from others for long. With natural delicacy and reserve, she hesitated to say anything. Indeed how could Mary reveal to a suspicious world, or even to Joseph, an experience that must have seemed utterly impossible?

And then came that awful day when Joseph became aware of her condition, and though he may have said nothing, she knew he doubted her. Or she may have told him her story, but how could he believe it? Despite her great faith, that night must have been dark indeed with only the light of her knowledge that she was pure and innocent of any wrong.

It must have been a black night also for Joseph. There is evidence that he was much older than Mary, and she was his first real love. His discovery could only have left him crushed and bewildered. Yet, despite his grief, his thoughts were on how he could help the poor girl in the hour of shame that seemed to be upon her.

> "Then Joseph her husband, being a just man, and not willing to make her a publick example, was minded to put her away privily" (Matt. 1:19).

To Joseph there seemed only one thing left to do—to make some arrangement whereby Mary could be sent away from the village to have her baby and thus be spared the humiliation and embarrassment of bearing the child in Nazareth. But God had not forgotten Mary, the holy virgin, for the child she was to bear was the very Son of God. At that fateful moment, the angel of the Lord appeared to Joseph in a dream and said, "Joseph, thou son of David, fear not to take unto thee Mary thy wife: for that which is conceived in her is of the Holy Ghost. And she shall bring forth a son, and thou shalt call his name Jesus: for he shall save his people from their sins" (Matt. 1:20-21).

When dawn came, what a morning it must have been for both Joseph and Mary! Joseph was at her door, his face beaming with joy and reassurance to tell her he knew all, and that all was well.

There are some who have exalted Mary above her position. Others have reckoned her only as common and ordinary. Neither view is correct. Mary was a person not lacking in energy and strong character. She possessed the gifts and graces that make for womanly greatness. Because some have exalted her beyond her place, we must not allow this to keep us from granting her full due. The record of her in the Scriptures, even though relatively brief, shows her to be a woman of unusual spiritual depth and piety. The fact that she conducted herself well in the presence of the angel showed her to be a person of courage and nobility of spirit.

Faith was a great element in Mary's character. If it is hard for some to believe in the Incarnation, it would have been far more difficult for her. Yet she believed it with all that was within her. Jesus Himself said that no mighty work could be done where there was unbelief (Mark 6:5-6). Therefore, her faith must have had a part in the great miracle of the Incarnation. It was the greatest of all miracles performed in the history of the human race. So it was for her as Elisabeth had said, "Blessed is she that believed: for there shall be a performance of those things which were told her from the Lord" (Luke 1:45).

Mary's humility is another of her striking virtues which manifested itself, not so much in self-depreciation, as in an utter forgetfulness of self. She did not seem to think of herself as either worthy or unworthy. Her soul was lifted away from herself, and she thought of God only.

Standing at the forefront of Mary's greatness was her purity as is revealed in the Magnificat. There is no confession, but a wonderful joy. Only the pure heart rejoices when God is near.

Mary's life was filled with mysteries that were beyond her. Yet she never ceased to ponder them as she waited their unfolding. When possible she was nearby to watch the developments in her son's ministry. She witnessed the soul-piercing scenes of the crucifixion. She shared in the first revelations on the resurrection morn.

She waited with the 120 in the Upper Room. She with the others received the blessed baptism of the Spirit.

There was a patience in Mary in her long years of waiting. After the birth of her child, there were no more angel choirs, strange stars, or miraculous escapes. No pilgrims came to Nazareth to search Him out; no kings came to do Him obeisance. Silence fell on the scene as thirty years came and went. What were Mary's thoughts in those days? Through all those years she pondered in her heart the things that the angel had spoken. She never doubted. And when the day of His ministry began, she turned to those who were serving and said, "Whatsoever he saith unto you, do it."

Chapter 13

The Birth of Jesus

Mary, according to the genealogy given in Luke, was the daughter of a man by the name of Heli. The family was poor, though we may assume that their standard of living was not much different from that of their neighbors. They came from a devout stock. Mary and Elisabeth were cousins, although we do not know that they were first cousins. It is hardly possible because of the differences in their ages that their fathers were brothers.

On each Sabbath day Mary went with her parents to the synagogue to listen to the Scriptures. She little realized at the time that certain of those Scriptures referred to her personally (Isa. 7:14). She did not quickly forget what she had heard (Luke 2:51). We do not have a record of what kind of education Mary received, though probably it was little. Nevertheless, her song in Luke 1:46-55 indicates that she was by no means unlearned.

What kind of man was Joseph? As far as the record shows, he was only a humble carpenter, probably much older than Mary, but the Scriptures describe him as a "just man." Like his ancestor Joseph, after whom he was named, he too seemed to have a special gift of dreams. Several times the revelations he received in dreams gave him information of the utmost importance.

Where did Mary first meet Joseph? Was it at the spring in Nazareth where she went to draw water? Or did she first meet him at the carpenter's shop? No doubt she admired his skill as a craftsman, and on that day her parents told her that Joseph had asked for her hand, her face probably lit up with joy. We can see Joseph bringing some gift which he had fashioned in the carpenter's shop. From that time Mary began making simple preparations for her wedding. Then began the strange events that were to change her life completely—events that almost tore her heart apart, but which in the providence of God had a happy ending.

In the city of Rome on the great throne sat Augustus Caesar, the ruler of an empire that was more vast than any the world had ever known. It might be supposed that this powerful figure was complacent in his victory in the great power struggle for control of the world. But actually he was puzzling over the problem of financing his unwieldy kingdom. The cost of maintaining the army and his far-flung administration required great sums of money. Many provinces were paying tribute, but Palestine was among those that were not. The emperor decided that each country must share its part of the burden. So it was that Augustus set the wheels in motion for carrying out his plan of universal taxation. This decree went down from one official to another until eventually the news reached the ears of Joseph and Mary. They realized that they immediately would have to go to the city of their ancestors, despite the fact that Mary was far advanced in pregnancy.

It was a familiar road, for Mary had returned on the route just six months before from her visit to Elisabeth. She was seated on the back of a donkey; and with Joseph leading, they began their trip down the road that led to the plain of Esdraelon. Not all the people on the route were friendly. While passing through Samaria, no hospitality was offered them. At Shechem they saw Ebal and Gerizim, the mountains of curse and blessing where the Samaritans worshipped. Perhaps they stopped and refreshed themselves at the well of Sychar, the one that Jacob dug. Then they went on, passing Shiloh, Gibeon, and Bethel. At last as they drew near Jerusalem, the magnificent temple burst into view. Though it was still in the process of building, the outer courts shone with a dazzling whiteness.

It was an unforgettable experience to visit Jerusalem, but they were not yet at their destination. Bethlehem was still five miles away. Within an hour after leaving the outskirts of Jerusalem, they were in view of the city. In another half hour, they were passing the tomb of Rachel, and then finally they entered the city. They had been frugally saving their money, so that they could hire a room at the inn. But alas, they found that many visitors were there ahead of them for the same purpose. Every spare room was taken. Joseph, almost in despair, at last found a manger which the innkeeper permitted them to use. The best that Mary could have was a rug and a little covering thrown over the straw. And thus the humble couple who would some day be the world's most famous family laid down to rest.

Some time in the night Joseph may have awakened. If so, he probably saw a star shining more brightly than all the rest, and it seemed to be hanging over the stable. His rest was soon to be broken again. Mary was not sleeping. She was in severe pain. The pangs of childbirth were upon her. What pitiful circumstances these were in which a mother should have to give birth to a child! Bravely Mary faced the situation, and despite all the discomforts the child was brought safely to birth with Joseph's poor help. Who could believe that in that humble surrounding the greatest event of history had just taken place!

Was Christ Born in the Winter?

The traditional date of the birth of Christ is December 25, but of course the Bible does not say this and the evidence is against its being at this time. Jerusalem and Bethlehem are at an altitude of 2500 feet. Snow often falls in this area. The winters were severe enough for Christ to have warned the Jews who were to flee the Romans when they surrounded Jerusalem to pray "that your flight be not in winter" (Matt. 24:15-22). The weather at that time of the year would have been very severe for a prospective mother to travel the long distance from Nazareth to Bethlehem. The child Jesus was born in an open manger, and it must be noted that the shepherds were on their own volition out in an open field. It was not customary for shepherds to be out with flocks at night in the winter. Historical evidence indicates that Christ was born in October.

The Visit of the Angels

"And there were in the same country shepherds abiding in the field, keeping watch over their flock by night. And, lo, the angel of the Lord came upon them, and the glory of the Lord shone round about them: and they were sore afraid. And the angel said unto them, Fear not: for, behold, I bring you good tidings of great joy, which shall be to all people. For unto you is born this day in the city of David a Saviour, which is Christ the Lord. And this shall be a sign unto you; ye shall find the babe wrapped in swaddling clothes, lying in a manger. And suddenly there was with the angel a multitude of the heavenly host praising God, and saying, Glory to God in the highest, and on earth peace, good will toward men" (Luke 2:8-14).

The visit of the angels to the humble shepherds was an interesting event, but it may be asked, Why did the angels not appear instead to the priests at Jerusalem who sat in Moses' seat? The priests indeed were informed of the event, but they were not interested enough to make the journey of five miles to Bethlehem to find out for themselves (Matt. 2:4-5). Why did the angels appear to the shepherds? Undoubtedly the shepherds, like Simeon, were among those who were watching for the consolation of Israel. In the quietness of their occupation they had time to meditate and prepare their hearts for

77

the great event. Nevertheless, the effect of the sudden heavenly visitation was to make them "sore afraid."

After the angels had gone back to heaven, "the shepherds said one to another, Let us now go even unto Bethlehem, and see this thing which is come to pass, which the Lord hath made known unto us. And they came with haste, and found Mary, and Joseph, and the babe lying in a manger" (Luke 2:15-16).

They of course told the remarkable story of the visitation to Mary and Joseph. We are sure for many a day to come they were to repeat the story to any and all who would care to listen.

The Poverty of Christ

The Scriptures tell us that He who was rich became poor that we might through His poverty become rich. By our standards today the family of Jesus was poor indeed, although probably not much poorer than the average family of Nazareth.

One incident occurred in the temple which gives us a glimpse of Joseph's financial condition. When it came time for the circumcision of the child, the Law required that the parents bring a lamb and offer it for an atonement. But the Scriptures taking due notice of the exigencies of the poor added, "And if she is not able to bring a lamb, then she shall bring two turtles, or two young pigeons" (Lev. 12:6-8). The poverty of the family of Jesus is thus evident. The devoted couple would have certainly brought a lamb had their means permitted. The most they could afford was two turtledoves.

By reason of their limited finances they could have scarcely made their way to Egypt to escape from Herod. Only because in the providence of God the Wise Men had brought gifts—gold, frankincense, and myrrh, were they able to make the trip.

The Visit of the Wise Men

"When they heard the king, they departed; and, lo, the star which they saw in the east, went before them, till it came and stood over where the young child was. When they saw the star, they rejoiced with exceeding great joy" (Matt. 2:9-10).

The Wise Men and the Star of the East are inseparably associated with the birth of Christ. What was this Star of Bethlehem? The verses above indicate that the Wise Men saw the star at different times—first in their homeland in the East and then later after they left Jerusalem on they way to Bethlehem. Since Christ was born in 4 B.C., the Wise Men saw the star at least two years earlier according to Verse 16. This would mean that the date that they first saw it was 6 B.C., or perhaps late 7 B.C.

Was this star a comet with its bright tail sweeping across the sky? Comets have always made a deep impression upon men's minds. They were believed to portend special events. It would not be surprising that men of that day would consider an especially brilliant comet as presaging some extraordinary event. Comets, however, do not linger long in the sky. Drawn by the powerful attraction of the sun, a comet revolves around that massive body, and then after gathering great momentum, it swings out into space. It would not have reappeared two years later.

History records a brilliant comet in 44 B.C., just before the Ides of March when Caesar was assassinated. Another appeared in 66 A.D., just before the Christians fled to Pella to escape the siege of the city of Jerusalem by the Romans. Halley's comet appeared in 12 B.C. and is described in great detail by Chinese astronomers. This, however, is too early to be associated with the birth of Christ in 4 B.C.

Astronomers inform us, however, that there was a conjunction of planets at about this time. Jupiter, Saturn, and Venus came so close together in the year 7 B.C. that "they appeared as one." But such a planetary configuration lasts only a few days. Matthew 2:9 declares that "the star, which they saw in the east, went before them, till it came and stood over where the young child was." This wording would indicate that the star actually appeared to change its position as they travelled from Jerusalem to Bethlehem, much as the Pillar of Cloud and the Pillar of Fire arose from the tabernacle and went before the children of Israel.

And who were the Wise Men, or Magi, as they are sometimes called? They were a priestly class from a region of Persia, who specialized in interpreting dreams and supernatural visitations. It is hardly possible that they were Jews since they did not seem to be familiar with the Old Testament Scriptures. When they reached Jerusalem, they went to the temple priests to inquire where Christ the King was to be born. The Wise Men were typical of the great multitude of Gentiles who were to believe on Him.

It is strange that the Wise Men of the East should travel all the way to Bethlehem to see the newborn babe, while the scribes and chief priests in Jerusalem only five miles away who knew where He was to be born, did not bother to investigate the report of His birth.

There was one person, however, who took their quest seriously. This was none other than Herod the king. Slowly dying in his bed, he hoped to perpetuate his dynasty and would stop at no cruelty to accomplish his purpose. To maintain his grip over the country, Herod had spies stationed everywhere to bring him news of anything that might jeopardize his interests. When word of the Magi's arrival came to him, he sent for the scribes and the priests to learn where Christ was to be born.

> "And they said unto him, In Bethlehem of Judea: for thus it is written by the prophet, And thou Bethlehem, in the land of Judea, art not the least among the Princes of Judea: for out of thee shall come a Governor, that shall rule my people Israel" (Matt. 2:5-6).

Having obtained this information, he called for the Wise Men. He told them he knew where the King of the Jews was to be born. They were to go to Bethlehem and search out diligently where the child was. Then craftily he asked them to return and give him the information as to where the child was so that he might also worship Him.

> "Then Herod, when he had privily called the wise men, enquired of them diligently what time the star appeared. And he sent them to Bethlehem, and said, Go and search diligently for the young child; and when ye have found him, bring me word again, that I may come and worship him also" (Matt. 2:7-8).

The Magi turned and left the palace of Herod. They took their gifts they had brought from Persia and mounted their beasts for the short trip from Jerusalem to Bethlehem. The Star they had seen in the East went before them and led them directly to the place where the child was.

By this time Joseph had found a house. Mary was no longer occupying a stable. And when the Wise Men came in, they fell down on the floor and worshipped the Babe. Then they took their gifts of gold, frankincense, and myrrh and laid them at His feet.

But as they were ready to return to Jerusalem, one of them was visited by a dream which warned them not to return to Herod, and they departed down the valley east of Bethlehem and returned to their country another way.

Naturally the Wise Men conveyed knowledge of their warning to Joseph and Mary. While Joseph was pondering this strange matter, he too had a dream. In the vision he received a warning to take the child and His mother and flee at once from Herod and go down to Egypt. There was no time to be lost. Herod had a fortress palace close to Bethlehem, and at any hour the word might go out to slay the child. Joseph knew enough about Herod that as soon as he discovered that he had been mocked by the Wise Men, his fury would know no bounds.

In the dead of night Joseph sat Mary and the child upon the back of the animal and they began the trek south to Egypt. By morning light they would not be far from the valley of Elah where Mary's ancestor David once fought the giant Goliath. It was not easy for Mary to hold the child in her arms hour after hour all through the night, but it had to be done. Every mile brought them closer to safety. By the time they reached Beersheba, they had put danger well behind them.

Meanwhile in Jerusalem, Herod waited impatiently for the return of the Wise Men. At last a messenger brought him the disconcerting news that the Wise Men had defied his command and returned to their country by another way. Filled with rage, Herod determined on a fiendish act which was in keeping with his cruel spirit. His officers were to go to Bethlehem and slay all the children in that part of the country from two years old and under. Then was fulfilled the prophecy of Jeremiah:

> "In Rama was there a voice heard, lamentation, and weeping, and great mourning, Rachel weeping for her children, and would not be comforted, because they are not" (Matt. 2:18).

This is a remarkable prophecy, and it refers to Rachel, Jacob's wife. In her earlier years of marriage she had been barren and had once cried out to Jacob, "Give me children, or else I die" (Gen. 30:1). At length her prayer to God was heard, and she gave birth to Joseph and later to Benjamin. Rachel's passionate love for children seemed to project itself down the ages to her descendants, and so it is said that the cry of mourning over the slaughter of the innocents is spoken of as "Rachel weeping for her children, and could not be comforted because they were not."

It was one of the last acts of the wicked Herod. To the very end of his life, the fiendish cruelty of his nature could not be satisfied. He ordered fires to be kindled in Jerusalem, and forty-two students were consigned to the flames. About the same time he wrote a letter to his son Antipas, asking him to come home. When the boy arrived, Herod made terrible accusations against him. After putting him in prison, he sent word for him to be put to death. As Herod's death drew near, spies came and told him that the people were rejoicing. Furious over this, he gave a command that when he died soldiers were to kill all who rejoiced at his death—a command that was never carried out. The agonies of the dying king were beyond description. Finally when he died, the people breathed a sigh of relief.

Archelaus Reigns, and Joseph and
Mary Return to Israel

"But when Herod was dead, behold, an angel of the Lord appeared in a dream to Joseph in Egypt, Saying, Arise, and take the young child and his mother, and go into the land of Israel: for they are dead which sought the young child's life. And he arose, and took the young child and his mother, and came into the land of Israel. But when he heard that Archelaus did reign in Judea in the room of his father Herod, he was afraid to go thither: notwithstanding, being warned of God in a dream, he turned aside into the parts of Galilee" (Matt. 2:19-22).

Herod, altogether, had made four wills. At his death, Archelaus was chosen as king of Judea, while the other sons, Herod Antipas and the half-brother Philip, inherited other provinces of the kingdom. All this, of course, had to be ratified by Emperor Augustus. But even before Archelaus could get away to Rome, violent demonstrations broke out in Jerusalem with the rioters demanding special concessions from Archelaus. The ringleaders of the mob were captured and burned alive.

Joseph and Mary of course did not intend to remain in Egypt. As soon as the angel of the Lord appeared to him in a dream, assuring him that Herod was dead, he made the decision to return.

When the family had crossed the desert and began to climb the hills of Judea, Joseph received word of further events occurring in Judea. He heard the terrible news that thousands of pilgrims who had gone to the city had been massacred by the soldiers.

It did not appear safe to pass through the land. When he learned that Archelaus was king over Judea, he decided to follow the road that went up the lowlands and around Mt. Carmel. From there he crossed the Plain of Esdraelon to Nazareth where their former home had been.

Chapter 14

The Boy Jesus

The city of Nazareth was to be the home of Jesus until He was thirty years of age. Writers of the life of Christ generally deplore the fact that so little is recorded about His youthful days. There was, however, a reason for this. The early life of Jesus was divinely intended to be little different from that of any other boy in Israel. Although it is probable that people recognized that Jesus was an unusual child, it was certainly furthest from their thoughts that the youth who dwelt in their midst was the very Son of God, whose impact on the world would be greater than any other person who ever lived.

The inhabitants of Nazareth may have noticed that although all children at times are given to misbehaving, yet they could never re-call Jesus acting improperly. Those who were especially close to the family probably observed His devotion to Mary and Joseph. Others perhaps marked His unusual interest in the Scriptures. Yet, He made mistakes that any boy makes, such as missing the party when they began the trip back to Nazareth. It seems probable that Jesus grew up in Nazareth without attracting any extraordinary attention.

The Apocryphal Gospels

Although the gospels have little to say about the boyhood of Jesus, some of the apocryphal New Testament gospels profess to push back the curtain of mystery that shrouds this period of His life. It is natural that where God is silent, the curiosity of man should attempt to fill in the blanks. In the days of Paul there were evidently those who sought to delve into the early life of Jesus. The apostle cautioned against too much zeal in this saying, "Yet, though we have known Christ after the flesh, yet now henceforth we know him no more" (II Cor. 5:16). It was His ministry and message that were significant, not His boyhood days.

The apocryphal gospel of Thomas records a number of miracles that were supposed to have transpired during Jesus' childhood. These are nothing but fabrications, and poor ones at that. Not a single historian considers them anything but fiction. These fables only show how unequal the imagination of man is to such a task. The stories are crude caricatures in comparison to the majestic narratives of the four gospels. They make Jesus a worker of frivolous and useless marvels. According to these apocryphal stories, Jesus made birds of clay and caused them to fly. He was supposed to have raised a boy from the dead to prove he was innocent of a crime. He changed playmates into animals. In short, the apocryphal gospels are compilations of mere chaff and some of the tales are not only incredible but tinge on the blasphemous.

Such miserable concoctions of fantasy warn us to stay clear of trying to peer too far into the hallowed enclosure of His early life. It was the purpose of God that Jesus should grow up quietly in an obscure village and draw to Himself no special attention. We are told that He grew in wisdom and stature and in favor with God and man, thus passing through all the stages of normal development.

As for the miracles which were supposed to have been performed during His boyhood, the gospel of John specifically tells us that the first miracle of Christ was that of turning the water into wine (John 2:11).

Childhood Experiences

Despite the lack of specific information in the Scriptural account, we can reconstruct in general outline the scenes of Christ's boyhood from our historical knowledge of the times.

It is probable that when Joseph and Mary departed from their home in Nazareth to go to Bethlehem, they left their house in the hands of relatives, possibly in the care of Mary's father. Perhaps they thought at the time that they might establish their home in Bethlehem where the child as He grew would have special educational opportunities afforded those who lived near Jerusalem. Subsequent developments which involved Herod's murderous decree to slay the children of Bethlehem and the oppression of the people by Archelaus changed any such plans if they existed. The decision was made to go back to their quiet home in Nazareth after they learned of Herod's death.

The family home, if it was similar to others in the city, was made of stone. It probably had a flat roof supported by rough hewn beams. Steps outside led to the roof which served as additional space for the family.

When Joseph and Mary began housekeeping in Nazareth, Jesus was probably only a toddling child, just old enough to accompany

His mother when she went to the village spring for water. Each day Mary went to this fountain several times. She filled her jar with water, and then balancing it on her head, she returned home.

Outside the house there probably was a stone mill. One millstone revolved above another. Grain was poured in a hole in the center of the top stone. As the stone turned, the kernels were crushed into flour. The flour was gathered into a vessel, mixed with water and a little leaven until it became dough. The mixture was set aside until the bread had risen.

In another part of the courtyard was a large oven made of baked mud and clay. Into the oven Mary thrust a layer of grass, shrubs, and small sticks. When the fuel was set afire and consumed, the gray ash which was left was raked away. Then Mary took the dough, patted it into the shape of pancakes and laid the cakes on the hot stones at the bottom of the oven. A lid was placed over the oven. When the bread was baked, it was eaten with cheese, olives, dates, and honey — commodities common in that country.

By our standards today, the family of Jesus was poor indeed. However, Joseph and Mary were probably neither richer nor poorer than the average family of the village.

As Jesus grew up in Nazareth, He was alert to all that was happening around Him. He watched the children as they played in the market place (Luke 7:32). He observed the corn merchant and the customers as they haggled over prices. He noticed the flowers, the trees, the sparrow that fell to the ground, and the foxes in their dens. He heard the shepherd call the sheep by their names (John 10:3). He learned the lore of the weather (Matt. 16:2-3). He watched the vine dresser as he pruned the branches of the vine, so that it would bear more fruit (John 15:1-2). All these things He saw, remembered, and used as illustrations when He began His ministry of teaching.

The Home of Jesus

The home of Jesus was a godly one. Joseph was a righteous and just man, although probably considered a peasant by the upper classes. He performed his tasks faithfully in the carpenter's shop and acquitted himself as an honest son of toil, supporting his large family to the best of his ability. As Jesus and each of His brothers grew older, they undoubtedly joined Joseph in the shop to help in the task of providing for the family.

As we have seen Mary was a superior person. She was certainly a woman of faith as was shown by her beautiful response

85

to the angel Gabriel (Luke 1:38). She showed a knowledge of the Scriptures, possessed poetic genius, yet was an exquisitely humble woman. She was keenly conscious of the great and utterly unexpected honor that had been conferred upon her as mother of the Messiah.

Despite her large family, she no doubt took special time to teach the children all she knew about spiritual things. The Great Secret she kept in her heart spurred her to do everything possible for her Firstborn. In return we know He was devoted to her, and even during the last hours of His life He was thinking of her welfare and making provision for her. While He suffered on the cross, He told John His disciple that he was to be a son to her. Outside of her home, however, Mary was reticent and said little about these matters. We are told that "His mother kept all these sayings within her heart" (Luke 2:51).

The Synagogue School

About the age of eight Jesus was sent to the teacher of the synagogue who taught the children from the sacred rolls of the Scriptures. The teacher would write Aramaic letters in the sand with a pointed stick, and the students sitting down cross-legged repeated together the letters that were spelled out. The teacher also read to the boys stories of the Bible characters, such as Abraham, Isaac, Jacob, and Joseph. Jesus listened to these stories with rapt attention. He let nothing that was read from the Scriptures fall to the ground.

On the day before the Sabbath, Joseph put away his saw, his chisel, and his hammer, and as night came on, the men of the village went to the synagogue. On the following morning, the boys and girls attended special services. The ruler of the synagogue usually appointed someone to read the Scriptures. Anyone who could read was qualified to take his turn at this task. The cylinder that contained the sacred scroll was brought out and unrolled. Then the one appointed chose a certain portion of the Scriptures to read to the congregation.

When the Scriptures were read Jesus took the greatest interest. While other boys might have thought that the sessions were sometimes dull, Jesus eagerly gave attention to them. It was during these hidden years at Nazareth that His mind became richly endowed with the knowledge of the Old Testament.

It appears from Luke 4:16 that the reading ability of Jesus as He became older was so superior that it fell to Him on numerous occasions to perform his task. "And as his custom was, he went into the synagogue on the Sabbath day and stood up for to read."

The Feasts of Israel

There was another activity in which Jesus participated that must have had an unusual interest for Him — the annual feasts of Israel.

The Jews of this period were very faithful in the observance of these feasts. One of these was the Feast of the Dedication of the Temple, or the Feast of Lights. This occurred during the winter time. People lit their lamps, and the young men marched down the streets with blazing torches. On the following day they went to the synagogue and sang joyful songs. The people recounted the stirring stories of the great hero, Judas Maccabeus, who vanquished Israel's enemies and purified the temple. The temple once had been defiled by the wicked Syrian tyrant Antiochus Epiphanes, and the Jews celebrated its purification by this eight-day Feast of Dedication.

There were other festivals, including the Feast of Purim, in which they remembered how Queen Esther overthrew the wicked Haman who plotted to destroy the Jews from the face of the earth. During this feast, the story of Esther was read from a scroll in the synagogue.

Then of course, there was the greatest of all feasts, the Passover. This feast was held each year at about the same time as our Easter. Many pilgrims went to Jerusalem to celebrate this notable event. Those who remained home ate the Passover feast in their houses with unleavened bread. Following the Passover was the feast of Pentecost, a little over a month later. Finally in the fall was the Feast of Booths or Tabernacles. People left their houses and camped out in the open under the branches of trees. This was something a small boy would relish. And so these various feasts in which the people celebrated the goodness of God were important events in the lives of the people of Israel. It was a time when parents would teach their children about God and about His peculiar dealings with their nation. We may be sure that the Boy Jesus gave all these occasions His most thoughtful attention. Each of these feasts had a meaning to Him, and He let nothing get past Him.

The Rebellion of Judas

When Jesus was about ten years of age, news reached Nazareth that Archelaus had been removed by Augustus as king of Judea. Archelaus had apparently inherited the worst traits of his father Herod, and at the same time he lacked his political finesse. Having little interest in trying to help the impoverished subjects of his kingdom, Archelaus embarked on an extravagant building program. He divorced his wife and married his brother's spouse. At last the news of his misgovernment reached the ears of the Emperor Augustus. The emperor had Archelaus recalled to Rome and then exiled to Vienne where he died a few years later. Augustus decided he no longer would have a king over Judea, but a governor. Thus it was at the trial of Jesus that Pilate the governor ruled instead of a king.

The year following the removal of Archelaus there was a rebellion in Galilee. News had come to Nazareth and other Galilean cities that the Roman government had ordered a census taken. Great anger was aroused among the Galileans. In every town and village young nationalist patriots arose and gathered in groups to curse Rome and swear revolt. In the neighboring town, Sepphoris, only three miles from Nazareth, a man by the name of Judas raised the standard of revolt (Acts 5:37). Young men throughout Galilee poured into the city to gather around Judas. They shouted the cry of war and vowed to give their lives to free the Jews from the Roman yoke. Ten thousand of them marched across the land to Tiberias, the new city where Herod's palace was soon to be built, and after overpowering the guards broke into the armory and appropriated the spears, swords, and shields. Then they went out to face the Romans.

The news of the revolt quickly reached the ears of Varus, who commanded the Roman legions in the hills above Gadara. His veterans marched against the undisciplined mob that Judas had gathered. There could only be one result. The raw Galilean recruits broke and fled. Then Varus went to Sepphoris and set fire to the town. That night every person in Nazareth went to the summit of the hill to see the whole city of Sepphoris going up in flames. By morning nothing was left but a smoldering ruin. The people of the city were driven like cattle to the sea coast. There they were forced to board ships to be taken to the slave markets. Two thousand of the young prisoners were crucified on crosses.

But the saddened Jews that survived hoped on. Some day the Messiah would come, and He would drive out the hated Romans and set up the kingdom of God on earth. But the boy Jesus who even then was learning what the prophets had taught knew that freeing the land of the Romans was not the Messiah's first task. Even then He must have been thinking of the possibility of the cross. Soon He would have His first opportunity to go to Jerusalem, and there learn from the teachers of the temple more about the hopes and aspirations of His countrymen.

Chapter 15
The Visit to Jerusalem

In the days of Jesus the thirteenth birthday of a Jewish boy marked a great milestone in his life. He then became "a son of the Law." At that age the responsibility for the keeping of the Law shifted from his father to him. He stepped over the threshhold into a new world. It was the greatest day in his life. When a boy reached thirteen years of age, it was customary for pious parents to take him with them to Jerusalem to celebrate the Passover. In the case of Jesus who was probably born in October, his twelfth birthday had occurred about six months before the Passover. Although not yet thirteen, He was allowed to go with Joseph and Mary.

Ever since the crescent of the new moon had appeared in the western sky, there was great activity in Nazareth. Pilgrims were making preparations for the journey to Jerusalem before the full moon of the Passover came. Joseph and Mary, like many others, were getting ready for the journey. The donkey besides carrying Mary also bore sleeping mats and the food that was needed.

The journey to Jerusalem was a long trip for a boy of twelve, but we may be sure that Jesus looked forward to it. Despite the artists who tend to make the boy Jesus appear weak and frail, He must have been of a strong constitution. During His ministry, He constantly made long trips from one part of the country to the other. The record says, "The boy grew and waxed strong in spirit" (Luke 2:40).

When all preparations had been completed, the family of Jesus met with the other pilgrims at the village spring. Water skins were filled at the fountain and fastened to the backs of the donkeys and camels. The beasts drank their fill, and the signal was given for the procession to start. Friends who remained behind waved goodbye, and the smaller boys, too young to go, stared wistfully as the caravan began to move. Dogs barked, and the babies taken along for their dedication at the temple cried.

The road from Nazareth led steadily downhill to the plain of Esdraelon. As the procession passed the bluffs, the pilgrims could see other caravans moving southward far down the valley. By the time they were well into the plain, the noon hour had come, and the whole company paused for lunch. Then they moved on. As night neared, the caravan leader called a halt. By this time they were into the foothills of Samaria. The evening meal was eaten; prayers were said, and the people laid their mats on the ground and were soon asleep.

The Samaritan people were generally hostile and had no dealings with the Jews, but if a caravan was large, there was little danger that any of the Samaritan raiders would attempt to attack the party. As the first rays of dawn were seen in the east, the caravan was astir.

Late in the afternoon of the second day they came to the city of Sychar which stood between Mount Gerizim — the mount of blessing — and Mount Ebal — the mount of cursing. Nearby was Jacob's well where Jesus later was to meet and talk with the Samaritan woman.

As they continued on the third day to journey southward, they passed many historic spots. There was the Valley of Ajalon where Joshua commanded the sun and moon to stay their courses. Further south were the ruins of Bethel where Jacob dreamed of a ladder reaching to heaven. Other places marked historic events in the lives of Saul and Samuel. These varied scenes must have attracted the interest of the boy Jesus. At last Jerusalem came into view. The weary but happy travelers ate their meal and then began preparations at once to rest. As many of the pilgrims as possible camped on the Mount of Olives where a magnificent view of the temple and its court could be had.

The Passover must have been a time of intense interest to Jesus. There was the visit to the temple — that dazzling edifice built by Herod which stood almost as one of the wonders of the world. Joseph and Jesus walked into the outer court and looked around, admiring the magnificent architecture. They continued until they came to the inner court. There was a sign carved in Greek letters, "Let no foreigners enter within the screen and enclosure around the holy place. Whosoever is taken in so doing will himself be the cause of the death that overtakes him."

This meant of course that God was only for the Jews. Since He was only a young lad, Jesus could go no further than the Court of the Women. Joseph, however, was allowed to go into the inner court where the heads of families offered their lambs for sacrifice. He received the sacred parts of the Passover lamb and came out again through the Gate Beautiful. Then they went to a place where the family and others of the Nazareth company celebrated the Passover supper.

Only two days were required for the essential observances of the Passover feast to be completed. Many might have wished to stay longer. Others were eager to get back home, since it was nearing the time of the wheat planting. Joseph's carpenter shop was without its master. At an agreed time, many of the Nazareth pilgrims started on their homeward journey, and Joseph and Mary joined the group. They took for granted that Jesus was with the other boys. Jesus as other lads naturally desired to be with those of his own age. All day long the company moved northward. As they neared a village (today called Ramaliah), the caravan prepared to halt for the night. It was then that Joseph and Mary discovered to their great alarm that Jesus was not with them. They ran quickly throughout the whole company inquiring anxiously of everyone as to His whereabouts. But not one had seen Him. What if something had happened to Him? The very thought almost drove them frantic. Would not the wrath of heaven be visited upon them if through their carelessness something had happened to Him?

But there was nothing to do but to wait for the morning to come. At the dawn they started to retrace their steps, reaching Jerusalem before the day was over. But neither that day nor the next could they find the lost boy. Their search was apparently without plan; they just went from one place to another walking and looking. An increasing dread came upon them. Finally on the third day they went to the temple, and there to their unbounded relief, they saw Him talking with the doctors and elders.

What had happened? The Passover supper had absorbed the whole soul and spirit of the boy Jesus. He felt that He had to contact the minds of the religious leaders as to what they believed was God's will and plan for the nation. It was His golden opportunity to ask them questions that were pounding in His soul. As He went into the temple, He found one of the groups of rabbis who were teaching. For a while He said nothing but listened quietly. Then the questions leaped from His lips. The rabbis were astounded by His insight and comprehension and in turn began asking Him questions. Though we do not know all the matters that were discussed, we do know that the burning question of the hour was when and how the Messiah would come and usher in the new age. Was He to be a warrior who would drive out the hated Romans? Or was He,

91

as Isaiah foretold in the 53rd chapter, to come to make an atonement for the sins of the nation? Most of the people, the rabbis included, held to the first view.

One day passed, then two. On the third day suddenly Jesus heard a familiar voice. It was His mother reproaching Him for not being in the company (Luke 2:48). The answer that the young lad gave marks the beginning of a new era in the life of Jesus. They are Jesus' only recorded words before He began public ministry. "How is it that ye sought me? wist ye not that I must be about my Father's business?" (Luke 2:49). Christ's humanity clearly shows here. He had not meant to displease His mother. He had tried to make the most of His trip to Jerusalem, and when He finally left the doctors and lawyers in the temple and returned to the camp, He found that His family had already left. There was nothing for Him to do but to await their return. When Mary and Joseph found Him, He dutifully returned with them to Nazareth. But from that time on there was a change in His life. He began to think about His mission in the world.

The next eighteen years in Nazareth are called the silent years, but they were by no means idle years. Jesus worked with His hands at the carpenter's trade and at the same time He was making preparation for His life's work. When that was completed He would go forth in His ministry which in three short years would profoundly change the destinies of the human race.

Chapter 16

Return to Nazareth

Joseph and Mary had returned to Nazareth from Jerusalem with Jesus, their son. At this point the eighteen silent years began. From the time of this visit to Jerusalem they perceived that a notable change was taking place in the young lad. His interests were rapidly turning away from childhood matters. Jesus was still Mary's son, but He appeared to be a little apart from her life. He seemed to be thinking thoughts that even she could not share. The consciousness of His identity and mission was making its full impact upon His being. There was that ever-present feeling that He must be about His Father's business.

No doubt Jesus longed to remain in Jerusalem where He might sit at the feet of the great masters. Nevertheless, it was not God's plan. Joseph and Mary naturally expected Him to return to Nazareth, and return He did. The writer of the Hebrews said, "Though he were a Son, yet learned he obedience by the things which he suffered" (Heb. 5:8). It would seem that in Christ's return to Nazareth, God was teaching men that simple obedience and faithfulness in discharging the normal duties of a son while growing to manhood was considered high and holy in His sight. Here is a pointed lesson to those who chafe at what seems to be the dull routine of life. Luke says:

> "And he went down with them, and came to Nazareth, and was subject unto them: but his mother kept all these sayings in her heart" (Luke 2:51).

The eighteen years which would run their course were not to be idle years. Jesus had to learn the carpenter's trade. The morning after He returned to Nazareth He was seen with Joseph on the way to the carpenter's workshop. He learned first by watching, and then by practicing with His hands. He had to learn to saw a board square, and how to use the plane to smooth a panel. He had to get the knack of driving a nail straight, and how to use the chisel.

We can believe that Joseph was honest, skillful in his carpenter's trade, and a hard worker. He had a large family to take care of, so he had to work long hours to make ends meet. His young apprentice would be a welcome help to him.

The houses of Nazareth were in the main constructed of stone, but they used considerable wood in the beams, the roof, the doors and windows. Shops and counters required shelves and chests for holding goods. Furniture such as chairs and tables were needed in the homes. We shall assume that any spare time Joseph and Jesus had was given to providing furniture for their own home. Certainly Mary would have appreciated some nice things in her house. Then there were yokes to make for the oxen, and the threshing flail for the reaper.

We can be assured that Jesus did good work. He could say to a farmer as He sold him a yoke, "This yoke I have made is easy" (Matt. 11:28-30). The plough also called for highly skilled workmanship. In time Jesus became well-acquainted with most of the people of the village and even of the country roundabout as they came and went from His shop. Perhaps He assisted in the rebuilding of the city of Sipphoris, three miles away. It was this city that Varus had destroyed when he overthrew the rebellion led by Judas of Galilee. The shepherds came in to have their crooks repaired. A boastful landlord wanted a bigger barn perhaps. Later, that same man's sons came around for a coffin for their father (Luke 12:16-21).

All in all, the carpenter's workshop was a school where Jesus learned many of the lessons of life; and from observations made there He would later frequently draw His illustrations.

Then one day Jesus was alone in the workshop. Joseph was home ill. He did not get better. His wife Mary watched him steadily grow worse. Jesus came home one evening to a sad family. Mary was weeping, for Joseph was dead. Jesus wept with the others, even as He would do someday at Lazarus' grave. Though He was to be the Resurrection and the Life, nevertheless as He said to Martha, His time had not yet come. It was His Heavenly Father's will that Jesus should taste and share all the sorrows of the human race, including death, the great enemy of man. Someday He would come to grips with this enemy and destroy its power forever.

How do we know that Joseph died during the years that Jesus spent at Nazareth? For one thing, he appears no longer in the gospel narrative. Mary, His brothers and sisters do, but not Joseph. When they attended the wedding at Cana of Galilee, Mary went but Joseph was not seen. Mary is mentioned several times in the gospel narrative, but never Joseph after the visit to Jerusalem. When Christ went to the Cross, He said to John the Beloved, "Behold thy mother!" And then turning to her, He said, "Behold thy son!" (John 19:26, 27).

The main responsibility of supporting the home then fell to Jesus. For eight days He remained at home with His mother during the mourning period. Then He went back to the workshop to take over the tasks. Perhaps He had the assistance of some of the younger brothers. He now learned what it means to be a father. Jesus knew what it was to toil long hours and earn His bread by the sweat of His brow. Indeed He was known in the community as the "carpenter" and the "carpenter's son" (Mark 6:3; Matt. 13:55).

Thus we see that Jesus in His days in Nazareth had all the experiences of home life, which were an important part of His training. He was the oldest son of a rather large family, as Mark 6:3 shows:

"Is not this the carpenter, the son of Mary, the brother of James, and Joses, and of Juda, and Simon? And are not his sisters here with us? And they were offended at him."

The neighbors were quite unable to see that the family of Jesus was any different from any other family.

As we have noted, responsibility for the support of Christ's younger brothers and sisters rested largely upon Jesus as the breadwinner of the family. He learned from experience the anxieties of the poor. Perhaps in His own family He heard the word which He later repeated in the Sermon on the Mount, "What shall we eat? or, What shall we drink? or, Wherewithall shall we be clothed?" He too had to learn to put His whole trust in the Heavenly Father, Who knew what those needs were. He too learned by experience that if He sought "first the kingdom of God, and his righteousness . . . all these things shall be added . . ." (Matt. 6:33).

Later after His ministry began, His peculiar ways would bring upon Himself the disapproval of the family who was sensitive to what the neighbors thought:

"And when his friends heard of it, they went out to lay hold on him: for they said, He is beside himself . . . There came then his brethren and his mother, and, standing without, sent unto him, calling him. And the multitude sat about him, and they said unto him, Behold, thy mother and thy brethren without seek for thee . . . For neither did his brethren believe in him" (Mark 3:21, 31-32; John 7:5).

In business Jesus would have inevitably become familiar with the petty side of human nature. There would have been the usual hagglers seeking to drive hard bargains. Like all other workmen in business for themselves, He would have had to face dealing with those who were given to bickering over prices. There were probably delinquent debtors to dun. Yet whenever possible He would have been quick to forgive debts in hardship cases.

Perhaps there were years when the family would struggle to keep afloat, and other times when it would get ahead. Probably He was in the market at intervals looking for those who were in need of employment.

Jesus participated in the social life of the village. He was present at weddings. This was later to bring upon Him the charge that He "came eating and drinking." He mourned with those who mourned, and wept with those who wept. When death came to other homes, He probably remembered the day when He and His family walked behind the bier of their father.

It is likely at times He became restive under the tedious teaching of the scribes in the synagogue, as He perceived that their unimpassioned and dull reading was not reaching the people. We may imagine that His soul burned within Him, as with Jeremiah, while He waited for the hour when He could deliver His message to the people.

All the things that He saw and experienced were contributing to His increase of knowledge of God's plan. He knew what life ought to be. More and more He discerned between the ways of man and those of God. He recalled the fate of Judas of Galilee and the revolutionaries from the village of Sipphoris, three miles distant. He Himself had been a witness to the terrible massacre of the Jewish patriots, a sacrifice which had accomplished nothing. No doubt some of the bright young men who marched away to engage in the hopeless battle were among those Jesus had known. His own heart must have been deeply saddened when the report reached Nazareth that 2,000 men had been crucified.

Having taken into consideration all these events and circumstances that went into the formation of the character of Jesus, there is still something unaccounted for. There was an original dimension of personality that was not given Him by any part of His environment. It was His spirit-awareness that whereas His body was entirely human, nevertheless, His spirit was something more than human. He was conscious that God was His Father in a way different from that of anyone else. He was the only begotten Son of the Father. But the full significance of truth, the great purpose of His mission, the exact manner by which that mission would be accomplished, all had to be worked out.

We must not overlook the fact that Joseph and Mary went up *every year,* not just the one time recorded, to celebrate the Passover at Jerusalem (Luke 2:41). It was on these journeys that Jesus may have made some of His dearest friendships. It was customary for pilgrims arriving in Jerusalem to camp on the Mount of Olives. Over toward the east and south only a short distance was the village of Bethany. It was on a road on the other side of the hill that led down to the Jordan River. In Bethany was a family which included a young man by the name of Lazarus. Jesus and Lazarus formed a mutual friendship for each other that may be classed with that of Jonathan and David. Lazarus' two sisters, Mary and Martha, were both devoted women, although quite unlike in temperament. Martha, probably the elder of the sisters, took the lead as the homemaker. She was a practical and unemotional person, and strove for perfection in her household. Mary, on the other hand, was impassioned and imaginative. Mary, starry-eyed, hung on every word that Jesus spoke, and seemed to understand Him better than any other woman. Jesus loved that home and often made His headquarters there when He was near Jerusalem.

During these trips that the family made to the Holy City it is likely that Jesus repeated His visits with the doctors and learned rabbis of the temple. There He would get a close understanding of the feelings and expectations of the people concerning the Messiah. It was then that it became evident to Him that the popular expectation and the divine plan for the Messiah were something quite different. Thus, very early in His life Jesus could see that when His ministry was to be revealed many of the people would be deeply disappointed.

During the years Jesus lived in Nazareth He had not yet received the fullness of the Spirit. Nevertheless, He was in continual communion with His Heavenly Father. We are told that "Jesus increased in wisdom and stature, and in favor with God and man" (Luke 2:52). Later in the days of His ministry, we find Him oftentimes retreating into the vastness of the mountains or the desert where He could commune with His Father. During those eighteen silent years, we may be certain that there were many such seasons in which He was alone with God. Thus, little by little, the whole plan and purpose of His mission became unveiled to Him.

During these years, no doubt many young maidens stirred with approaching womanhood watched Him covertly, noting His stalwart form, His kind eyes, the gentle and courteous manner in which He treated them. Yet while aware of His attractive personality, they must have felt lifted out of themselves and above their natural emotions into a spiritual realm when they came into His presence, something they themselves were unable to account for.

· Mary, His mother, for her part treasuring the secret of the virgin birth, naturally watched Him closely, seeking for signs of what her own spiritual intuition told her was coming. Not until He reached manhood, probably, did she tell Him her great secret. And then on a suitable occasion, with womanly delicacy she told him the story of the Angel Gabriel's visit to her home and how he brought the message of the impending supernatural birth. She no doubt also related the dream that Joseph had. And then after making these disclosures, she probably looked expectantly at her Son to note His reaction. We can imagine His answer was a smile that showed that He fully understood. For Jesus had known from childhood that He was from above and had come to fulfill a great purpose in the world. His knowledge of the book of Isaiah, which must have been one of His favorite books (Luke 4:16-20), had shown Him years before that Immanuel was of virgin birth (Isa. 7:14). Nonetheless, the confirmation by His mother must have been welcome.

From time to time, Jesus went out on the hilltop above Nazareth. Mary saw Him go and watched Him return, but what took place in His visits to the summit she did not know. She probably noticed with a pang that there was a widening gulf — a realm that her Son was entering into that she herself could not invade. Yet His attitude toward her was always the same — one of great love, gentleness, and deference.

Chapter 17
Jesus and the Scriptures

As we have noted, there can be no doubt that Jesus from His early childhood was aware of His divinity, but all that this involved, the manner and methods of His future ministry, and how He should go about the fulfillment of His mission to the world, He would discover by the means appointed to Him.

Jesus must have realized early that His great source of knowledge of the divine plan of God was to be found in the Scriptures, access to which He had at the synagogue in Nazareth. That He did carefully study the Scriptures is one of the most obvious facts of His hidden years. His constant reference to what Moses and the prophets had written, His absolute belief in their inspiration, and that not one jot nor tittle should pass away till all be fulfilled, proves this.

To what extent were the Old Testament Scriptures able to enlighten Him on the character and manner of His future ministry? Would this enlightenment make it possible for Him, upon whose shoulders rested the fate of the world, to orient His life to His great calling?

Before we answer these questions, we should first take note of what Jesus had learned by the time He had reached manhood, concerning Israel's expectation of the advent of the Messiah. Regular attendance at the annual festivals at Jerusalem made Jesus intimately familiar with the nature of the Jews' religious worship. His keen perception saw Judaism in its stark reality. He perceived Israel as a nation moved by a fierce nationalism and a proud contempt for other peoples.

There was also a hardening of the moral life of the nation into a system of formality and rituals. There was the outward offering of sacrifice, but no inward piety. The people as a whole were ignorant and superstitious, yet faithful to such ideals that they had.

When Jesus on His occasional trips to Galilee visited the hot baths on its shores, He witnessed the heart-breaking scenes of human misery and physical suffering. He saw revealed the little world of men, women, and children, worn and wasted with sickness and disease. It produced a great compassion in His heart for those who so suffered.

In the area on the west shores of the Sea of Galilee, the great trade routes of the nations crossed. From the foreigners and pilgrims He had opportunity to know something of the customs of the pagan religions. He learned of India's travail and the moral reform inaugurated by Buddha. Travelers from Persia informed Him about Zoroaster who had set up another system of religion. From the West He would have heard about the mystic religions and the principles of Greek philosophy. He learned also of the darker cults which made gods of men, worshipped indecency, and practiced indescribable vileness.

Thus a vision of the world as it really was formed in His mind — a world lost and perishing, yet with possibilities. He felt the weight of its wretchedness, its suffering and its unavailing sorrow. He saw the failure and despair of the race. He witnessed its violence, its lust for riches, the desire for luxury, and the selfish pursuit after pleasure. He saw also the patient toil, the servitude, the poverty of the downtrodden, and the desire for better things. He was made to know the longing in the human heart for immortality on one hand, and the cynicism and materialism that existed on the other. And ever in the background were the sorrows of a race that had fallen, the sobbing of women and little children, the grief of the bereaved who stood beside the cold form of their loved one.

Some say Jesus never laughed. Certainly this was not true, but in view of the great weight of human suffering, laughter left Him— how could He laugh before this piteous picture of a sad and forlorn world? But His smile became all the sweeter because of His understanding of the sorrows and griefs of mankind.

W. P. Livingston in his volume *The Master Life* sums up what Jesus saw and His interpretation of the need of the human race whose burdens He was to share and whose souls He had come to rescue:

> "That world needed no political potentate, or military colossus, who would strut through a petty hour of blood and triumph and then vanish into the abyss. Nor did it need a master of learning who would expound the philosophy of the universe or the constitution of matter or the solution of economic and industrial problems, or the principles underlying art. These things did not touch its essential life. They left

unaffected its spiritual palate. They were appropriate to the intellectual sphere and it was the privilege of man to enlighten himself ... but to inform him out of season, regarding the origin and physical history of the earth, the processes that shaped it into being ... would be inviting the natural evolution of mind and interfering with the divine scheme."

What then was to be the nature of the mission of Christ? What was needed was someone who could speak with authority and tell mankind what was truth, the purpose for which people were born, how they might live in accord with the law of their being, and how they might have immortality. Jesus was to be God's evangelist proclaiming to the world the principles of the kingdom of God and of eternal life. In Him was the desire of all nations. He was the One who had come to redeem men from sin and set them free.

Jesus then would reveal God to mankind, show them His real nature, that God was a Father to whom every child could go. He would show men that before they could enjoy heaven, heaven had to first be born within their hearts. He would make them to know that before the visible kingdom of God would appear on the earth, that kingdom must first be set up in the human heart. He would declare to them that the soul was worth more than the body which would soon perish, and that men could not live by bread alone but by every word that proceedeth from the mouth of God, that loss of the body meant little, but the loss of the soul was catastrophic.

Nonetheless Jesus was becoming increasingly aware that this was not the message for which Israel was looking. It was rather Judas of Galilee that had caught the imagination of the people, even though he led many to their death. Men were impatient for the throne of Israel to be set up. Thus the task of Jesus would be very difficult due to their twisted thinking. The Messiah they were looking for was not one who would teach, but one who would lead them to victory on the battlefield. There was little desire for a purely spiritual kingdom.

What wisdom Jesus would need to present His message to the people! How He would have to make allowance for their ignorance and shallowness. He would have to acquiesce in their religious customs. He would have to use simple illustrations such as those from nature, so that they could understand. And above all, He would have to lead them back to the Scriptures to lay a foundation for His teachings.

Jesus knew He was born to be a king. Later when Pilate asked Him the question, "Art thou a king then?" He would answer, "To

101

this end was I born . . ." But at the same time He would also say that His kingdom was not of this world.

"Jesus answered, My kingdom is not of this world: if my kingdom were of this world, then would my servants fight, that I should not be delivered to the Jews: but now is my kingdom not from hence" (John 18:36).

Jesus recognized in Jacob's prophecy a reference to the sceptre of Israel descending to Him.

"The sceptre shall not depart from Judah, nor a lawgiver from between his feet, until Shiloh come; and unto him shall the gathering of the people be" (Gen. 49:10).

In Balaam's prophecy He saw Himself as a Star arising out of Jacob who would someday overthrow the enemies of Israel.

"I shall see him, but not now: I shall behold him, but not nigh: there shall come a Star out of Jacob, and a Sceptre shall rise out of Israel, and shall smite the corners of Moab, and destroy all the children of Sheth" (Nu. 24:17).

But it was also clear to Jesus that He had to come first as a prophet, a Saviour to save the nation from her sins. He first had to reign over the people's hearts before He could rule over them as a kingdom. This great truth must have come to Him very early. He certainly knew all the facts of the terrible power struggle that had taken place in the establishment of the Roman Empire. Judas' insurrection and the ghastly consequences were an illustration close to home that the kingdom of God could not be established by those methods. Jesus undoubtedly foresaw that there would be attempts to make Him King, as indeed there were, and He would have to be on His guard against them (John 6:14-15).

Jesus, therefore, saw that His ministry was to have its beginning as a prophet. And indeed He referred to Himself as a prophet when He spoke to Nazareth saying, "No prophet is accepted in his own country." He must have carefully studied the life of Moses, for He saw Himself typed in the Scriptures by this prophet:

"The Lord thy God will raise up unto thee a Prophet from the midst of thee, of thy brethren, like unto me; unto him ye shall hearken; According to all that thou desiredst of the Lord thy God in Horeb in the day of the assembly, saying, Let me not hear again the voice of the Lord my God, neither let me see this great fire any more, that I die not. And the Lord said unto me, They have well spoken that which they have

102

spoken. I will raise them up a Prophet from among their brethren, like unto thee, and will put my words in his mouth; and he shall speak unto them all that I shall command him. And it shall come to pass, that whosoever will not hearken unto my words which he shall speak in my name, I will require it of him" (Deut. 18:15-19).

At Sinai, God had spoken directly to the children of Israel. But this approach had frightened them, and they besought Moses that henceforth God should speak to him rather than directly to the people. However, Moses was only the prototype who portrayed the prophet that was to come. As did Moses, so did Jesus in His time speak the words of God to the people of Israel.

Jesus saw His own life in Moses; He was imperiled at birth, rejected by His brethren, and chosen of God to deliver Israel. He saw Moses as an intercessor, as the giver of the Law of God, as leading the children of Israel up to the very doors of the Promised Land, yet not as being permitted to go over himself. So He, the deliverer of Israel would lead His people into a land of rest and of plenty, but at the price of His own life.

The Ministry of the Messiah

It must have come early to Jesus the type of ministry that He was to have. He saw that it was a ministry of deliverance not to rid the nation of the Romans, but to set free the spirits and bodies of men from sin and sickness. The book of Isaiah, which refers so often to the Messiah must have held His attention. The passage in Isaiah 61:1-2 was one that He must have pondered often and indeed it was the text He chose for His first recorded sermon:

> "The Spirit of the Lord God is upon me; because the Lord hath anointed me to preach good tidings unto the meek; he hath sent me to bind up the brokenhearted, to proclaim liberty to the captives, and the opening of the prison to them that are bound; To proclaim the acceptable year of the Lord, and the day of vengeance of our God; to comfort all that mourn."

This prophecy told Him many things. First, He was to receive a special anointing of the Spirit, by which He would be given power to perform the work that lay before Him. It reminds us of the words He spoke to His own disciples after His resurrection, when He gave them the Great Commission: "But' ye shall receive power after that the Holy Ghost is come upon you: and ye shall be witnesses unto me..." (Acts 1:8).

Jesus was not merely to speak words as all the other religious teachers and reformers before Him had done, but He was to demonstrate His authority by a ministry of power. How His heart must have gone out to the sick lying about the warm-water springs near Tiberias. As the Messiah, He would restore sight to the blind, heal the brokenhearted, give liberty to those that were bruised; and to those bound by Satan's power He would bring deliverance.

His Rejection

But just as certainly as the poor and the down-trodden were to receive this ministry with joy, just so surely was it made plain to Him from the prophecies that the religious authorities would reject Him. In Chapter 53 of Isaiah, He saw His fate foretold clearly and unmistakably. Many of the Psalms also revealed the sufferings and peculiar destiny of the Messiah.

Looking backward in time we today are able to see how perfectly all these prophecies were fulfilled in the vicarious suffering, death, and resurrection of Jesus Christ. To us they proclaim salvation and redemption. To the Youth who had reached manhood in Nazareth, they spelled out the many sorrows and griefs that He was to bear in fulfilling His appointed mission.

That we might see through the eyes of Jesus as He studied the prophecies and communed with His heavenly Father during the days He was in Nazareth, we list these prophecies of His betrayal, trial, death, resurrection, and their fulfillment. When Jesus read them they were not yet fulfilled. He knew that before they should fail fulfillment, the very heavens must fall. It was these solemn things that were on Jesus' heart and mind, thoughts which He could not convey to His mother as the days of His active ministry swiftly approached.

Let us notice some of these prophecies that related to Christ's ministry and their later fulfillments:

The Prophecy   The Fulfillment

1. The Messiah was to be rejected.

"He is despised and rejected of men; a man of sorrows, and acquainted with grief: and we hid as it were our faces from him; he was despised, and we esteemed him not" (Isa. 53:3).

"He came unto his own, and his own received him not" (Jn. 1:11).

104

2. The Messiah was to be betrayed by one of His close followers and friends.

The Prophecy	The Fulfillment
"Yea, mine own familiar friend, in whom I trusted, which did eat of my bread, hath lifted up his heel against me" (Psa. 41:9).	"And Judas Iscariot, one of the twelve, went unto the chief priests, to betray him unto them" (Mark 14:10).

3. The Messiah was to be sold for thirty pieces of silver.

"And I said unto them, If ye think good, give me my price; and if not, forbear. So they weighed for my price thirty pieces of silver" (Zech. 11:12).	"And said unto them, What will ye give me, and I will deliver him unto you? And they covenanted with him for thirty pieces of silver" (Matt. 26:15).

4. The Messiah was to be silent before His accusers.

"He was oppressed, and he was afflicted, yet he opened not his mouth: he is brought as a lamb to the slaughter, and as a sheep before her shearers is dumb, so he openeth not his mouth" (Isa. 53:7).	"And the high priest arose, and said unto him, Answerest thou nothing? what is it which these witness against thee? But Jesus held his peace. And the high priest answered and said unto him, I adjure thee by the living God, that thou tell us whether thou be the Christ, the Son of God" (Matt. 26:62, 63).

5. The Messiah was to be smitten and spat upon by His enemies.

"I gave my back to the smiters, and my cheeks to them that plucked off the hair: I hid not my face from shame and spitting" (Isa. 50:6).	"And some began to spit on him, and to cover his face, and to buffet him, and to say unto him, Prophesy: and the servants did strike him with the palms of their hands" (Mark 14:65).

6. The Messiah was to bring healing to the people.

"Surely he hath borne our griefs, and carried our sorrows: yet we did esteem him stricken, smitten of God, and afflicted. But he was wounded for our transgressions, he was bruised for our iniquities: the chastisement of our peace was upon him; and with his	"And when Jesus was come into Peter's house, he saw his wife's mother laid, and sick of a fever. And he touched her hand, and the fever left her: and she arose, and ministered unto them. When the even was come, they brought unto him many that were possessed

The Prophecy	The Fulfillment
stripes we are healed" (Isa. 53:4-5).	with devils: and he cast out the spirits with his word, and healed all that were sick: That it might be fulfilled which was spoken by Esaias the prophet, saying, Himself took our infirmities, and bare our sicknesses" (Matt. 8:14-17).

· 7. The Messiah was to be mocked and taunted.

"But I am a worm, and no man; a reproach of men, and despised of the people. All they that see me laugh me to scorn: they shoot out the lip, they shake the head, saying, He trusted on the Lord that he would deliver him: let him deliver him, seeing he delighted in him" (Psa. 22:6-8).	"And they that passed by reviled him, wagging their heads, And saying, Thou that destroyest the temple, and buildest it in three days, save thyself. If thou be the Son of God, come down from the cross" (Matt. 27:39-40).

8. The Messiah was to suffer with transgressors and pray for His enemies.

"Therefore will I divide him a portion with the great, and he shall divide the spoil with the strong; because he hath poured out his soul unto death: and he was numbered with the transgressors; and he bare the sin of many, and made intercession for the transgressors" (Isa. 53:12).	"Then were there two thieves crucified with him, one on the right hand, and another on the left" (Matt. 27:38).

9. The Messiah's hands and feet were to be pierced.

"For dogs have compassed me: the assembly of the wicked have inclosed me: they pierced my hands and my feet" (Psa. 22:16).	"Then saith he to Thomas, Reach hither thy finger, and behold my hands; and reach hither thy hand, and thrust it into my side: and be not faithless, but believing" (John 20:27).

10. The Messiah was to be given gall and vinegar.

"They gave me also gall for my meat; and in my thirst they gave me vinegar to drink" (Psa. 69:21).	"Now there was set a vessel full of vinegar: and they filled a sponge with vinegar, and put it upon hyssop, and put it to his mouth" (John 19:29).

11. Messiah's side was to be pierced.

"And I will pour upon the house of David, and upon the inhabitants of Jerusalem, the spirit of grace and of supplications: and they shall look upon me whom they have pierced, and they shall mourn for him, as one mourneth for his only son, and shall be in bitterness for him, as one that is in bitterness for his firstborn" (Zech. 12:10).

"But one of the soldiers with a spear pierced his side, and forthwith came there out blood and water" (John 19:34).

12. They were to cast lots for the Messiah's garments.

"They part my garments among them, and cast lots upon my vesture" (Psa. 22:18).

"And when they had crucified him, they parted his garments, casting lots upon them, what every man should take" (Mark 15:24).

13. Messiah was to be buried with the rich.

"And he made his grave with the wicked, and with the rich in his death; because he had done no violence, neither was any deceit in his mouth" (Isa. 53:9).

"When the even was come, there came a rich man of Arimathaea, named Joseph, who also himself was Jesus' disciple: He went to Pilate, and begged the body of Jesus. Then Pilate commanded the body to be delivered. And when Joseph had taken the body, he wrapped it in a clean linen cloth, And laid it in his own new tomb, which he had hewn out in the rock: and he rolled a great stone to the door of the sepulchre, and departed" (Matt. 27:57-60).

14. Messiah was to be a sacrifice for sin.

"But he was wounded for our transgressions, he was bruised for our iniquities: the chastisement of our peace was upon him; and with his stripes we are healed. He was taken from prison and from judgment: and who shall declare

"The next day John seeth Jesus coming unto him, and saith, Behold the Lamb of God, which taketh away the sin of the world" (John 1:29).

his generation? for he was cut off out of the land of the living: for the transgression of my people was he stricken. Yet it pleased the Lord to bruise him; he hath put him to grief: when thou shalt make his soul an offering for sin, he shall see his seed, he shall prolong his days, and the pleasure of the Lord shall prosper in his hand. Therefore will I divide him a portion with the great, and he shall divide the spoil with the strong; because he hath poured out his soul unto death: and he was numbered with the transgressors; and he bare the sin of many, and made intercession for the transgressors" (Isa. 53:5, 8, 10, 12).

15. Messiah was to be raised from the dead.

"For thou wilt not leave my soul in hell; neither wilt thou suffer thine Holy One to see corruption" (Psa. 16:10).

"And as they went to tell his disciples, behold, Jesus met them, saying, All hail. And they came and held him by the feet, and worshipped him" (Matt. 28:9).

16. Messiah was to ascend to the right hand of God.

"Thou hast ascended on high, thou hast led captivity captive: thou hast received gifts for men; yea, for the rebellious also, that the Lord God might dwell among them" (Psa. 68:18).

"And he led them out as far as to Bethany, and he lifted up his hands, and blessed them. And it came to pass, while he blessed them, he was parted from them, and carried up into heaven" (Luke 24:50-51).

When Was The Messiah To Come?

There was one more prophecy in the book of Daniel that must have held a tremendous interest to Jesus. That concerned the time that had been appointed for the Messiah to come. What must have been the thoughts of the young Man when He first read the prophecy of Daniel 9?

"Know therefore and understand, that from the going forth of the commandment to restore and to build Jerusalem unto the Messiah the Prince shall be seven weeks, and threescore and two weeks: the street shall be built again, and the wall, even in troublous times. And after threescore and two weeks shall Messiah be cut off, but not for himself: and the people of the prince that shall come shall destroy the city and the sanctuary; and the end thereof shall be with a flood, and unto the end of the war desolations are determined" (Dan. 9:25-26).

Here the prophet Daniel received word by the archangel Gabriel as to the very date that the Messiah was to be cut off — or put to death. Was Jesus born at the right time that the prophecy mentioned? It said that the Messiah was to be cut off just 69 weeks after "the going forth of the commandment to restore and to build Jerusalem" (Dan. 9:25). The event for the restoration of Jerusalem was clearly predicted by Isaiah in the Edict of Cyrus:

"That saith of Cyrus, He is my shepherd, and shall perform all my pleasure: even saying to Jerusalem, Thou shalt be built; and to the temple, Thy foundation shall be laid" (Isa. 44:28).

Its fulfillment was recorded in Ezra 1:1-4. How long a period is the 69 weeks that were to begin with this event? If it were days, the period would only be a little over a year — far too short a time. In Genesis 29:27, we see that a "week" of years is seven years. Sixty-nine weeks of years is, therefore, 483 years. Jesus using such chronologies as were available in His time, saw that indeed He had come on the scene at the exact time! Of course He knew that He was the Messiah, as much as He knew anything. But it is notable that Jesus always supported His faith by the confirmation of the Scriptures. The knowledge that these 483 years were almost up must have spurred Him to renewed prayer and preparation. Apart from this, the prophecy declared the Messiah was to be cut off! He was to consummate His ministry with death!

The Priesthood of Jesus

The Scriptures also showed Jesus that He was to function as a priest, not as one of the tribe of Levi, for He was not of that tribe, but after the order of Melchizedek:

"The Lord hath sworn, and will not repent. Thou art a priest for ever after the order of Melchizedek" (Psa. 110:4).

109

Jesus saw that the Levitical priesthood and the Law made nothing perfect (Heb. 7:11; 18-19). The Levitical priesthood died and did not continue. Therefore, the Messiah became a priest after the order of Melchizedek (Heb. 7:17).

> "But this man, because he continueth ever, hath an unchangeable priesthood. Wherefore he is able also to save them to the uttermost that come unto God by him, seeing he ever liveth to make intercession for them" (Heb. 7:24-25).

As priest, Christ would mediate the better covenant (Heb. 8:6), which would take the place of the old covenant (Heb. 8:13). But before Christ could become priest, it was necessary that He reach the age of thirty, the time when a priest was accepted for service (Numbers 4:3). If He entered His ministry at thirty, how many years would that leave Him before the prophecy said the Messiah would "be cut off" or die? Only about three years! Jesus would have to fulfill His tremendous task in the amazingly short period of three years! It would have been enough to stagger Him, to overwhelm His humanity were it not for His great faith in God. As it was, a few times He bent under the weight of His gigantic task. And so it was that little by little, as Jesus pondered the Scriptures, the form and nature of His ministry was taking shape in His soul. Yet He was not limited to the Scriptures only, for indeed the Spirit of God was upon Him from the beginning to teach Him, and to bring all things to His remembrance. Notwithstanding, during the pre-ministry years He did not yet have the great and unlimited measure of the Spirit that He would have after His baptism:

> "For he whom God hath sent speaketh the words of God: for God giveth not the Spirit by measure unto him" (John 3:34).

The Scriptures were the basis of the ministry of Christ, although the Spirit dwelling with Him made the Word alive and powerful and guided Him into all truth.

It is interesting to follow the gospel narrative of the four evangelists and observe the manner in which the events in Christ's life were again and again related to a fulfillment of Old Testament prophecy. To the people He said, "Search the scriptures; for in them ye think ye have eternal life: and they are they which testify of me" (John 5:39). And to the unbelieving Jews He said, "For had ye believed Moses, ye would have believed me: for he wrote of me" (Verse 46). To the Sadducees He said, "Ye do err, not knowing the scriptures, nor the power of God" (Matt. 22:29). And after the resurrection when He opened the understanding of certain of His disciples, "He said unto them, O fools, and slow of heart to believe all that the prophets have spoken: Ought not Christ to have suffered these things, and to enter into his glory? And beginning at Moses and all the prophets, he expounded unto them in all the scriptures the things concerning himself" (Luke 24:25-27).

Chapter 18

The Divinity of Christ

One day during the ministry of Christ, Jesus asked the Pharisees the question, "What think ye of Christ?" (Matt. 22:42). They answered that they believed He was the son of David, which according to Christ's humanity was true. But Jesus was considering the question of His divinity, and He called attention to the fact that David in the Spirit had called Him Lord. How could He then be His son?

The question of who Christ is has been answered in many ways. Some have considered Jesus only as one of those especially gifted individuals who come into the world from time to time. They say He was a man with a unique personality and possessed with unusual talents, but still only a man. This view has been tenaciously held by a certain school of thought from the days of Christ on down to the present. It has a special hold upon those types of thinkers who commonly go under the name of Unitarians. The Unitarian holds that the physical laws of nature are invariable and constant and that all true knowledge is a product of the observation of these physical laws. This view, of course, excludes all miracles and denies the divine inspiration of the Scriptures. If followed to its logical consequences, it destroys all grounds for belief in angels, spirits, and the immortality of the soul. Indeed, it denies the very possibility of the government of God. God is to them the unknown and unknowable. Such a position inevitably leads to atheism.

There is a second class of people who look upon Christ as more than human, but less than Divine. They admit the grandeur of Christ's nature and the excellence and sublimity of His teachings. They exalt Him above the angels but not to the level of deity. This belief is a theory of compromise.

Then there is the medieval view that is still held by some that Jesus had a double soul — a human soul and a divine soul in one body. This view represented a groping for the truth, and is a closer approach to truth than the first two. It is however a cumbersome

112

theory. The real truth, as we shall see, is actually very simple. Let us now turn to the Scriptures and see what they have to say on this all-important matter.

1. The Word Was Made Flesh

John the apostle tells us that "the Word was made flesh, and dwelt among us." This is the explanation given by John who was the closest to Christ. The simple meaning of the above words is that the divine Spirit clothed Himself with a human body and in that condition took on the limitations of a man.

2. Made in the Likeness of Men

> "Let this mind be in you, which was also in Christ Jesus: Who, being in the form of God, thought it not robbery to be equal with God: But made himself of no reputation, and took upon him the form of a servant, and was made in the likeness of man: And being found in fashion as a man, he humbled himself, and became obedient unto death, even the death of the cross" (Phil. 2:5-8).

From this Scripture, we see the pre-existence of Christ in the form of God, and that He took upon Him the form of man. In other words, Jesus being a divine person took on a human body and became subject to all its laws and conditions.

3. Took on Sinful Flesh

> "For what the law could not do, in that it was weak through the flesh, God sending his own Son in the likeness of sinful flesh, and for sin, condemned sin in the flesh" (Romans 8:3).

Here we are told that Christ took on sinful flesh. He took on human nature through Mary, so that in all respects His body was the body of a man beset with the same temptations, yet without sin.

The fact is that these Scriptures simply teach that the Son of God came into the world in the person of Jesus. In so doing, He veiled His royalty and emptied Himself of the powers that belonged to Him in His pre-incarnate state. He did not bring with Him in the incarnation the attributes of deity; although after He was baptized in the Holy Ghost He manifested by degree the glory of the eternal.

Jesus, after He had received the baptism of the Spirit at the River Jordan, "being found in fashion as a man," became subject to the gradual unfolding of those powers He once had. He came back to His original self little by little. As Henry Ward Beecher said in his *Life of Jesus, the Christ*:

> "Who shall say that God cannot put Himself into finite conditions? Though as a free spirit, God cannot grow, yet as fettered in the flesh, He may. Breaking out at times with amazing power in single directions, yet at other times feeling the mist of humanity resting upon His eyes, He declares, 'Of that day and that hour knoweth no man, no, not the angels which are in heaven, neither the Son, but the Father.' This is just an experience we should expect in a being whose problem of life was, not the disclosure of the full power and glory of God's attributes, but the manifestation of the love of God and of the extremities of self-renunciation . . ."

Some early theologians believed suffering to be inconsistent with divinity. With such ideas of the divine nature, how could they believe that Jesus, a Man of suffering, was divine? The fact is man's nature and God's nature do not differ so much in kind as to the degree of their attributes. Love and mercy and goodness are the same in God as in man. When God created man, He said, "Let us make man in our image, after our likeness" (Gen. 1:26).

Yes, Christ was very much God. When clothed with flesh and made subject to physical laws, He was then a Man of the same moral faculties, of the same mental powers, subject to the same physical weaknesses, trials and temptations — only without sin. A human soul is not something different from a divine soul. What Christ was like on earth in His sympathies, tastes, friendships, we shall find in Him in heaven — only amplified to an infinite degree.

But now the question is: When did Christ know He was divine? Isaiah 7:15,16 shows that Christ came to consciousness the same as any other child. "For before the child (Immanuel) shall know to refuse the evil, and choose the good . . ." (Verse 16). This verse makes it plain that His own human consciousness in which memory would play a part would not occur much before the age of three. Yet once consciousness had come, there must have come simultaneously the consciousness of His pre-existence.

Christ was very emphatic of His pre-existence in His personal testimony. Here are a few typical statements He made on the matter:

> "Jesus said unto them, If God were your Father, ye would love me: for I proceeded forth and came from God; neither came I of myself, but he sent me . . . Jesus said unto them, Verily, verily I say unto you, Before Abraham was, I am . . .

I came forth from the Father, and am come into the world: again, I leave the world, and go to the Father . . .And now, O Father, glorify thou me with thine own self with the glory which I had with thee before the world was . . . Father, I will that they also, whom thou hast given me, be with me where I am; that they may behold my glory, which thou hast given me: for thou lovedst me before the foundation of the world" (John 8:42; 58; 16:28; 17:5, 24).

Not only did He testify of His pre-existence; but He declares His actual deity:

"I and my Father are one . . . Believest thou not that I am in the Father, and the Father in me? the words that I speak unto you I speak not of myself: but the Father that dwelleth in me, he doeth the works . . . Jesus saith unto her, I that speak unto thee am he . . . Jesus heard that they had cast him out; and when he had found him, he said unto him, Dost thou believe on the Son of God? . . . All things are delivered unto me of my Father: and no man knoweth the Son, but the Father; neither knoweth any man the Father, save the Son, and he to whomsoever the Son will reveal him . . ." (John 10:30; 14:10; 4:26; 9:35; Matt. 11:27).

"Saying, What think ye of Christ? whose son is he? They say unto him, The son of David. He saith unto them, How then doth David in spirit call him Lord, saying, The Lord said unto my Lord, Sit thou on my right hand, till I make thine enemies thy footstool? If David then call him Lord, how is he his son?" (Matt. 22:42-45).

That Christ knew of His divinity in His childhood is shown in His one recorded saying before manhood. It was made while He was in the temple conversing with the elders and the doctors. Mary, His mother, found Jesus after a three-day search and said, "Son, why hast thou thus dealt with us? behold, thy father and I have sought thee sorrowing" (Luke 2:48). Mary had referred to Joseph who was His nominal father. Immediately Jesus in a gentle tone, but in a way impossible not to understand, called their attention to the fact that it was God who was His father. Mary should never forget that.

"And he said unto them, How is it that ye sought me? wist ye not that I must be about my Father's business?" (Luke 2:49).

115

He was not only emphasizing that they should know by now that He ought to be about His Father's business, but that indeed God was His true Father.

The eighteen years having been expired, it was time for Christ's public ministry to begin.

Chapter 19

The Temptations in the Wilderness

"And Jesus being full of the Holy Ghost returned from Jordan, and was led by the Spirit into the wilderness, Being forty days tempted of the devil. And in those days he did eat nothing: and when they were ended, he afterward hungered" (Luke 4:1-2).

Of what happened during the forty days in the wilderness, the Scriptures maintain an almost complete silence. Since the Lord has kept His counsel as to what occurred during that time, it is not ours to speculate. But of that which took place when the forty days were over, we have a detailed account.

It is evident that Satan's appearance was at the right psychological moment. It took place when Christ, after the long days of fasting, was at His weakest. This strategy of the devil is not a matter to be overlooked, for most of us have moments of exhaustion and depression. It is well that we know the time when Satan usually chooses to attack.

The devil's first words are significant. "If thou be the Son of God," he said. He began the battle over the question of the Sonship of Christ. He tried to inject a doubt concerning His divinity. He knew that if ever there were a time in which he could get Christ to doubt the fact, then was the time. Great as are the benefits of a long fast, it is toward the end that the most serious danger exists. This is a time when people sometimes "go off the deep end" as a result of wrong impressions and hallucinations.

When we hear Satan saying to Jesus, "If thou be the Son of God," we are witnessing a bold attempt on his part to confuse Christ's sense of His divinity by appealing to the human side of His nature. Only once again would this temptation strike Him with the same force; that was on the Cross when He cried, "My God, my God, why hast thou forsaken me?" (Mark 15:34).

There is a remarkable parallel between Satan's words to Christ, "If thou be the Son of God," and those spoken by the serpent to

117

Eve in the Garden of Eden, "Ye shall be as gods." The temptation in each instance was a suggestion to make a reach upward for self without regard to God's Word or His will. Whereas Adam and Eve yielded to the temptation to become as gods by giving way to their appetite, Christ refused to arrogate deity to Himself in the way that the devil prompted.

The Sonship of Christ was and still is the great battle area in God's plan to bring His salvation to mankind. God gives that truth to men by revelation of the Spirit and not through spectacular demonstrations that the devil suggested. The devil's strategy was to incite Christ to attempt to prove His Sonship in a way contrary to the will of God. Nor did the devil ever, to the last hour, give up his efforts to ensnare Christ. Even on the cross we hear voices flinging at Him the words, "If thou be the Son of God, come down" (Matt. 27:40). The importance of the temptation is seen in its persistent recurrence. If the devil at any time could have tied Him to a line of conduct that would ill-befit Him, he would have accomplished his purpose.

It was essential that the Lord not assert His divinity after a carnal way, but it should be accomplished in the Heavenly Father's way. At the river Jordan, Jesus had received the fulness of the Godhead bodily (Matt. 3:16-17, Col. 2:9). What He was doing in the wilderness was emptying His human will in order that the will of God might be fully operative in His. It was in this emptying of Himself that room was made for the fulness of God.

The First Temptation:
The Snare of Bodily Hunger

The devil is exceedingly subtle in his temptations. This fact is seen in the first words by which He addressed Christ. He suggested that the Lord prove His divinity by making stones into bread. During a long fast, the desire for food is almost absent, but as it ends, appetite returns. The devil wanted to prompt Christ into making an unwarranted display of His power. It was an insolent challenge on his part to provoke Christ into an abortive attempt to prove His diety.

It is a fact that with the sense of physical weakness that follows a fast, there is also a feeling of spiritual power. There was the temptation of cutting the devil down by a demonstration of that power. In one God-like act, He could have silenced the taunts of Satan. Moreover, the temptation was rational. Since Christ was so weak from exhaustion, he could have preserved Himself and His life for God's work. Such was the temptation that beset Esau and caused him to fail. He said, "Behold, I am at the point to die: and what profit shall this birthright do to me?" (Gen. 25:32).

There is also a deeper side to the temptation. Christ came not to do His own will, but the will of the Father. He came into the world to be a man, to act like a man, to be limited as a man, and not to perform prodigies for His own personal benefit. When Christ answered Satan, He answered him not as the Son of God whose rights had already been established on earth, but as the Son of Man, and He quoted the Scripture, "Man doth not live by bread only, but by every word that proceedeth out of the mouth of the Lord" (Deut. 8:3). Thus He is showing His trustful reliance on God to meet His necessity.

It was certainly not a matter whether the stones could be turned into bread, for as John the Baptist said, "God is able of these stones to raise up children unto Abraham" (Matt. 3:9). It was simply that the method that Satan suggested was false. In Eden we see Eve turning from the revealed word and the Tree of Life to satisfy her pride and her appetite. Christ, on the other hand, turned from appetite to the will of God that He might lead men back to the Tree of Life. Thus we see the choice in Eden was reversed by the second Adam.

There is a saying of Christ that has significance here. He said, "If a son shall ask bread of any of you that is a father, will he give him a stone? . . . or if he shall ask an egg, will he offer him a scorpion?" (Luke 11:11-12). In this Christ was speaking the language of His experience. He once had been in the desert hungry, in a stony place where scorpions and serpents lurked. The devil pointed to a stone and said that in it He would find the answer to His need. If He took the stone, it might be bread in His hand. But Jesus indignantly rejected the insinuation that His heavenly Father would answer in that manner.

Christ had to meet this temptation more than once in His life. He might have been ensnared by a natural desire to satisfy the physical hunger of his fellow men. Having fed the five thousand, they sought to make Him king by force, but Jesus knew that their real motive had been inspired because of the loaves and fishes they had eaten:

> "Jesus answered them and said, Verily, verily I say unto you, Ye seek me, not because ye saw the miracles, but because ye did eat of the loaves, and were filled. Labour not for

119

the meat which perisheth, but for that meat which endureth unto everlasting life, which the Son of man shall give unto you: for him hath God the Father sealed" (John 6:26-27).

To desire to end poverty is a noble thought, but how insignificant the feeding of the body is to giving men the "meat which endureth to everlasting life." Christ never really touched the problem of the world's hunger and its need for physical bread. Not that this does not have its place, but He was concerned with something of vastly more importance:

"Therefore I say unto you, Take no thought for your life, what ye shall eat, or what ye shall drink; nor yet for your body, what ye shall put on. Is not the life more than meat, and the body more than raiment?" (Matt. 6:25).

It was in these teachings that Christ offered His listeners the Bread of Life (John 6:41, 66). If He had only chosen a bread policy, He would have saved Himself from the death of the cross.

It is interesting to note what the bread policy later did for Rome. The emperor put his people on the dole and gave them bread and circuses. In time the treasury was drained and Rome became a city of effete sightseers. And little by little, the empire rotted away until finally Caesar's throne fell. That is the fate the devil designed for Christ. But in failing to bring the world its bread, Christ brought the Bread from heaven which if any man eat, he shall have everlasting life. Man needs bread, but not bread alone. His higher life and his moral and spiritual capacities must be provided for. They have a far greater importance than the mere physical wants.

The Temptation of the Fourth Dimension

The second temptation of Jesus was different from the first, and it involved an occurrence which some describe as a temptation of the fourth dimension. By some strange means, the person of the Lord was conveyed from the wilderness to the pinnacle of the temple in Jerusalem. To some people this incident offers difficulty, and they are inclined to regard the physical transportation to Jesus as an imaginary one — that is, it was supposedly a scene vividly presented to His imagination.

While the event was contrary to the laws of the natural world, this should not stumble us. There are laws of nature which have remained hidden through the ages which have only recently been discovered. As to the laws in the spirit world, our knowledge is extremely limited. But we do know in this atomic age that energy transcends matter, and life transcends both and controls both. The method by which Christ was transported to Jerusalem is outside the bounds of our present knowledge, but this does not remove it from the sphere of possibility. The fact is that such an experience belongs in the realm of the fourth dimension. Scientists laboring with the theory of relativity now agree there is a realm in which the fourth dimension operates, although admittedly they have a difficult time explaining it.

In a sense, matter is a bondage. Our material embodiment is a great limiting factor as to what we can do. Man is engaged in the tremendous undertaking of going to the moon. To break away from the earth's gravitation requires a rocket's thrust to overcome its powerful attraction.

The physical body is a cumbersome house, despite the fact that it is a wondrous mechanism. Our minds can roam the universe far faster than the speed of light. But the body must travel at a clumsy gait and be left far behind as the mind goes soaring in flights of fancy. After the resurrection, Christ received a glorified body that was able to accomplish those supernatural feats of transportation. Since Satan possessed certain powers in the spirit realm, he was able to escort Jesus to the pinnacle of the temple, there to suggest a second temptation to Him. Again, it was the temptation as in the Garden. "Ye shall be as gods." It was a temptation of the soul.

As the serpent offered Eve a new realm of knowledge, so he offered the Lord a new realm of experience:

> "Then the devil taketh him up into the holy city, and setteth him on a pinnacle of the temple, And saith unto him, If thou be the Son of God, cast thyself down: for it is written, He shall give his angels charge concerning thee: and in their hands they shall bear thee up, lest at any time thou dash thy foot against a stone. Jesus said unto him, It is written again, Thou shalt not tempt the Lord thy God" (Matt. 4:5-7.)

Jesus was to cast Himself down from the temple and thus gratify the vulgar desire of the crowd for wonders. The idea was to do some sensational and startling miracle that would get their ear and enable Him to awe them into obedience. If by the power of God His descent to the ground was stopped and He did not crash to instant death, the crowds would listen to Him as a superman from heaven. Then if He said, "I am the Messiah," the world would be at His feet. It was a plan to force the hand of God to reveal Christ's Sonship in a spectacular way. It was to achieve a short-cut to power through a miracle.

The devil again addressed Jesus, "If thou be the Son of God." The prince of the power of the air had just escorted Christ to the pinnacle of the temple in the Holy City. Then the thought was, "You have been brought safely hither; shall not God also protect you in the short flight to the ground?"

In the temptation Jesus was made to feel His humiliation as the Son of man. Why should He not overthrow this bondage? Why should God's Son be forced to walk? The prince of the power of the air had demonstrated his power by the swift flight. Why shouldn't He, God's Son, show that He had a power as great, if not greater, than the devil's? Satan in effect was pointing the finger of scorn at the Godhead walking.

Nevertheless, Christ bore the insult, and refused to be pushed into making a rash or vulgar display of the power of God. He accepted His human limitation and did not seek to emulate the proud flight of Satan. He simply answered, "Thou shalt not tempt the Lord thy God" (Matt. 4:7).

Once when Herod sought His life, certain Pharisees told the Lord to depart, "for Herod will kill thee." But Jesus answered them saying, "Go ye, and tell that fox, Behold, I cast out devils, and I do cures to day, and to morrow, and the third day I shall be perfected. Nevertheless I must walk to day, and to morrow, and the day following" (Luke 13:31-33).

Thus did Jesus declare that He must walk until His mission was completed. He could not evade the perils and hardships to purchase comfort at the expense of the fulfillment of God's will.

There were several occasions when Jesus was tempted to use His power in a way inconsistent with His lowly position as the Son of man. At Nazareth, some of the citizens attempted to throw him over the brow of a cliff, but "He passing through the midst of them went his way." When they took up stones to stone him, "Jesus hid himself . . . and so passed by." From this we may understand that He did not employ supernatural means to escape, but rather put His trust in the providence of God.

Satan never ceased to tempt Christ in this matter. Even at the last hour of His life, the words were flung at Him, "Come down from the cross." Though Jesus could have done this as the Son of God, He could not as the Saviour of men.

After His resurrection, when He had cast off the restraints of His humiliation, He exercised quite freely those powers that the tempter solicited Him to use for an untimely display. Christ would not accede to the devil's proposal that He become a world's superman. He would not put on a theatrical display of His powers to win the awe and admiration of the fickle populace.

As Morris Stewart says in *The Temptations of Jesus:*

> "But Jesus left the great wealth that was His, in the grasp of His Father's hand; and He took nothing from its store save with the sanction of His will and the bidding of His word .... But for Jesus to step from the temple ledge would have been to dictate to heaven instead of waiting its command. Such abandonment of His dependence would have shifted the poise of His divinity which was steadied by the fingers of God; and His descent would have cast down the path of salvation from life to death and the shock of its fall have shaken the throne of God in all the earth."

The Temptation to Receive the Kingdoms of This World

The first two temptations of Jesus appear to be almost trivial beside the third. The first was refusal to use His power to make bread. The second was the suggestion to trust God to save Him in the deadly leap. Yet trifling as they appear to be, most men who fall yield to temptations such as these.

But altogether different from the first two was the third temptation that confronted Christ:

> "Again, the devil taketh him up into an exceeding high mountain, and sheweth him all the kingdoms of the world, and the glory of them; And saith unto him, All these things will I give thee, if thou wilt fall down and worship me. Then saith Jesus unto him, Get thee hence, Satan: for it is written, Thou shalt worship the Lord thy God, and him only shalt thou serve" (Matt. 4:8-10).

The devil took Jesus to a high mountain and showed Him the kingdoms of the world in a moment of time, and then said, "All these things will I give thee, if thou wilt fall down and worship me." Here was a change of strategy. The devil no longer challenged His Sonship. He was given a dazzling demonstration of Satan's temporal power. Satan, long skilled in temptation, believed that the manhood of Christ preponderated over His divinity. With blasphemous insolence, the devil paraded before the eyes of Jesus his tremendous power and the greatness and glory of his world kingdoms.

Since there is no mountain in the world that commands such a geographical view as the one mentioned, this scene too was a supernatural demonstration performed on the part of Satan. In the spiritual realms, Christ was able to take in this stupendous panoramic view which transcended time and space.

The offer was manifestly real. For in a profound sense the kingdoms of this world belong to Satan. Adam originally had been given the dominion; "And God said, Let us make man in our image, after our likeness . . . and *let them have dominion*" (Gen. 1:26).

But Adam and Eve disobeyed God and obeyed Satan, thus transferring their allegiance to him. Satan now claims it and the claim was not disputed by Christ. Indeed all through the Scriptures, we find hints of the sovereignty of Satan. John the apostle says, "And we know that we are of God, and the whole world lieth in wickedness (Margin. "wicked one" — I John 5:19).

The tenth chapter of Daniel clearly shows that the evil archangels of Satan dominate and control the great empires of the earth.

It is true that in the days of Israel's kingdom, God had attempted to found a theocracy, and the throne of Judah was the throne of the Lord (I Chron. 29:23), but the endeavor at that time because it involved Israel's obedience had achieved small success. When Christ went to the cross, He said to the unbelieving Jews, "This is your hour, and the power of darkness" (Luke 22:53).

God, of course, has never abandoned His plan to rule over the earth, and in due time, the kingdoms of this world will become the kingdoms of the Lord Jesus Christ (Rev. 11:15). Yet at the moment, the devil's boast of mastery was not unwarranted. He was king of the world, and not a figurehead, or endowed with only a shadowy rule. The power of the world was in his grasp wherewith he could dazzle the eyes of men. The temptation was an intensely real one.

Satan thus looked upon Christ's coming on the scene as an invasion of his own domain, and that his whole kingdom was imperilled by His presence. He knew that Christ's purpose was to incite men to revolt from Satan's power. As Paul said concerning the matter, "And that they may recover themselves out of the snare of the devil, who are taken captive by him at his will" (II Tim. 2:26). Jesus had plans to build the Kingdom of

Heaven right within the bounds of Satan's principality! And of the Church He would build He said, the "gates of hell" should not prevail against it. The follower of Christ indeed has to wrestle against these diabolical powers:

> "For we wrestle not against flesh and blood, but against principalities, against powers, against the rulers of the darkness of this world, against spiritual wickedness in high places" (Eph. 6:12).

Now apparently, Satan realizing the grave peril that he was facing, was willing to surrender his whole domain into the hands of Christ upon the sole condition that He bow down and worship him. It is a commentary on Satan, wise as he is, that he had hopes that his offer would be accepted. It was dazzling, alluring, but he had not measured the steel that was in the One who was "meek and lowly of heart," the One he sought to tempt. Christ gave the offer no consideration; He did not ponder over it, nor weigh its possibilities. Indeed, His whole being revolted against the evil suggestion, and He answered the devil in the only way he could understand, saying, "Get thee hence, Satan: for it is written, Thou shalt worship the Lord thy God, and him only shalt thou serve" (Matt. 4:10). Christ's use of the Scriptures to defeat Satan is so consistent that the significance cannot be ignored. The Word of God has a force infinitely greater than the mere combination of sounds upon which that power is conveyed.

Satan's hold over mankind is based on catering to the material desires of unregenerate men. Men hold on to this world's goods with strained hearts and a desperate grasp. Their attention is so engrossed in these temporal things that the treasures of heaven have little or no attraction for them. Christ came to reverse this order, that men instead of grovelling in the earth might aspire to heaven. It was Satan's object to turn the Lord aside from this purpose. Therefore, he led Him into the "sphere of earth's power and glory" and invited Him to take all it contained and with that be content.

But since Christ had subjected His own will entirely to that of the Father at the river Jordan, there was nothing in Him that responded to Satan's temptation. The Lord left ivory palaces to come to this world, giving up His heavenly riches that we through His poverty might become rich. Yet He had a long, hard pull before Him to turn men from the attractions of this world to the riches of the one to come.

The temptation that Jesus met in the wilderness was to be experienced again and again. All Israel had a Messianic expectation. The throne of David was empty as far as could be seen. If He would but occupy it, the nation was ready to back him as a man. All that Christ had to do was to speak the word. The nation was ready to make Him king during the early part of His ministry. Even His disciples expected Him to take the throne. Peter rebuked Him for His talk of the cross. Indeed that impetuous disciple was ready to fight for Jesus with His sword.

But it was not to be that way. Before Christ could rule over the earth, He first had to rule over the hearts of men.

Later the Medieval Church was to fall for the very temptation that Christ had rejected. It pandered to riches and the wealth of this world; it laid claim to the temporal power over the kingdoms of earth — the very thing that the devil offered Christ and which He rejected. What would have happened had Christ accepted the devil's offer, may be seen in the history of the Medieval Church. The temporal power it attained, instead of bringing blessing to the world, ushered in the Dark Ages, wherein the true light of heaven was almost extinguished.

The climax came when Satan said to Jesus, "Fall down and worship me." At that moment, Jesus turned His eyes from the tempter's brilliancy and said, "Get thee hence." This final incitement to treason revolted Jesus to His depths. This appalling suggestion of disloyalty to His Father caused Him to turn to God to escape from the grasp of the tremendous evil that had assailed Him. At that moment the devil went, and the angels came. Christ recoiling from the inducements of hell sought the fellowship of heaven. As Morris Stewart says, "And when Satan said, 'Fall down and worship me,' we see Jesus turn away in godly horror lest His fainting body should succumb and fall prone in the semblance of the unlawful homage! With the last strength of His manhood, He stretched out hands of appeal to God, and sent to heaven an urgent call that the arm of God would take and hold Him!"

Deep called to deep, and the angels came. It was not the angels which wrought the deliverance of Jesus. Their chief ministry to Him was their radiant company. They came not to succor Him during the battle, but to minister to Him after the battle was won. For it was a battle that Jesus fought and won single-handedly.

126

Chapter 20

The Cana Miracle

It is significant that immediately after conversing with Nathanael, Jesus went to Cana of Galilee about twenty miles from Capernaum. This was the home of Nathanael (John 21:2). Is it possible that the meeting with Nathanael had something to do with the trip to Cana? Did Nathanael have some information about Jesus' mother who may have been looking for Him? Did he know about the wedding that was about to take place? Surely in so small a village as Cana, Nathanael would probably know both the bride and the groom.

It is generally believed that because of Mary's prominence in the story and her anxiety about the wedding arrangements, her knowledge of the family's resources, and the position she occupied in being able to address the servants indicate a kinship to the family. Either the bride or the bridegroom may have been a near relative of Jesus. Since Cana is quite near to Nazareth, it is likely that Jesus knew the bride. And she, admiring Jesus, wanted Him to be present at her wedding.

Some think that Jesus went to the wedding as a sort of a clergyman ready to speak a word in season to the guests. Jesus, however, went also to enjoy the fellowship, and during His brief ministry, He was present at many such social gatherings. As a matter of fact, some thought He did too much visiting with publicans and sinners.

Did Jesus Turn Water into Fermented Wine?

Before we can enter into a study of this beautiful incident in the ministry of Christ, we shall surely be asked the question, whether Jesus at this wedding, turned water into fermented wine? It is necessary to find the right answer to this question in order to understand what happened that night.

There are those who insist that Christ at the wedding at Cana made fermented wine. Building on this assumption, they take it as a matter of course that Christians have a right to drink fermented liquors. Is this reasoning correct?

Those who take this position quite ignore the fact that it has been abundantly proven that the Bible speaks of more than one kind of wine. It refers both to fermented wine and unfermented wine. One is a delightful and wholesome beverage. The other is a poison which degrades human beings and makes alcoholics out of many of them. As we shall see, the wine that Jesus made was certainly fresh, pure, unfermented wine.

Those who hold that Christ made fermented wine disregard the fact that the Old Testament consistently disapproves of the use of alcoholic beverages. They would have the Lord disobeying the injunction of the Scriptures which declares, "Look not upon the wine when it is red, when it giveth his color in the cup, when it moveth itself aright" (Prov. 23:31).

Furthermore, they would place the Lord in disagreement with the command which teaches that those in the holy service must abstain from alcoholic wine (Lev. 10:9). They would have Christ at the wedding feast manufacturing a hundred gallons of alcoholic beverages, sufficient to result in the drunkenness of the entire company at the marriage.

Moreover, they ignore the obvious fact that wine, when freshly made, has no alcoholic content at all. For wine to become alcoholic, a lapse of time is necessary for the fermentation process to take place. Or, is it possible that the Lord fermented the fresh wine that He made? God forbid! If such be true, the Lord performed the same work as the breweries do.

Because the master of the feast mentioned that the wine that Jesus made was "the good wine," advocates of drinking fermented spirits say, that this proves that the wine must be alcoholic! This is assuming the very thing to be proven. To most people grape juice is an exquisite drink. Fermented wine is drank, not so much for the taste, but for the reaction it produces when it gets into the bloodstream. Actually, intoxicating wine has a rather bitter and unpleasant taste when first drank. The only "good wine" is non-alcoholic wine.

The Truth About the Turning of Water to Wine

Now it is said that Jesus went to the wedding for the purpose of turning water into fermented wine, and thus to show for all time that He was in favor of His disciples drinking. What a travesty on truth!

Obviously, the most important purpose of Christ's attending the wedding of Cana was to give sanction and approval to marriage, an institution which had been debased by man's shameful perversion of sex — a circumstance for which liquor must bear heavy responsibility. Christ's presence at the wedding as one of the first acts of His public life was to establish in the minds of men the sanctity of marriage.

But while placing His approval upon that institution, was Christ at the same time giving His sanction to the drinking of alcohol and to drunkenness?

We believe that any such interpretation is a gross perversion of the Scriptures. If Jesus had come to the wedding for the purpose of turning water into fermented wine, it would in effect negate the many texts in the Bible which teach against the use of intoxicating beverages.

Christ's Startling Answer to His Mother

That Jesus was by no means endorsing the drinking of alcohol is seen in His startling answer to His mother, Mary, who had said to Him, "They have no wine." Jesus replied in words that have been considered harsh, "Woman, what have I to do with thee? mine hour is not yet come" (John 2:4). Yet, in the light of the context, these were the very words demanded by the occasion. Christ, the Holy One, must react sharply to the implied suggestion that He make more of the kind of wine the company had been drinking — alcoholic wine! So degrading are the results of drinking alcohol, that an implication that Christ become party to its manufacture must call forth a rebuke, even if His mother were the one who was responsible for calling it forth.

We will not challenge the contention of those who claim that there may have been some fermented wine at the wedding. Perhaps some of the guests were already giddy by the time the wine gave out. If so, such a scene was certainly exceedingly distasteful to Christ; yet He bade His time. He awaited the propitious moment to show His attitude toward it. That moment arrived when the supply of wine failed. Perhaps the fact that Jesus said nothing in reference to wine-drinking during the festivities caused Mary to think that He was giving His silent approval to the proceedings. Since the wine had given out, her host was in an embarrassing situation. She turned to Him saying, "They have no wine." Was this a suggestion on her part that Jesus should produce more of the same kind of wine (if it was the fermented kind) they had been drinking? If so, was it not this that caused Jesus to say, "Woman what have I to do with thee?"

Notice that the unclean spirit, when addressing Christ in the synagogue, used the same phrase, "What have we to do with thee?" (Mark 1:24). The phrase in Greek is *"ti emoi kai soi."* Simply it means, "What have we in common?"

Certainly the demons had nothing in common with Jesus. But in the case of Mary, we would at first thought, that she and Jesus had everything in common, until we consider her words, "They have no wine." Then the difference becomes clear. The point of view of Jesus and that of His mother Mary on this subject were quite different.

However, with the rebuke the Lord did find a way to grant Mary's request. He turned the water, not into fermented wine, which could clearly have been an invitation to drunkenness, but to the sweet pure wine of the grape. This fruit of the vine was indeed a type of the blood He was to shed on the cross for mankind. But of this, He said, "Mine hour is not yet come" to fulfill that appointed purpose of His life. Still, in changing the water into wine, He would give the people a symbol of the covenant of His redeeming blood. Later, He would say, "Drink ye all of it; For this is my blood of the new testament, which is shed for many for the remission of sins" (Matt. 26:27-28). So while the time had not yet come for the actual fulfillment of these things, He could and did grant them a miracle that evening— which would be the type of His glorious redemption.

Now having considered the event in its relation to Christ's alleged making of alcoholic wine, we now look at the significance of the incident in its other aspects.

Christ's presence at the wedding shows us that God wants His people to be joyful. The source of that joy, however, must be consistent with God's holiness and righteousness. Nothing can more totally destroy happiness than sin. It is important that the sinner understand this. Religion would be a far more attractive thing to people if they learned it from Jesus' point of view.

As we have seen, an unfortunate circumstance developed at this wedding. The parents of the bride were poor people on whom the wedding would be a drain on their finances. In the midst of the wedding, the festivities came to a painful pause. Perhaps a larger number of guests than expected were present, causing the supply to run out more quickly than was anticipated. Peasant people, though poor, have a proud sensitiveness and they would feel a shame in failing in hospitality at this most important day in their daughter's life.

The mother of Jesus came to Him and whispered, "They have no wine." Did she expect Him to perform a miracle? It is impossible to answer the question fully. Some see in Mary's request a motive which conceivably could have had a bearing on the events of the evening. Certain people in Nazareth evidently knew that Mary had conceived Jesus before she was married to Joseph. It is probable that Mary and Joseph tried to explain what had taken place to some of their closest neighbors with not too great a success. It was one of those swords which pierced her heart about which Simeon spoke (Luke 2:35).

It can be well understood that adverse rumors went around the village of Nazareth, and the story that Mary told would be considered by the profane as a joke. Through the years Mary, innocent as she was, had to bear the reproaches cast against her as best as she could. Can we blame her for longing for the day when her Son would begin His ministry and show to the nation His true identity and thus vindicate her innocence and her virtue? Therefore, did her request at the wedding in Cana spring from a hope that now at last was the time for her Son to show forth His glory to the nation? And did not His reply caution her that the time had not yet fully come?

However this may be, the answer of Jesus shows that she expected Him to do something. Apart from the matters we have discussed, Mary believed that somehow Jesus would find a way to remedy the embarrassing predicament that the family was in. The events of recent weeks could not have been hidden from her, and their import suggested a possibility of power she did not fully understand.

Not many weeks before, Satan had suggested to Jesus that He make bread out of stones. Jesus had refused to make bread at Satan's command. His mother had made a similar request, albeit for a far different motive. What should Jesus do?

Jesus decided the circumstances warranted that He do something. Had He been a guest of the high and mighty, it is probable He would not have performed the miracle of turning the water to wine. But among these humble unsophisticated people who in their simplicity trusted in his kindliness and goodness, He would meet their need. Nevertheless, He was careful to make certain that His act was interpreted correctly.

His answer to his mother was also a reminder to her that there had come a change in their relation. She must no longer presume that things were the same as when He "came to Nazareth, and was subject unto them." He had a great mission to perform. There were things on His mind that she could neither understand nor share. It would be a hard lesson for her as a mother to learn.

Nor are we to think that the words, "Woman, what have I to do with thee?" spoken by Jesus were unduly severe. At that time, persons of the highest rank were so addressed. The word "woman" which sounds harsh to us was a mode of address which Christ used to His mother when He spoke to her when on the cross, "Woman, behold thy son." Nor did Mary appear hurt or rebuffed by what He said at the wedding. She knew Him too well for that. She did not know what He would do, but she told the servants, "Whatsoever he saith unto you, do it."

We do not believe that it would be irreverent to suggest that when Jesus came to the wedding, He had no intention of performing a miracle. Jesus had bound Himself with human limitations. This problem with which He was confronted was something that was unexpected; and He was being pressed to come to a sudden decision, just as we on occasions are forced to make unexpected decisions.

As Jesus waited for the leading of the Spirit, His course of action became plain. Although it was not the moment for the full revelation of His glory, still God whose compassion can always be touched, recognizing the need of the poor people, gave Jesus permission to perform His first miracle. But He must do it without fanfare or any ostentation.

Once the decision was made, Jesus gave instructions to the servants not to say anything to the guests, not even to the governor of the feast, as to where the supply of wine came from — at least until the wedding was over. His mother, as we have seen, had given explicit command to the servants that they follow his instructions. Everything was to be done naturally and without undue display. The servants were to fill up the waterpots with water, and then draw out and give to the guests. The governor of the feast evidently was somewhat of a philosopher, for he called the bridegroom and said, "Every man at the beginning doth set forth good wine; and when men have well drunk, then that which is worse: but thou has kept the good wine until now" (Verse 10).

In the miracle at Cana we see foreshadowed the nature of the ministry of Jesus. His work was to be a work of transformation, a ministry of blessing, a ministry of the supernatural. Nor did He disdain the innocent gaiety of homely pleasure. He was not against laughter. He was not the advocate of a sad countenance. Indeed, He was later to say of the Pharisees who fasted with long faces, "Be not, as the hypocrites, of a sad countenance" (Matt. 6:16).

In this we see a difference between Jesus and His forerunner. John was solitary, unsocial, and stern in his denunciation of sin that he might get men to flee from it. The Messiah by contrast entered into men's lives to share their joys, their problems, their sorrows, and to give them victory over sin.

In His attendance at the wedding, Jesus set His seal on marriage, as an institution ordained of God to promote the happiness and welfare of man. It has been well said that it is a sad thing that Jesus is not invited to all weddings. The marriage ceremony of the church declares marriage to be a high and holy estate signifying the mystical union between Christ and the church; therefore, it is not to be entered into lightly or wantonly, but reverently, soberly, discreetly, and in the fear of God.

We are told that in this miracle, Christ "manifested forth his glory; and his disciples believed on him" (John 2:11). Miracles were a part of His ministry, and they should have a definite place in the ministry of the church. Yet miracles are not for ostentatious display; they are a manifestation of God's compassion for suffering humanity. Christ never demonstrated miracles to satisfy curiosity, to dazzle the eyes of the crowd, to prove Himself to unbelief, or to excite mere wonder; He performed them to meet the needs of suffering humanity whom He came to heal and bless.

> "This beginning of miracles did Jesus in Cana of Galilee,
> and manifested forth his glory; and his disciples believed on
> him" (John 2:11).

According to the above, this was the first miracle that Jesus performed, indicating that the miracles recorded in the apocryphal books, alleged to have occurred in His boyhood days were pure fiction.

Chapter 21
The Cleansing of the Temple

After the wedding at Cana, Jesus and His mother and His brethren went down to Capernaum. Perhaps the brothers of Jesus thought to look over the city of Capernaum with the opportunities in that area for their carpenter trade. Little Nazareth might not be able to supply sufficient business for all of them.

> "After this he went down to Capernaum, he, and his mother, and his brethren, and his disciples: and they continued there not many days" (John 2:12).

At this particular time, Jesus did not remain long in Capernaum, but decided to go to Jerusalem to be there at the time of the celebration of the Passover, as had probably been His custom since the first Passover of His boyhood.

The natural route southward would have been to walk around the lake and down the gorge made by the Jordan River. Three days of steady travelling would have brought Him and His disciples to the crest of the Mount of Olives. By the time He reached there, thousands of pilgrims would have been swarming about the mount and in the valley below.

The visit of Jesus to Jerusalem at that time would have been different from any he had made previously. On other occasions He had been a pilgrim, but this time He came to the city — not yet to proclaim His Messiahship — but as a reformer. It was the capital of a nation where public opinion was formed, and if the people of Jerusalem received Him, the city would be the natural center for His ministry. The officials and leaders of the nations could have the first opportunity to accept His ministry.

It was at this Passover that the words of Malachi were fulfilled which spoke of the coming, of both Christ and His forerunner. John the Baptist had already come, and then suddenly the Messiah presented Himself at the temple.

> "Behold, I will send my messenger, and he shall prepare the way before me: and the Lord, whom ye seek, shall sud-

134

denly come to his temple, even the messenger of the covenant, whom ye delight in: behold, he shall come, saith the Lord of hosts. But who may abide the day of his coming? and who shall stand when he appeareth? for he is like a refiner's fire, and like fullers' soap" (Mal. 3:1-2).

Unfortunately, as we shall see, the Jews were not to delight in Him, for Christ came as a refining fire. Power and privilege lay in the hands of an ecclesiastical aristocracy, and they were well satisfied with things as they were and had no desire for change.

To Jesus, the temple was a sacred place. It was a symbol of His Father's presence even at the age of twelve, when in the temple He had felt that He "must be about his Father's business." But year after year as He had come to Jerusalem for the Passover, He had seen the temple desecrated by the money-changers who exploited the worshippers that came to Jerusalem. The avarice of the priests had turned the temple into a great money-making machine.

The pilgrims as they made their way to the temple had to pass through a large crowd of vendors and hawkers, who were busy selling their wares in the streets. This trafficking near the temple, while not altogether seemly, would perhaps be excusable. But the Court of the Gentiles, which was a part of the temple, had become a stockyard filled with cattle with its accompanying stench and filth. This could not be condoned. In the enclosure, there were men with wicker cages filled with doves, sitting under the shadow of the arcades. Finally, there were the money-changers. They performed the function of changing the various kinds of money of heathen governments, money defiled with heathen symbols and heathen inscriptions, into local currency. Once they had carried on their business outside the walls; but in time the space inside the Court of the Gentiles had proved too tempting to their greed, and they moved inside.

Thus it was that the place which should have been a house of prayer for all nations had been degraded into a shambles and a bustling bazaar. The lowing of the oxen and the bleating of the sheep, the cry of the huckster, the clink of the money, made the place a great babel of confusion, disturbing the worshippers, as well as drowning out the prayers of the priests.

It was necessary, of course, to have cattle markets and money-changers, but to bring all this into the temple grounds where the people were waiting to worship was a desecration of the Holy Place. It showed a lack of reverence.

On this day of which we speak, there was a strange commotion at the gate. A young man, stern, masterful, having an air of authority, came to the door of the temple. In His hands was a scourge of cords, and after pausing a moment, He began driving out the sheep and oxen and those who attended them. Then going over to the money-changers, He overturned their tables with the money that had been carefully stacked in piles, causing them to fall and the pieces to roll all over the floor. He did not overturn the tables of the dove-sellers lest the birds be injured, but to them he said, "Take these things hence."

> "And when he had made a scourge of small cords, he drove them all out of the temple, and the sheep, and the oxen; and poured out the changers' money, and overthrew the tables; and said unto them that sold doves, Take these things hence; make not my Father's house an house of merchandise. And his disciples remembered that it was written, The zeal of thine house hath eaten me up" (John 2:15-17).

Certainly this was a startling turn of events! Who was this young man who presumed to do such things? Nevertheless, no hand was lifted to stop Him. Soon the cattle and their drivers had disappeared. The money-changers staring angrily at the man who had interfered with their profitable business and had "insulted" them, looked around for someone to champion their cause, but no one volunteered. There was something in the stern eye of Jesus that caused everybody to back up. Muttering dark threats, the money-changers gathered up their coins and shambled off.

The chief priests of the temple were offended and dismayed. Their authority had been publicly challenged. It was something they could never forget nor forgive. When they had recovered from their astonishment, they came to Jesus, not daring to condemn what He had done, yet in no little indignation they asked Him by what authority He had done these things:

> "Then answered the Jews and said unto him, What sign shewest thou unto us, seeing that thou doest these things? Jesus answered and said unto them, Destroy this temple, and in three days I will raise it up. Then said the Jews, Forty and six years was this temple in building, and wilt thou rear it up in three days? But he spake of the temple of his body. When therefore he was risen from the dead, his disciples remembered that he had said this unto them; and they believed the scripture, and the word which Jesus had said" (John 2:18-22).

These words were quite beyond their comprehension. "Destroy this temple, and in three days I will raise it up." Although they did not understand the meaning of this, it made a powerful impression upon them that they never forgot. Why the very idea! It was forty-six years since the temple had begun building. Herod the Great had lavished his resources on the temple to ingratiate himself with the Jews. Ten thousand workmen had been employed to hew and fashion the stones. One thousand priests in sacred vestments lay the stones after they had been hewn. The temple with its colossal construction of marble, its costly mosaics, the magnificent sculpturings, the embroidered veils, and the ornamentation of precious stones had made it to rival the Seven Wonders of the World. Now this unknown stranger from the hills of Galilee had declared that if they destroyed it, He could raise it up again in three days!

The Jews might have realized that there was a hidden meaning behind those words but it suited their purpose to take them to mean the literal temple. Three years later during the time of Christ's trial, they would quote Him on this more than any other statement He made. In so doing, they distorted what He had said to, "I will destroy this temple that is made with hands, and within three days I will build another made without hands" (Mark 14:58). Jesus, of course, had never used this expression, but the maddened Jews were aware that it was best adapted to bolster their charge of sedition.

Yet, even His disciples did not fully understand what He meant at the time, nor did they realize until after the resurrection that He had spoken of the temple of His body. Hitherto there had been one temple of the living God, the one which had enshrined the Shekinah glory. But now the Spirit of God was dwelling in a temple made without hands. And this great truth was involved in the building of the mystical Body of Christ, the church (Acts 7:45-48; I Cor. 6:19).

Nevertheless, it is likely that the Jews had more insight into what Jesus really meant than they chose to let on. For when Jesus lay dead and buried in the tomb, they came to Pilate with the strange story saying, "Sir, we remember that that deceiver said, while he was yet alive, After three days I will rise again" (Matt. 27:63). It seems improbable that they had gotten this information from any other source than from this occasion. Since the disciples had not themselves believed that Jesus was going to die, they certainly would not have been the ones to volunteer this information.

Yet while Jesus had never said that He would destroy the temple, was not the worldly-minded priesthood doing this very thing? Were they not destroying its purpose and significance by allowing the temple to be profaned and commercialized, so that God would have to allow it to be removed out of His sight, and a new temple — the temple of the Church — to grow up in its place?

There is something about this picture of Christ in the temple that the artists have overlooked. Jesus was not always the meek lamb. There were times when He was angry. He became angry when the bigoted Jews sought to bring up their petty little rules to keep Him from healing a man on the Sabbath day. He exposed with fierce anger the hypocrisy of the Jews that held men back from seeking God and who "devoured widows' houses." He called them whited sepulchres, blind guides, and a generation of vipers! God is vexed at the hypocrisies of men. Men might mock Christ, might spit on Him and crucify Him, and He would show no personal resentment. He would have His disciples turn the other cheek to evil. But if the cheek of a helpless innocent was smitten, that was another matter.

The book of John informs us that other miracles were performed while Jesus was in Jerusalem, although we are not told what they were (John 3:2; 4:45). But Jesus apparently saw that there was not a deep enough work accomplished in the hearts of the people of that city that He could trust them. Jerusalem was not a place in which He could establish a sure foundation for His ministry. He would return to Galilee. But before He began His journey back, He was to have an unusual visitor, a man by the name of Nicodemus, a ruler of the Jews, who came to Him under cover of darkness.

Chapter 22
The Night Visitor

One can imagine the excitement in Jerusalem that night after Jesus had cleansed the temple. This Galilean prophet had challenged the chief authorities of the nation. Everyone was talking about what had happened. Those of the established order were hostile and critical. But there were those even among the Pharisees who were impressed by the young man. It is also possible that John the Baptist's declaration about His being the Messiah had reached the ears of those at Jerusalem. The Baptist had a powerful influence throughout Judaea.

Whatever the Pharisees were, they were alert to what might affect their own interests. When news came of John the Baptist's ministry in the wilderness, they immediately dispatched a deputation of priests and Levites to meet him and ask him whether he were Elijah or the Christ (John 1:19-27). It appears possible, therefore, that they sent Nicodemus to Jesus for the purpose of ascertaining more about Him, and just what His claims were. They had already asked Him to show them a sign as proof of His authority (John 2:18), but the reply they had gotten was by no means satisfactory. Perhaps Nicodemus could elicit further information from Him.

Nicodemus seemed to be well suited for such a delicate mission. He was a ruler of the Jews, a member of the Sanhedrin. Although not a bold man, he was known as one who stood against injustice. While it is possible that Nicodemus was acting on behalf of the Jewish rulers, many believe that Nicodemus made the visit without knowledge of the other members of the Sanhedrin. Whether he went as a messenger, or on his own accord, we know he went secretly, not wishing people of the city to know of His visit.

Where did this memorable interview of Nicodemus with Jesus take place? Probably on the Mt. of Olives, or its vicinity, since we have no record that Jesus passed the night within the city's gates. Nicodemus had to ascertain earlier in the evening where Jesus and His disciples lodged. Then at nightfall, under the cover of darkness, he went to see Him. Covered from head to foot with his cloak, he stood knocking at the door of the house where Jesus was staying. He was invited in and cordially received. Since the upper part of a house was often used for private conversations, it is probable that they went up to the roof to talk. There Nicodemus made known the purpose of his visit.

> "The same came to Jesus by night, and said unto him, Rabbi, we know that thou art a teacher come from God: for no man can do these miracles that thou doest, except God be with him" (John 3:2).

It is clear that Nicodemus recognized Jesus as a prophet, and had probably spoken to his colleagues in His favor. Later, he was to defend Christ at a time when it was dangerous for him to do so. But he was not a bold man, and he had a constitutional timidity that he had difficulty in overcoming. Nicodemus acknowledged that Jesus was of God, although he probably was not prepared to accept Him yet as the Messiah. He intimated that some of the others of the Sanhedrin were of a favorable opinion, although they had reservations about some of the things that He did, such as perhaps His act of cleansing the temple.

Nicodemus recognized the miracles that Jesus had performed. Indeed the miracle is the universal language understood by all. And it is by the miracle that the gospel was to be introduced to the heathen and preached in all the world (Mark 16:15-18). The miracle was the sign of the Messiah, and of the approach of the Kingdom of God. Nicodemus wanted to hear about that kingdom that the Messiah would establish. He expected as all others did that it would be a temporal kingdom, glorious and prosperous. Every Israelite by birth would be a member of it. So understood Nicodemus. It is just possible that the kindly old man, situated in his high position, thought that his counsel might be of value to the young enthusiast, and perhaps keep Him from making rash moves such as the one that occurred in the temple.

What Nicodemus might have said further, we can only conjecture, for Jesus brushed aside the line of thought of His visitor, and without formalities started with the uncompromising statement, "Verily, verily I say unto thee, Except a man be born again, he cannot see the kingdom of God" (John 3:3). We have only fragments of the conversation, but we can assume that Jesus explained further, that the Kingdom of God was not a kingdom of politics and earthly power. Something more was needed than Jewish birth to enter it. Men needed to be born again, born of the

Spirit of God. That was the only way they could enter into the Kingdom.

This declaration of Jesus amazed Nicodemus. He had known about the heathen needing conversion, but not Jews. The idea was abhorrent to this Pharisee's instincts. In a kind of querulous surprise, he chose to interpret the words of Jesus in an absurd physical sense. "How can a man be born when he is old? can he enter the second time into his mother's womb, and be born?" (Verse 4). Jesus did not pause to notice this kind of argument, and He repeated, "Except a man be born of water and of the Spirit, he cannot enter into the kingdom of God" (Verse 5). Here was an allusion to the work of John the Baptist and his baptism in water unto repentance.

The cool breezes of the mountain blew about them, as they sat there talking. Jesus showed that the work of the Spirit was as real as the wind that blew, although it was a mystery: "The wind bloweth where it listeth, and thou hearest the sound thereof, but canst not tell whence it cometh, and whither it goeth: so is every one that is born of the Spirit" (John 3:8).

Nicodemus was so puzzled by all this that he could say little more. Jesus half sorrowful and half reproachful, went on to explain to him about spiritual things. He even divulged His mission to him — that He was to give his life that men might be saved.

> "For God so loved the world, that he gave his only begotten Son, that whosoever believeth in him should not perish, but have everlasting life. For God sent not his Son into the world to condemn the world; but that the world through him might be saved. He that believeth on him is not condemned: but he that believeth not is condemned already, because he hath not believed in the name of the only begotten Son of God. And this is the condemnation, that light is come into the world, and men loved darkness rather than light, because their deeds were evil. For every one that doeth evil hateth the light, neither cometh to the light, lest his deeds should be reproved. But he that doeth truth cometh to the light, that his deeds may be made manifest, that they are wrought in God" (John 3:16-21).

Nicodemus left the place a bewildered man. Yet he felt irresistibly compelled to believe in the young man who had given him that memorable interview. Twice more we hear of Nicodemus. Each time he acts with caution; nevertheless, he takes the side of Jesus. Once when the Jews were bent on violence, Nicodemus said, "Doth our law condemn a man without a hearing?" And finally when Jesus was dead, he came again bringing his gift of spices, the last gift he could give to the Friend he had come to believe in.

Shortly after this, Jesus left Jerusalem. Jerusalem was not the place to make His home. He departed out of the city and went down to the Jordan River. John had not yet been cast into prison and he was baptizing in Aenon near Salem. We are told that the disciples of Jesus also began to baptize and make disciples. Why they baptized is not explained in the gospels. We do know that as soon as John was put in prison the disciples ceased this type of ministry — until Christ gave them the Great Commission, after His resurrection. It is obvious that earlier baptism was but a transitory phase of the opening ministry of Christ. Jesus probably did not consider it wise to make an abrupt change while John was still active. His baptism that He would authorize would be distinctly different from John's.

Already John's star was waning. His crowds were diminishing — a large part of his former audience was flocking to the baptism of Christ's disciples. The jealousy that could not move the Baptist did, however, affect the hearts of John's followers. A certain Jew who seemed glad to sow dissension in John's camp said, "Rabbi, he that was with thee beyond Jordan, to whom thou barest witness, behold, the same baptizeth, and all men come unto him" (John 3:26). The resentment that another should be a successful rival of their champion who had once so stirred the people, is seen in this irritable address. In John's answer, his essential greatness shines forth. He could not and would not enter into the petty rivalries of men. To him God was the sole source of all good gifts. He reminded his disciples that he had always said that he was not the Christ, but only the friend of the Bridegroom.

The news eventually got around to Jesus that the Pharisees were using the success of His ministry to create jealousy in John's camp. Therefore, out of regard for the wounded feelings of John's followers, he thought it advisable to leave Judaea.

But even as He prepared to depart, word reached Him that John had been taken by Herod's soldiers (Matt. 4:12). In making his trip to Galilee, he decided to go through Samaria. It would not do for Him under those circumstances, to meet John as he was being escorted in chains to the fortress of Machairus. He would never see John again during this earthly life. With the Baptist's ministry terminated, a new era in the ministry of Christ began.

Chapter 23
The Woman of Samaria

"He left Judaea, and departed again into Galilee. And he must needs go through Samaria. Then cometh he to a city of Samaria, which is called Sychar, near to the parcel of ground that Jacob gave to his son Joseph. Now Jacob's well was there. Jesus therefore, being wearied with his journey, sat thus on the well: and it was about the sixth hour. There cometh a woman of Samaria to draw water: Jesus saith unto her, Give me to drink. (For his disciples were gone away unto the city to buy meat.) Then saith the woman of Samaria unto him, How is it that thou, being a Jew, askest drink of me, which am a woman of Samaria? for the Jews have no dealings with the Samaritans" (John 4:3-9).

At the time of which we are speaking, most Jews had ceased taking the route through Samaria because of the bad feelings between Jews and Samaritans. These people of Samaria were of mixed blood, part heathen and part Israelite. At the time of the early captivities, they had been brought over by the Assyrian king to re-people the country (II Kings 17:26-27). Their religion was a mixture of Judaism and heathenism. The sacred record declares, "So these nations feared the Lord, and served their graven images, both their children, and their children's children: as did their fathers, so do they unto this day" (II Kings 17:41).

In the days of Nehemiah, they had volunteered their services to help build the walls of the city of Jerusalem; and since their services were refused, they had become the implacable enemies of the Jews.

Shortly after the birth of Christ, a new feud developed between the Samaritans and the Jews. The Samaritans had always refused to recognize the primacy of Jerusalem and claimed that their sacred Mount Gerizim was the place to worship. But beyond this, the Samaritans minded their own business. Then a serious incident occurred. During the days of the Passover, the custom of closing

143

the gates of the city of Jerusalem at night was not observed because of the many visitors who had come long distances and had no place to lodge except outside the city walls. Some of the Samaritans, resolving to defile the temple, brought in fragments of dead bodies and scattered them about the temple area. Nothing could have angered the Jews more than this. From that time on, the Samaritans were excluded from the temple grounds. The incident resulted in a complete estrangement of the two peoples. They no longer had dealings with one another of any kind. Most Jews when making the journey north to Galilee did not take the shorter way through Samaria, but took the longer route up the Jordan valley. But Jesus decided to go on the old way. John records the statement that "he must needs go through Samaria."

Starting early in the morning in order to secure as many hours of daylight as possible, He and His disciples left the Jordan area on their journey north, stopping at length for rest and refreshment at a well located near the town of Sychar in Samaria. This well was famous in that it had been dug by the patriarch Jacob many centuries before. The well was a hundred feet deep, but its waters were unusually excellent and the inhabitants of the city preferred the quality of its water over that which came from the calcareous springs of Mt. Ebal. Jesus, being wearied with His journey, sat down on the well under the shelter of an alcove built overhead. Since it was the noon hour, it was arranged that the disciples should continue on into the city to purchase provisions (John 4:8).

While Jesus was waiting for the return of the disciples, His solitude was broken by the approach of a Samaritan woman. Turning about, He saw the woman coming to the well to draw water, her earthen vessel gracefully poised on her head. The woman's appearance at this hour was unusual, for ordinarily the people of the East draw their water in the morning or the evening. The fact that she came at high noon indicated that she was not on good terms with the women of the city. She was apparently an outcast of society, having been married five times, and at that time was consorting with a man who was not her husband. She must still have had traces of beauty, or she would not have attracted so many husbands. But there was also a look of sadness and disillusionment upon her face as of one from which hope had faded.

The Lord hailed her approach. Thirsty and fatigued Himself, He observed her pitcher and since He had no means of reaching

144

the cool water that glimmered below, He said to her, "Give me to drink." The attire of Jesus and His accent were sufficient to show the woman that Jesus was a Jew. This startled her, and half in surprise and half in irony, she responded saying, "How is it that thou, being a Jew, askest drink of me, which am a woman of Samaria? For the Jews have no dealings with the Samaritans."

Jesus responded saying, "If thou knewest the gift of God, and who it is that saith unto thee, Give me to drink; thou wouldst have asked of him, and he would have given thee living water." She pointed at the well, a hundred feet deep. He had no vessel to draw with, how then would it be possible for Him to draw water? Was He greater than their father Jacob who had dug the well and drank of it? Jesus had met the same unimaginative dullness among the learned, but spiritually unperceptive. The woman could only think of common water, while He was speaking of the water of everlasting life that quenched thirst forever.

This seemed to be a sheer absurdity, yet though the woman was puzzled by his words, and despite her own prejudices, she found herself beginning to have confidence in the stranger. So she said, "Sir, give me this water, that I thirst not, neither come hither to draw." If she could drink of this wonderful water, it would not be necessary for her to come all the way from the village at the hot noontide to draw water from this well.

At this moment, the Lord made what appeared to be a startling change of conversation. He asked her to go and call her husband and return. In the decorum of the East it was improper for Him to hold a conversation with a strange woman. But the purpose of His request was to awaken the conscience of the woman. For He could not give her the water of life, until that was accomplished. Jesus' words forced her to answer ,that she had no husband, and the Lord acknowledging her confession, bared her loose and sinful life.

> "The woman answered and said, I have no husband; Jesus said unto her, Thou hast well said, I have no husband: For thou hast had five husbands; and he whom thou now hast is not thy husband: in that saidst thou truly" (John 4:17-18).

Here we see the working of the gift of the Word of Knowledge. Christ as a man did not have omniscience, but the gift in its operation disclosed pertinent information about the woman which would be helpful in the arousing of her conscience. Jesus was not there to accuse and condemn her. Nevertheless, it was necessary that her conscience be awakened before He could help her.

The woman was then convinced that Jesus was a prophet. Not eager to linger on the facts of her own history, her mind leaped to the great question that agitated the passions of her people, and which was the basis of the fierce controversy between her race and the Jews. It was, as it were, the age-old question that has been fought over thousands of times, "Which church is the true church?"

Since chance had given her this golden opportunity to speak to a prophet, was not this, she thought, the time to settle the question whether Gerizim, the place where Joshua had uttered the blessings, or Jerusalem, where Solomon had built the temple, was the place where men ought to worship? Her question received an answer, but one different from what the woman expected:

> "Our fathers worshipped in this mountain; and ye say, that in Jerusalem is the place where men ought to worship. Jesus saith unto her, Woman, believe me, the hour cometh, when ye shall neither in this mountain, nor yet at Jerusalem, worship the Father. Ye worship ye know not what: we know what we worship: for salvation is of the Jews. But the hour cometh, and now is, when the true worshippers shall worship the Father in spirit and in truth: for the Father seeketh such to worship him. God is a Spirit: and they that worship him must worship him in spirit and in truth" (John 4:20-24).

The Jews were unquestionably right in their contention that Jerusalem was the place where God had chosen to put His name. Compared to Judaism, the worship of Samaria was hybrid and defective. But Jesus skillfully avoided the controversial issue and carried the matter beyond the temporal and provincial aspect by saying that the time had come when true worshippers might worship God at any place and any time.

The woman was deeply moved, but how could she change her whole belief on the words of a passing stranger? She merely sighed and said, "I know that Messiah cometh, which is called Christ: when he is come, he will tell us all things" (John 4:25).

Then in sudden and startling revelation, Jesus chose to reveal to this outcast the secret of His identity and the reason for His coming into the world! He said, "I that speak unto thee am he."

At this moment, the disciples had returned with the provisions they had procured at the village. They stood aghast as they listened to Jesus conversing with the Samaritan woman. Ordinarily, a Jew might not talk to a woman on the street, even if she were his own wife or daughter. The downgrading of women is one of the

146

features of Judaism, as well as the heathen religions. In the *Vinaya* a *Bhikshu of Buddhism,* a man is not only forbidden to speak to a woman, but he may not hold out his hand to his own mother if she should be drowning. The disciples, therefore, might well marvel that the Master would converse with this Samaritan woman. Yet accustomed to His strange and unexpected ways, they did not remonstrate with Him or make comment on His conversation with her.

The woman herself gave the disciples no heed. Overwhelmed by the tidings she had heard, she hurried away, forgetting to take her water-pot. The disciples after producing the provisions they had brought, invited Jesus to partake. But all hunger had been satisfied in His exaltation of winning a soul. He merely said, "I have meat to eat that ye know not of" (Verse 32). Here was the explanation of the words He had spoken when the evil one tempted him, "Man shall not live by bread alone, but by every word that proceedeth out of the mouth of God."

The disciples still did not know what He was referring to, and they asked each other, whether while they had been absent someone had brought Him food. Patiently the Lord explained what He meant. He pointed to the people of the city of Sychar who were now coming out to Him because of the Samaritan woman's testimony, "Come, see a man, which told me all things that ever I did: is not this the Christ?" (Verse 29).

Jesus told His disciples not to say to themselves that there were four months yet before the harvest, but to look at the fields already white unto harvest. Jesus intimated that while He sowed in sorrow, they would be joyful reapers of the harvest in time to come.

Now this woman (who incidentally was the first woman to preach the gospel in the Christian dispensation) in the joy of her discovery, forgot the ostracism and scorn to which she had been subjected, and went boldly to the people and told them that she had found the Messiah. Her words apparently made a remarkable stir. It should also be remembered that a few months before, the whole region had been moved by the preaching of John the Baptist. The people had probably heard John's announcement that the Messiah had come. Therefore, upon hearing the words of the woman that a wondrous prophet had come to their neighborhood, they poured out to meet Him.

When Jesus saw the people rushing toward Him, and saw their eager faces, He longed to bless them. It was a welcome contrast

147

to the poor reception He had received in Jerusalem. When He saw the hunger in their hearts, He no doubt chafed at the limitations of His mission that confined His ministry to that of Israel. He scarce could refrain from putting in the sickle, then and there, as He longed for the day when the river of His grace could break all bounds and stream out to a thirsty world. But it was only His to sow; later the disciples would reap.

> "I sent you to reap that whereon ye bestowed no labour: other men laboured, and ye are entered into their labours" (John 4:38).

Thus, in these words Jesus congratulated the disciples that for them was reserved this high ministry, this great hope and consummation for which the prophets had dreamed and toiled.

Nevertheless, so great were the importunities of the people that Jesus consented to tarry with them two days. Although He performed no miracles there, the people received Him joyfully and believed that He was the Christ, the Saviour of the world.

> "And many more believed because of his own word; And said unto the woman, Now we believe, not because of thy saying: for we have heard him ourselves, and know that this is indeed the Christ, the Saviour of the world" (John 4:41-42).

Those two days that Jesus tarried bore abundant fruit, and the results were firstfruits of the great Gentile harvest that was to come. No doubt it was the teaching of these two days that played a large part in the rich harvest of souls that took place a few years later when Philip went down to Samaria and preached Christ to them (Acts 8). Jesus might have tarried longer in Samaria, and other cities in that vicinity might have received Him just as enthusiastically. But a public demonstration in His favor in Samaria at this time would surely have prejudiced His future work in Jewry; so reluctantly He bade them goodbye, and He turned His footsteps toward Galilee.

Chapter 24

The Visit at Nazareth and Cana

"And he came to Nazareth, where he had been brought up: and, as his custom was, he went into the synagogue on the sabbath day, and stood up for to read. And there was delivered unto him the book of the prophet Esaias. And when he had opened the book, he found the place where it was written, The Spirit of the Lord is upon me, because he hath anointed me to preach the gospel to the poor; he hath sent me to heal the brokenhearted, to preach deliverance to the captives, and recovering of sight to the blind, to set at liberty them that are bruised. To preach the acceptable year of the Lord. And he closed the book, and he gave it again to the minister, and sat down. And the eyes of all them that were in the synagogue were fastened on him. And he began to say unto them, This day is this scripture fulfilled in your ears" (Luke 4:16-21).

Jesus and His disciples continued their journey northward until they reached Galilee. It appears that He stayed there only a short time, and then went on to Nazareth. He was well received in Galilee, for some of the people had been in Jerusalem at the Passover Feast, and they had seen the miracles that Jesus had performed there. Upon returning to Capernaum, they had spread His fame abroad (John 4:45).

This was not altogether to Christ's liking. He was becoming known as a "wonder-worker" before He had an opportunity to preach to them the gospel of the Kingdom. People were wanting healing for their bodies before healing for their souls. He did not desire to become an object of gaping wonderment. He decided, therefore, before He settled down in Galilee, that He would first go to His home town of Nazareth. Leaving His disciples behind so they could catch up on their fishing, He made the seven-hour journey.

In the years that Jesus had spent in Nazareth, it had been His custom to attend the synagogue on each Sabbath. Upon the next Sabbath day, He went with the others there to worship. Since He had previously been a reader in the synagogue, they brought out the scroll and gave it to Him to read. He took it and unrolled it until He came to Chapter 61 of Isaiah. Then the whole congregation stood to their feet while He read. Jesus did not read the whole passage, but stopped with an exquisite preciseness at the words, "the day of vengeance of our God." That part of the prophecy was not to be fulfilled at that time. This was not the day of vengeance, but "the acceptable year of the Lord."

Jesus went on to explain to the people that no prophet is acceptable in his own country. He reminded them that miracles were not limited to a geographical area, and He gave them examples of the healing of Naaman the Syrian, and the multiplying of the meal and oil for the widow at Sarepta, both Gentiles.

As He continued His discourse, it appeared to the people at Nazareth that He was saying that they were no better than Gentiles and lepers. This struck hard at their racial pride. It was intolerable that a mere carpenter grown up in their village should talk to them in this way. Their anger burst out into a flame. Rising up, some of the more vengeful citizens probably demanded an apology for His words, and securing none, "thrust him out of the city, and led him unto the brow of the hill whereon their city was built, that they might cast him down headlong" (Lk. 4:29). His hour, however, had not yet come; and suddenly Jesus asserted His mastery. "He passing through the midst of them went his way." It was not exactly a miracle, yet it was a demonstration of personal power. Something about His bearing overawed them. Under the spell of His presence, the mob which had intended violence involuntarily bowed before Him.

There would be other times when the Jews would take up stones to kill Him, but somehow each time they would fail to carry out their design. It was this same power that prevented the officers from arresting Jesus after they had been given a charge to do so by the Sanhedrin. It was that dominion of His Spirit that caused the soldiers to fall backward when they came to take Him after Judas had betrayed Him.

But was there no boyhood friend in Nazareth to stand by Him? Seemingly none. There were friends, however, in Cana of Galilee only a few miles away. That was the village where He had performed His first miracle of the turning of water into wine. At Cana He would probably stay at the home of Nathanael, one of

His first disciples. Yes, at Cana He would find a friendly reception awaiting Him. The little maiden whose wedding He had honored by His presence would be glad for His visit there. Those who were present at the wedding feast would all want to see Him. No doubt there was a great indignation at Cana when the news reached them of how rudely He had been treated by the citizens of Nazareth. The people of Cana had little use for those of Nazareth. Nathanael's response to Philip's news about the One who came from there was, "Can there any good thing come out of Nazareth?" (John 1:46).

The Healing of the Nobleman's Son

Jesus had not been in Cana long when a visitor from Herod's Court, hearing of His arrival, sought Him to come at once to Capernaum to heal his son. Not all of Herod's court had shown the spirit of Herodias. We know that Manaen, the foster-brother of Herod, was in after-years a believer, and indeed a prophet (Acts 13:1).

We also know that Joanna, the wife of Chuza, Herod's steward, was among the women who ministered to Jesus of their substance (Luke 8:3). It has been conjectured with some probability that the nobleman was none other than Chuza himself.

> "So Jesus came again into Cana of Galilee, where he made the water wine. And there was a certain nobleman, whose son was sick at Capernaum. When he heard that Jesus was come out of Judaea into Galilee, he went unto him, and besought him that he would come down, and heal his son: for he was at the point of death. Then said Jesus unto him, Except ye see signs and wonders, ye will not believe. The nobleman saith unto him, Sir, come down ere my child die. Jesus saith unto him, Go thy way; thy son liveth. And the man believed the word that Jesus had spoken unto him, and he went his way" (John 4:46-50)

It was at one o'clock in the afternoon when the nobleman arrived. This courtier was in sore trouble. His only son was lying sick of a deadly fever at Capernaum. The fame of Jesus' miracles at Jerusalem as well as those performed already in Galilee had inspired the father with a desperate hope. He had left the bedside of his dying child and had searched until he had located Jesus in Cana. Now he implored Him to come and heal his son.

The request did not altogether please Jesus. Everywhere the

151

talk of His miracles had spread, and it seemed to Him that there was no recognition or thought of the conditions by which healing might he received. And what about this courtier from Herod's court? Herod had just taken John the Baptist and imprisoned him in the fortress of Machairus. Although the nobleman seemed sincere, nevertheless, it was important that Jesus make clear that He was no mere miracle-worker or physician, ready to place His supernatural powers at the beck and call of anyone who wanted Him. It appeared that the nobleman's trip to see Him was a desperate resort after everything else had failed.

Every minister who prays for the sick has many such people to deal with. Some are desperate; they can think of nothing but the fact that their loved one faces death. They have to be shown that "healing is the children's bread," and that it is appropriated by faith.

Therefore, Jesus said unto him, "Except ye see signs and wonders, ye will not believe" (Verse 48). That was Herod's case. He had a sort of superstitious belief in the supernatural. When he heard of Jesus' ministry, he was sure that He was John the Baptist raised from the dead (Matt. 14:1-2). Later, when Jesus was on trial, Herod wanted Him to perform a miracle for him, which had He done so, Herod no doubt would have released Him. Jesus, however, would perform no signs to gratify the vulgar curiosity of the monarch.

Nevertheless, the nobleman's passionate entreaty caused Jesus to yield to his request, which illustrates how importunity will move the heart of God. The nobleman had more desperation than real faith, but even that desperation begat faith for healing. Jesus told the nobleman that his son would live.

It appears that Jesus' words calmed the anxieties of the father, for instead of going directly to Capernaum, he slept somewhere that night while on the road. He could have gotten back within five or six hours, but he believed the words of Jesus. The following day, while still on the way, he met his servants who brought him the wondrous news that his son was recovering. The father asked them when he began to amend. The servants replied that it was at the seventh hour of the previous day, the hour when Jesus spoke the word (John 4:51-53).

There is a great truth in this incident. Not all sick persons have faith for instantaneous miracles. But if they will only believe the word that is spoken, they will, as the nobleman's son, begin to amend from that hour.

Chapter 25

The Demoniac
in the Synagogue

From Cana Jesus went to Capernaum on the sea of Galilee, making the trip soon after the nobleman's son was healed. There has been some dispute as to where Capernaum was located, but it is generally believed that it was situated at the northwest corner of the Sea of Galilee. The lake is some 13 miles long and 8 miles wide, and shaped somewhat like a harp. It lies 682 feet below the level of the Mediterranean Sea, and thus basks in tropical heat. The water is crystal clear and teems with edible fish. In the Lord's day, the surface of the lake was dotted with the boats of fishermen of whom were Andrew and Peter and James and John. On its banks were thriving cities, Tiberias, Bethsaida, Chorazin, Capernaum, Magdala, and others. Capernaum means *Village of Nahum,* and tradition claims it was the burial place of the prophet.

Capernaum was a city of unusual prosperity. First of all, it was the principal center of the fishing industry. A suburb of the town was given to the salting of fish, which were packed in kegs and exported. South of the city is a fertile plain which brought forth figs, grapes, olives, and nuts in luxurious abundance.

One other important circumstance contributed to Capernaum's prosperity, and that was the fact that several of the great trade routes converged at this point. Caravans from the East and West, as well as from the North and South, crossed near Capernaum. This heavy stream of traffic made the city a great trade center. It was, therefore, more than a provincial town in Jesus' day; it was in fact fast becoming a cosmopolitan city. Capernaum, therefore, was well adapted and situated for the purposes of the Lord's ministry. Nowhere else could He have secured so extensive a hearing, except perhaps at Jerusalem, which, however, as we have already noted, responded only reluctantly to His revolutionary teaching.

It will be noted presently, the great number of sick people that were brought to Christ for healing, while He was in Galilee. Not far from Capernaum at Tiberias were hot springs where many sick folk congregated. The nobleman no doubt let it be known in Tiberias, how his son was healed. The news that this distinguished family had professed faith in Jesus would spread rapidly, and it is not surprising that the sick gathering around these spots would seek to have Christ lay hands upon them for healing.

The Meeting in the Synagogue

"And they went into Capernaum; and straightway on the Sabbath day he entered into the synagogue, and taught. And they were astonished at his doctrine: for he taught them as one that had authority, and not as the scribes. And there was in their synagogue a man with an unclean spirit; and he cried out, Saying, Let us alone; what have we to do with thee, thou Jesus of Nazareth? art thou come to destroy us? I know thee who thou art, the Holy One of God. And Jesus rebuked him, saying, Hold thy peace, and come out of him. And when the unclean spirit had torn him, and cried with a loud voice, he came out of him. And they were all amazed, insomuch that they questioned among themselves saying, What thing is this? what new doctrine is this? for with authority commandeth he even the unclean spirits, and they do obey Him" (Mark 1:21-27).

Christ's disciples, as we have noted, seem not to have been with Him at Nazareth and Cana, with the possible exception of Nathanael who lived in Cana. Apparently they remained in their homes while He went on to Nazareth. We find them at Capernaum and active in their occupations when the Lord returned.

Jesus stayed at the home of Peter for a time, but later it appears that He had His own house. Perhaps someone healed through His ministry asked Him to use it for the time (Mark 2:1-2). Regardless of who owned the house, it apparently suffered damage, when four men broke open the roof to let a palsied man down for healing (Mark 2:1-4).

After establishing His headquarters in Capernaum, Jesus began regular attendance at the local synagogue, where He was often invited to speak (Luke 4:31). The structure was of white limestone, some sixty feet wide and eighty feet in length, and was one of the finest synagogues in the land. It had been built by a wealthy centurion who was a friend of the Jewish people (Luke 7:4-5). The synagogue was later destroyed, perhaps by an earthquake, and built again only to suffer another devastation.

154

But the stones are still there today, and the site is considered one of the best authenticated places in Israel.

There was a women's gallery in the synagogue which was supported by stone pillars. The women and girls did not enter the lower part of the building to reach this gallery, but ascended an outside stairway of stone.

On the day that Jesus made His first appearance in the synagogue at Capernaum, we can fairly well trace the order of events. The morning service would have been at nine o'clock. Shortly before that hour, people from every part of the city could have been seen making their way to the new white synagogue. Farmers and fisher-folk came with their families. Zebedee arrived with his wife and their full-grown sons, James and John. Andrew came with Peter and his family. Perhaps Jesus walked along with them. Jairus, the ruler of the synagogue, was there with his wife and daughter. It is not improbable that "the nobleman whose son was sick at Capernaum" and whom Jesus healed was present. Many people had heard that the stranger who had been performing wonderful miracles was in town and was expected at the synagogue. By nine o'clock the place was crowded to the doors.

The service began. The chief minister rose to begin prayers. The whole congregation bowed their heads. When prayers were over, one of the rolls was taken out of the ark, and a rabbi or prominent person began to read. After that, the chief minister looked toward the visitor sitting next to Peter, and told Him that if He had a word of exhortation to come forward and speak. Jesus accepted the invitation and went to the front and sat in the chair of the rabbi. Every eye was fixed on Him as He began to speak. People had heard many rumors concerning Him. Who was He? What was His teaching? As Jesus began to speak, it was not in the dull conventional tone of the scribes. His words went forth with power and authority.

We do not have a record of the actual words Jesus spoke that day. But it is probable that His message was along similar lines to that which He preached on the Mount of Beatitudes. The reaction of the people to the sermon was nearly the same as that which occurred when He came down from the Mount (Matt. 7:28-29; Mark 1:27).

It was not the intention of Jesus that the people should get the idea that He was coming to overthrow the Law. He said, "Think not that I am come to destroy . . . but to fulfill" (Matt. 5:17). But He did show that He was lifting the Law to a higher and nobler plane. The following is probably an example of what He said:

> "Ye have heard that it was said by them of old time, Thou shalt not kill; and whosoever shall kill shall be in danger of the judgment: But I say unto you, That whosoever is angry with his brother without a cause shall be in danger of the judgment: and whosoever shall say to his brother, Raca, shall be in danger of the council: but whosoever shall say, Thou fool, shall be in danger of hell fire.... Ye have heard that it was said by them of old time, Thou shalt not commit adultery: But I say unto you, That whosoever looketh on a woman to lust after her hath committed adultery with her already in his heart" (Matt. 5:21-22, 27-28).

Jesus thus took the people far above the letter of the Old Law, telling them to "Love your enemies, bless them that curse you, do good to them that hate you, and pray for them which despitefully use you, and persecute you . . ." (Matt. 5:44).

Suddenly, while Jesus was in the midst of His discourse, there was a wild disturbance. A demon-possessed man had slipped into the congregation. Apparently this unfortunate person was not violent, except at times. However, when the evil spirit was disquieted, it would throw him into a spasm. Demons are very sensitive to the presence of divine power, as anyone who has had experience in casting out these evil spirits well knows. We can understand that the presence of Christ would be quickly felt in the spirit world. Demons writhe in agony when the power of the Holy Spirit is manifested in their vicinity. The evil spirit realized that his own security was threatened, and he cried out saying:

> ". . . Let us alone; what have we to do with thee, thou Jesus of Nazareth? art thou come to destroy us? I know thee who thou art, the Holy One of God" (Mark 1:24).

We notice that some who write on the life of Christ doubt the existence of evil spirits. David Smith in *The Days of His Flesh* says:

> "The idea is of course simply a fantastic notion of a dark age unskilled in natural science, and it was nothing strange that people in the New Testament should have entertained it. But it is disconcerting that it seems to have been entertained by Jesus also. He would address the supposed demon, rebuking it and commanding it come out of the man! That He should thus share the limitation of His age is at first blush somewhat of a shock of faith; yet, even if it be allowed, there is perhaps no real occasion for disquietude. When the Lord of Glory

156

came down to earth, He assumed the nature of the children of men, being made at every point like unto his brethren, and it might be accepted as a welcome evidence of the reality of the Incarnation if He were found to have shared the scientific and metaphysical conceptions of His contemporaries."

This weird exegesis on demons is a pitiful one, written as it is by one who evidently has had no practical knowledge of the reality of the spirit world. The activities of demon forces in the earth today have become so widespread that to deny their existence can only mark a professed Christian as a person of incredible ignorance. The above "explanation" is a miserable attempt to make Christ an ignoramus who fell in with the delusions of His time.

As the people of Capernaum that day listened to the speaker with mute astonishment, hanging on to His words with deep reverent admiration, the demon in the man disturbed by the presence of Christ, cried out in fear. Perhaps the evil spirit hoped to break up the meeting and thus bring discredit upon the speaker.

Many times in the writer's experience, we have witnessed demons distressed by the presence of an anointed minister. They may rave against him, demanding to be let alone. But Jesus recognized the source of the disturbance and spoke to the evil spirit, commanding it to come out of the man. Immediately the demoniac fell to the floor in a fearful paroxysm, screaming and convulsed. But it was soon all over. The man arose wonderfully healed and in his right mind.

It was a thrilling moment for the congregation. The ruler of the synagogue, as well as the other officials, had sat transfixed by this strange occurrence. They had seen the man, his face twisted and distorted, collapsing and writhing on the pavement. They heard the shriek of the baffled and tormented devil, while women in the gallery cried out with fear and terror. But the man was now in his right mind and could talk to the people in normal conversation. The deliverance of the demoniac was so remarkable as to command the astonishment and admiration of the entire audience.

The Healing of Peter's Mother-In-Law

The news of what happened, spread like wildfire through the community. People from a distance went back to tell other friends. By evening the whole region had heard about it. In the meanwhile Jesus returned to Peter's house with James and John.

157

"And forthwith, when they were come out of the synagogue, they entered into the house of Simon and Andrew,
with James and John. But Simon's wife's mother lay sick of
a fever, and anon they tell him of her. And he came and
took her by the hand, and lifted her up; and immediately
the fever left her, and she ministered unto them" (Mark
1:29-31).

Peter lived with his wife and her mother in a little house by
the seashore. When Jesus and the group reached the door of the
home, they were met by Peter's wife, who had distressing news
to tell. The mother-in-law, who had been feeling badly enough
not to have attended the synagogue services, had become ill with
a raging fever. Peter having witnessed the miracle at the synagogue, lost no time in requesting Jesus to come into the sick
woman's room. Jesus complied, and speaking to the mother, took
her by the hand and lifted her up. It is to be noted that Jesus did
not pray for the afflicted one. He exercised His authority and
commanded the sick to be well. The Lord in this case recognized
the presence of a spirit of oppression, and as Luke 4:39 declares,
"He . . . rebuked the fever." The woman at once felt the flow of
strength into her body, and at the same moment, the fever left.

Obeying the command to arise, she got up out of bed and began
to help prepare the dinner. "She arose and ministered unto them."
Faith is an act. The act of Peter's mother-in-law may well be
emulated by other sick persons. When they receive healing, they
should begin to repay the Lord with their grateful service.

The Lord then enjoyed a few hours of relaxation. It was the
Sabbath day and the rules of traveling about on that day were
very strict. Nevertheless, when the sun was set and the Sabbath
was over, there was great excitement in the city of Capernaum.
The eager multitude began to press about the doors of Peter's
home, bringing with them their sick and diseased.

"When the even was come, they brought unto him many
that were possessed with devils: and he cast out the spirits
with his word, and healed all that were sick: That it might
be fulfilled which was spoken by Esaias the prophet, saying,
Himself took our infirmities, and bare our sicknesses" (Matt.
8:16-17).

What a strange scene it was. Only a few steps away was the
Sea of Galilee, one of the most beautiful bodies of water in the
world, reflecting the glow of the evening sunset. But all around the
door were the hideous results of sin— not necessarily the sin of

the individual, but the sin of the race. For there was no sickness before the fall of man. How many times have we beheld similar heart-rending scenes of a multitude of sick folk who have come to a meeting where people are ministered to for healing? How sad is the sight — cripples, hydrocephalics, mentally handicapped, those with Down's syndrome, paralytics, the demon-possessed, others wasting away with an incurable disease. There are those who would tell such people that they are suffering for the glory of God. Peter, who saw Jesus heal that day, knew better. When he preached his sermon at the house of Cornelius, the apostle explained that sickness owed its origin to Satan rather than to God. He said that Jesus "went about doing good, and healing all that were oppressed of the devil."

> "How God anointed Jesus of Nazareth with the Holy Ghost and with power: who went about doing· good, and healing all that were oppressed of the devil; for God was with him" (Acts 10:38).

Far into the deepening twilight Jesus ministered to the sick and diseased. Tortured souls were brought forward. The evil spirits repeated the words of the one in the synagogue. They cried out saying, "Thou art Christ, the Son of God" (Luke 4:41). They had known Jesus in the ages before, when they were holy beings. The terrible recollection of lost opportunity must have swept through their minds in a paroxysm of despair and hopelessness; for they well knew they had long since crossed the line whereby no process of redemption could ever save them. Rejected of God, their corrupted natures had become irreversibly fixed. To come into the presence of Christ was, therefore, unspeakable torture, and they cried out in their anguish.

Jesus could do nothing for these evil spirits. They were beyond mercy, and it was His duty to close their mouths, lest they call attention prematurely to His deity. He, therefore, "suffered them not to speak." What a warning to sinners who carelessly ignore the call of Christ, who stands at their heart's door knocking. For the time must come when they too, if they reject His call, will be forever outside the pale of mercy, with the demons and lost spirits.

Jesus was touched with the infirmities of the afflicted, and laboring into the night, He ministered until every sick person had received deliverance. Matthew makes a significant remark. He says that Jesus healed these people "that it might be fulfilled which was spoken by Esaias the prophet, saying Himself took our infirmities, and bare our sicknesses" (Matt. 8:17). The meaning is unmistakable. Jesus bore our sicknesses upon Himself, even as He did our sins. Divine healing is in the atonement! Christ bore our sicknesses, and we need not bear them again!

At last Jesus had completed His task. He turned to the doorway of the house of His friend, Peter. But when He retired that night, it was not to sleep. He faced a problem that every man who has success in the healing ministry faces. That day He had been unexpectedly called upon to deliver a demon-possessed man. This led to the great multitude of sick folk coming for healing. Consequently, He had been unable to give any teaching concerning the kingdom. He knew that if that continued, people would soon come to look upon Him as a mere wonder-worker instead of "the Lamb of God which taketh away the sin of the world."

Healing of the soul must ever come before healing of the body. Healing is the children's bread. Yet deliverance of the sick was a part of Christ's ministry. It expressed God's compassion for the afflicted and the suffering. Moreover, it opened a great door, for it brought the people to Him.

Early the next day, long before sunrise, Jesus arose from His bed and without disturbing the rest of the household, departed for a solitary place. He needed communion with His Heavenly Father at that important moment.

> "And in the morning, rising up a great while before day, he went out, and departed into a solitary place, and there prayed. And Simon and they that were with him followed after him. And when they had found him, they said unto him, All men seek for thee. And he said unto them, Let us go into the next towns, that I may preach there also: for therefore came I forth. And he preached in their synagogues throughout all Galilee and cast out devils" (Mark 1:35-39).

When daybreak came and Peter and the other disciples arose, they found people already gathering at the door, but Jesus was nowhere to be found. We can understand Peter's dilemma when inquirers began trying to exact a promise from him that Jesus would minister to them.

What a crowd there must have been that morning on the street in front of Peter's house. No wonder when he and James and John finally found Jesus they said, "All men seek for thee." Jesus replied that it was necessary for Him to go to the other cities round about — although it may be that He yielded to the importunity of the multitude to minister to them before He and His disciples departed.

160

Chapter 26

The Healing of the Leper

Up until this time, the disciples of Jesus had not gone out into the full-time ministry. They accompanied the Lord on certain trips and then returned to pursue their fishing occupation. Now they were back again in Capernaum. Sometimes they worked at their trade far into the night, possibly to get caught up financially. On this particular occasion, they had toiled all night and had taken nothing.

Jesus in the meantime had secured a few hours of much needed rest. But while He slept the people surrounded the place where He was, and when He awakened, He found that a large audience was waiting to hear Him. Realizing that the house was not a convenient place to give the people instruction, He made His way to the seashore where some of His disciples had beached their boats after a fruitless night of labor.

But even there He could not speak with liberty. The people, eager to catch every syllable, or to touch Him for healing, began to crowd in closer and closer. Seeing that Peter's boat was nearby where he and his brother were washing their nets, Jesus beckoned to him to push his boat out a little from the land so that He might use it as a pulpit. Then as the people congregated along the shore, Jesus began to teach them the Word of God.

When He had finished His discourse, Jesus turned to Peter. Since there were no fish in either of the boats, He knew that Peter and his partners had spent an unprofitable night. He then requested that they push out into the deep a little way from the shore and cast in their nets one more time. Impetuous Peter always ready to say the first thing that came into his mind, reminded the Lord that they had toiled all night and had taken nothing. Nevertheless, at Christ's word, they would try once more.

When they brought up the net, they found that they enclosed a great multitude of fishes, so that the net began to break! They motioned for their partners, James and John, to come to their assistance, and soon they filled both boats with fish until the small craft were actually about to sink.

When they got the boats to the shore, Peter began to consider the extent of the miracle. What did he do? Did he give thanks to the Lord for the great catch? No, in his impetuosity he realized as he had not before, that Jesus was the very Son of God, and by contrast he was a sinful man. Indeed Peter had been a rough fisherman, one not above cursing when things did not go right. A flash of conviction told Peter that He was totally unworthy to be a companion of the Lord. Impulsively he cried out saying, "Depart from me; for I am a sinful man, O Lord." Yet, that was the last thing that Peter wanted — for the Lord to depart from him.

How differently the hearts of men react to the gospel! One of the thieves on the cross mocked the Lord, calling Him in effect an impostor. But the other, deeply penitent, rebuked the first and said to Jesus, "Lord, remember me when thou comest into thy kingdom." One thief went to the region of lost spirits, the other to paradise (Luke 23:42-43).

Herod wanted Jesus to perform a miracle to gratify his vulgar curiosity. There was no thought on his part of taking Christ as his Saviour. On the other hand, the miracle of the draught of fishes had the effect of making Peter aware of his sinfulness, and it filled him with self-loathing. Today miracles still have this dual effect, depending upon the individual. Some consider them as mere wonders to excite curiosity. Others see the hand of God in the miracle and are brought to the point of deep conviction of their sins.

But the words that came from Jesus to Peter were not those of self-reproach, but of great gentleness. He said, "Fear not; from henceforth thou shalt catch men" (Luke 5:10). It was Christ's call to Peter to leave everything behind and launch out into the full-time ministry. But there was work to do first. The boats had to be cleaned, the nets mended. The fish had to be packed in boxes for the caravans which would carry them north to Jerusalem or west toward the ships of the Great Sea. Finally, their task completed, they were ready to leave all and set out with Jesus in the great adventure of reaching a lost world for God.

The Healing of the Leper

We should note at this point that there is a difference of opinion among Bible scholars as to the exact chronological order of some of the events which transpired at this particular period in our

Lord's ministry. One such instance is that of the healing of the leper. We believe, however, that the exact sequence in which the miracle occurred is of no great moment. It is enough to know it happened at this particular time when Jesus was making a tour of the Galilean cities. The Lord had just come down out of the mountain where He had been teaching the multitude and had entered a town — probably Bethsaida or Chorazin. At this moment, He was met by a most forlorn creature, a man who was afflicted with the disease of leprosy. At one time the man had enjoyed good health and probably never thought that he would become the victim of so foul a plague. Then one day he noticed an inflamed spot on his flesh. What could it be? He dared not think of what it might mean; but before long, his worst fears were realized. Others noticed it, and he was reported to a priest, who after examining him, pronounced him a leper. From then on, he was doomed to a living death, cast out from the presence of others. For the rest of his life he would have to make his living as a beggar. Only death could give him surcease of his misery.

Then one day news came to him of the young man from Nazareth. He heard of people with incurable afflictions who had been healed by Jesus. A wild hope sprang up in his breast! But the question was, how could he meet Jesus? Because he was a leper, he was not allowed to mingle among the crowd. He could not go into the town. People would flee in horror if he approached them. Even the rabbis would throw stones at him if he came near them. The Pharisees when they saw a leper would cry, "Away to thine own place, lest thou pollute others."

Leprosy is a type of sin. It holds a fearful and tragic fate, once the disease gets seated in the blood. But the wild hope would not leave the poor beggar. He would watch for the moment when Jesus was separated from the rest of the people; then he would go up to Him and make his desperate appeal. And that is what he did. He cried out in a pleading voice, "If thou wilt, thou canst make me clean." And to his unbounded joy, the Lord put forth His hand without a moment's hesitation, and touching the leper said, "I will; be thou clean." Thus we see Christ's expression of God's will concerning sickness and disease. Some in their ignorance of the Scriptures, have taught that it is not God's will to heal. Thousands of sick and afflicted have gone through life patiently suffering because they have been told that God has sent the sickness upon them for some mysterious reason. Yet, Jesus taught that sickness was of the devil (Luke 13:11,16). The apostles

163

taught that Jesus healed those that were oppressed of the devil (Acts 10:38). The Scriptures teach that sickness is a curse (Deut. 28) and that Jesus Christ was revealed to redeem men from the curse (Gal. 3:13).

So Jesus Christ not only healed the leper, thus inferring it was God's will to do so, but He plainly said, "I will; be thou clean." The fact is that if sickness were the will of God, every physician who attempts to cure would be violating the divine will and every hospital would be a house of rebellion.

Yet it seemed a dangerous thing for Jesus to reach out and touch the man. According to the Law, He contracted ceremonial pollution. In pronouncing the man clean He had trespassed upon the province of the priest, and given the rulers a pretext for accusing Him of violating the Law. As has been said, it was a glorious violation of the letter of the Law, but it was at the same time a glorious illustration of the spirit of the Law, which declares that mercy is better than sacrifice. Christ was not polluted by touching the leper, but instead the whole body of the leper was healed and cleansed by the hand of Christ. So it is that Christ touching man's sinful nature cleansed it; yet at the same time He remained without sin.

Nevertheless, Jesus, even while healing the people, must fulfill the Law by perfect obedience. The miracle had not been witnessed by the multitude. He told the man to say naught to anyone, but to go and show himself to the priest and to offer the things commanded by the Law of Moses, and to secure the certification that he was clean.

The rites pertaining to the sacerdotal cleaning of the leper are fully described in Leviticus 13-14. The priest took the leper outside the town and performed an elaborate ceremony before pronouncing him clean. The man made an offering, shaved off his hair, bathed, and remained seven days out of his house. The ceremony was so elaborate and occupied a considerable period of time so that there would be no dispute over his actual cleansing.

Christ told the leper to show himself to the priest for a witness. For one thing, Jesus wanted to give the religious authorities of the nation ample evidence that His mission was of God. On the other hand, He enjoined the leper to say nothing to the people. There were two reasons for this. The people had already witnessed many of His miracles. There was danger of an over-emphasis, that people would get to look upon Him more as a miracle man than as a Saviour.

He healed the leper because of His compassion for him, but considered it advisable that nothing be said about the matter. He did not want to put such accent on miracles that men would be carried away by the spectacular and forget that He was calling them to humility and self-effacement

There was another reason. This miracle would excite the emotions of the people; they would press upon Him until He would no longer be able to minister to them. Jesus had no modern auditorium to preach in; there was no well-trained band of ushers to rope off the crowd; nor was there a waiting limousine which would pick Him up and whisk Him away to a place of rest.

Unfortunately, the leper in the exuberance and joy of deliverance overlooked this admonition. Failure to understand that obedience is better than sacrifice, the man instead of carrying out the Lord's instructions began to publish the news of his cleansing to everyone who would listen. As a consequence, "Jesus could no more openly enter the city, but was without in desert places" (Mark 1:45). Even so, we are told that the people came from every quarter.

Chapter 27

The Healing
of the Centurion's Servant

While Jesus was carrying on His ministry in the various cities of Galilee, He preached a sermon which is known as the Sermon on the Mount, on a hill north of Capernaum. In bringing His sermon to a conclusion, Jesus made some searching remarks that must have given His hearers serious thought:

> "Not every one that saith unto me, Lord, Lord, shall enter into the kingdom of heaven; but he that doeth the will of my Father which is in heaven. Many will say to me in that day, Lord, Lord, have we not prophesied in thy name? and in thy name have cast out devils? and in thy name done many wonderful works? And then will I profess unto them, I never knew you: depart from me, ye that work iniquity" (Matt. 7:21-23).

Lest the people suppose that supernatural demonstrations were always proof of holiness, or even of the person's right relationship with God, Jesus pointed out that on the day of judgment there would be some who would come to Him and say that they had prophesied in His name and cast out devils and did many wonderful works, but He would have to tell them to depart from Him, for they were workers of iniquity.

Many questions have been raised concerning these matters, and some frankly say that they cannot see how this could possibly be true, although since Jesus spoke the words they must be. That such cases exist, however, was proven by the acts of a man who was standing at the time a few feet from Jesus, listening to all He said. His name was Judas Iscariot.

We have every reason to believe that Judas healed the sick and cast out devils as did the other disciples. Acts 1:17 specifically declares that Judas "had obtained a part of this ministry." Jesus gave the sign of true discipleship, saying, "By their fruits ye shall know them" (Matt. 7:20).

The Healing of the Centurion's Servant

Now we are told that following His Sermon on the Mount, the Lord returned to Capernaum. Upon entering the city, He was met by certain elders of the Jews, who informed Him about the servant of a certain centurion who was ready to die.

> "Now when he had ended all his sayings in the audience of the people, he entered into Capernaum. And a certain centurion's servant, who was dear unto him, was sick, and ready to die. And when he heard of Jesus, he sent unto him the elders of the Jews, beseeching him that he would come and heal his servant" (Luke 7:1-3).

There are those who take exception to the accuracy of the story at this point, because of a trivial variation between the Luke and Matthew narratives. This, they claim, is a proof against the verbal inspiration of the Scriptures. They point out that Luke says that the elders of the Jews brought the message to Jesus, whereas in Matthew 8:5, it declares that it was the centurion that came to Him.

Those who find a contradiction here, merely quibble over words. That there are variations proves that there was no collusion of witnesses in the writing of the gospels. In the same chapter, it speaks of Jesus' healing the multitude at eventide (Matt. 8:16). Luke 4:40 says this took place when the sun was setting. Of course we know that the sun was not setting in the technical sense — it was the earth rotating on its axis that caused the effect. But does not everyone know what is meant?

A lawyer writes a legal document that spells out every technicality. God knew that the Bible would be more easily understood if it were written as it is, rather than as a legal or a scientific document. Words are skeletons of the thought. For example, John 4:1 says:

> "When therefore the Lord knew how the Pharisees had heard that Jesus made and baptized more disciples than John."

This verse states that Jesus baptized. Was this true? In the sense that Jesus permitted His disciples to do it, it was true. But that He actually performed the act Himself, technically, was not true, as the next verse states. "Though Jesus Himself baptized not, but his disciples" (Verse 2). The present instance is a similar case. The Matthew account tells about the centurion's request —

for it was his request — but the Luke account goes into detail and explains that the centurion did not actually go personally, but sent certain elders of the Jews as his messengers. It also explains why the centurion had not gone himself (Verse 7). But we are ahead of our story. Let us return to the elders who met Jesus as He entered the city of Capernaum.

The news of Jesus' return to Capernaum had brought joy to the heart of this officer who was not a Jew himself. He was a centurion of Herod's army who had probably heard of the miracle of the healing of the nobleman's son. Perhaps he had also been present in the synagogue on the Sabbath when Jesus had healed the demoniac. The centurion without actually becoming a proselyte, had reverence for the Jewish faith, for he had built for the people this beautiful synagogue, and had thereby won their gratitude.

There is another circumstance which shows the centurion to have been an unusually kind and gracious man. He treated his servants not as slaves as was common in those days, but almost as members of his family. The text says that a "servant, who was dear unto him, was sick, and ready to die" (Luke 7:2). So when the news went through the town that Jesus had returned, the centurion immediately called for certain of the elders of the Jews to entreat Jesus to come and heal his servant.

The elders being much indebted to the centurion for his beneficence in building them a place of worship, could hardly do otherwise than respond to his request. It was still early in the ministry of Christ, and the rulers of the Jews had not yet taken a public stand against Him. There are some who believe that these Jews feigned approval of the centurion's purpose and agreed to the request only because they did not wish to offend their benefactor. However, we hardly think this view is correct, for apparently the ministry of Christ at this time had deeply impressed the people of Capernaum. One of the rulers of the synagogue was Jairus who shortly would be seeking the services of Jesus to heal his daughter from a fatal malady.

At any rate, the deputation of elders met Jesus as He was entering into Capernaum. They informed Him about the centurion and to strengthen their petition, they said, "That he was worthy for whom he should do this; For he loveth our nation, and he hath built us a synagogue" (Luke 7:4-5).

Jesus made no comment on this extraordinary explanation as to why He should heal the centurion's servant. Nevertheless, He consented to go with them. It is true that by works men show forth their faith, but works are not a basis for receiving the gift of God, which is entirely by grace. No puny efforts of man can possibly purchase God's blessings.

It is not uncommon even today to hear people seeking healing or salvation on a similar basis. There are those who think God should answer their petition because they have been a Sunday school teacher, or have given to the poor, or performed other good works. No one is healed, or for that matter, saved by their good works. Nevertheless, Christ in His condescension overlooked their faulty understanding of the ways of God. Since He could not commend their theological views, He said nothing. In His own spirit, Jesus felt that the centurion was ready to receive His blessing, although not for the reason mentioned. And so He said, "I will come and heal him" (Matt. 8:7).

Now the centurion would likely have been horrified if he had heard the plea that the elders had made on his behalf. It seems that the delegation had scarcely left his house before he had misgivings. The soldier, although perhaps not well versed in the Scriptures, nevertheless, seemed to have an intuitive understanding of what was right and proper.

It occurred to him that he, a centurion engaged in commanding a band of Roman soldiers was not worthy that Jesus should come under his roof.

"Then Jesus went with them. And when he was now not far from the house, the centurion sent friends to him, saying unto him, Lord trouble not thyself: for I am not worthy that thou shouldest enter under my roof: Wherefore neither thought I myself worthy to come unto thee: but say in a word, and my servant shall be healed. For I also am a man set under authority, having under me soldiers and I say unto one, Go, and he goeth; and to another, Come, and he cometh; and to my servant, Do this, and he doeth it" (Luke 7:6-8).

The centurion had faith. Being under the direct authority of Herod, and familiar with those of Herod's court, he undoubtedly knew about the case of the nobleman's son, how Jesus had said the word and the boy was healed. His reasoning was that although he had only one hundred men under him, nevertheless, within the limits of his authority, he could speak the word and his command would be obeyed. Therefore, if Christ was Lord over principalities, did He not have power to issue a command and it would be obeyed? Let Jesus speak the word and ministering angels would carry out His orders.

Some have considered the centurion's statement "a grotesque and heathenish conception." But Jesus regarded it as a manifestation of faith greater than any that He had found in Israel. After telling the centurion's messengers that the servant was healed, Jesus made a most extraordinary remark:

> "And I say unto you, That many shall come from the east and west, and shall sit down with Abraham, and Isaac, and Jacob, in the kingdom of heaven. But the children of the kingdom shall be cast out into outer darkness: there shall be weeping and gnashing of teeth" (Matt. 8:11-12).

In these words, Jesus foresaw the self-righteous Jews rejecting the message of repentance and being cast away into the outer darkness, while on the other hand, Gentiles from the east and the west would come and sit down with Abraham, Isaac, and Jacob in the kingdom of heaven.

This statement of Jesus was obviously disturbing to the ears of the Jews. They conceded that the centurion who had built them a synagogue was worthy of some consideration, but to declare that Gentiles would be on par with Abraham, Isaac and Jacob, was to them a most unorthodox statement. It served to put them on the alert to watch Jesus carefully for any further statements of this nature.

Chapter 28

The Raising of the Son of the Widow of Nain

When the messengers of the centurion returned to the house, they found that the servant was made completely whole. It was impossible that this miracle occurring in such a prominent home, should not come to the attention of the whole city. Jesus could not stay long in Capernaum, so the next day (perhaps the translation "subsequently" is better), Jesus set out on the trip to the little city of Nain. He could not escape the people, for as He and His disciples made their way, "much people" followed Him.

The distance from Capernaum to Nain is about twenty-five miles. It lies on the west slope of Little Hermon not far from Endor where the witch who was visited by Saul once lived. By leaving early in the morning and sailing to the southern part of the lake, and then walking the rest of the way, they probably reached their destination some time in the afternoon.

A person standing on an elevated position near the city of Nain that day would have noted an interesting circumstance. There was a procession in the city that was making its mournful way toward the city gate, and another that was following Jesus; both groups were so moving that when they reached the gate, they would meet.

The procession moving out of the city was a funeral train making its way to some ancient burial caves which incidentally may still be pointed out today; they are located about a mile from the city.

A funeral is always a sad scene, but this procession had a pathos deeper than usual, for the young man being carried out was the "only son of his mother, and she was a widow." On the wicker bier lay the body of the dead lad. Even at a distance the wails of the mourners could be heard. The Jews, as was their custom at funerals, expressed their anguish for the poor widow in doleful cries.

The followers of Jesus stood aside to let the cortege pass. The

171

broken-hearted mother tottered by. She had no eyes for the Man who stood watching the sorrowful sight. The light had gone out of her life, and she was quietly sobbing out her grief.

Jesus looked on the tortured woman, and her grief moved upon His heartstrings. The sight of her sorrow appealed irresistibly to Him. Pausing only to say to the mother, "Weep not," He approached the dead lad. As He touched the bier, something about His presence caused the pallbearers to stand still. Then He spoke to the dead and said, "Young man, I say unto thee, Arise" (Luke 7:14). These words of authority went out into the spirit world calling the departed soul back into the body.

It was a moment of breathless drama. For a few seconds no one moved. The mourners ceased their wailing. The watchers were transfixed by the strange scene. Then it happened! As if awakened from a deep sleep, the lad sat up and began to speak. What a dramatic moment it was as Jesus delivered the youth to his mother! Tears of grief were suddenly turned into tears of uncontrollable joy. It was a rehearsal for the resurrection day when loved ones are brought together again. This great truth of life beyond the grave, Jesus unequivocally taught:

> "Marvel not at this: for the hour is coming, in the which all that are in the graves shall hear his voice, And shall come forth; they that have done good, unto the resurrection of life; and they that have done evil, unto the resurrection of damnation" (John 5:28-29).

And what about the audience? What undescribable awe must have settled upon them! Death is that veil that conceals from human vision that which goes on beyond the grave. Yet that veil had parted at the words of the man of Nazareth!

> "And there came a fear on all: and they glorified God, saying, That a great prophet is risen up among us; and that God hath visited His people. And this rumour of Him went forth throughout all Judaea, and throughout all the region round about" (Luke 7:16-17).

The writer once saw a young boy that had been killed in an accident, brought back to life through the prayer of faith. It was a scene that baffled description. He can understand something of the tremendous emotional experience the people must have had that day as they witnessed this amazing scene of the widow's son being brought back to life.

Chapter 29
Simon, Son of Jona

The hometown of Peter was Bethsaida, which probably was only a short distance from Capernaum (John 1:44). His father Jona, named him "Simon." During a Maccabean revolt, a high priest by the name of Simon had become a national hero. It is likely that Peter was named after him. There are many Simons in the New Testament—Simon the Pharisee, Simon of Cyrene, Simon the Zealot, Simon the brother of Jesus, and others.

We cannot be certain whether Simon was a full-blooded Jew. Galilee was part of the region where Assyria, centuries before, had replaced the inhabitants with pagans. Not until 104 B.C. did Aristobulus conquer Galilee and force the inhabitants to accept the Mosaic Law. Once Galilee was converted by force of arms, however, it became very loyal to the religion of Judaism. Galilean children were carefully trained in the Jewish religion. When eight days old, Simon was circumcised. At six, he was sent to school at the synagogue. There he and other boys would sit on the floor cross-legged listening to the teacher and chanting long passages of the Scriptures. He and his companions were also taught to read and write, both in the Aramaic and the Greek languages. Outside of the synagogue, no one spoke Hebrew.

Galilee was not a back-water area of ignorant peasants. It was a great commercial center, and children growing up received at least a modest education. Simon knew the history of his nation, as well as what was happening in the Roman world. He learned something of Greek literature; but most important of all, he gained a considerable knowledge of the Old Testament Scriptures while attending the synagogue school.

Knowing the impulsive nature of Simon Peter—we can well understand that he was no model scholar—Jesus took note of the headstrong spirit of his youth when He said, "When thou wast young, thou girdedst thyself, and walkedst whither thou wouldest" (John 21:18). In other words, he went where he wished.

Peter no doubt learned more outside of school than in. He was the type of person who always was alert to what was going on about him. Through his city of Bethsaida passed great caravans that came from distant countries. Roman legionnaires were continually about, ever ready to quell an uprising, one of which reached sizeable proportions during the revolt of Judas (Acts 5:37).

And there was the Sea of Galilee. As a fisherman's son, he would have been much on the water. Peter learned to swim, to set a sail, and to pull the oars. Certainly he spent much time in the boat of his father and other fishermen, as they made their living by fishing.

When Peter was about twelve years of age, he left school and started to work for his father. Jews of Galilee married young, so it is probable that he had a bride by the age of eighteen. According to the custom, a price was paid the father-in-law for the wife that he might be somewhat compensated for the expense he was out in bringing her up. Apparently Peter was fortunate in his choice, for she made a home for Jesus in their little house when He stayed with them. She kept the home fires burning and carried on when Peter was out on preaching missions with Jesus and the other disciples. Later she shared with her husband his missionary journeys (I Cor. 9:5).

It is possible that Peter's parents died while he was comparatively young. We have no word of them, but we learn that Peter moved to his wife's mother's house in Capernaum, taking his brother Andrew with him. There they earned their livelihood by plying their trade as fishermen. The Sea of Galilee was a rich fishing-ground, and the demand for fish in this busy commercial metropolis was brisk. Bread and fish were the staple foods of the nation. Besides this, a great quantity of fish was pickled and sent abroad in the export trade.

Peter owned his own boat which was large enough to accommodate the Lord and the entire twelve disciples. Since a dragnet required two ships to tow it, he and his brother Andrew had entered into a partnership with James and John and their father Zebedee. They would go out a distance to sea, and then row to shore gathering up the fish in their net as they came along. When they got near to shore, they would have to jump into the sea to maneuver the net to land. Some of the fish had sharp spines which cut the net, and thus they had the task of mending the nets after each expedition.

Peter was far from a model Jew. He was a rough man, on occasion given to profanity, and even after he became a disciple of Jesus, once under strong temptation he began to curse and swear (Matt. 26:74; Mark 14:71). How shall we assess the character of Peter except to say that in all ways he was very human? Good-hearted and generous, he was impetuous and prone to rebuke others, even the Lord on occasion.

Given to impulse, he once boasted that he was ready to go to prison and even to death for Jesus. Yet, with all his faults there was much good in Peter. Jesus saw in him a diamond in the rough.

On the eve of the Sabbath Peter and his companions would lay up their nets and haul their fishing boats up on the beach. In the morning he and Andrew would attend the synagogue services. The synagogue in Capernaum built by the generous centurion was one of the finest in Galilee.

Many of the sermons preached in the synagogues were dull and boring, dealing with the trivialities of the Law. But there was one subject that never failed to arouse Peter's interest. His face would brighten whenever it was mentioned—the coming of the Messiah and His kingdom. He and others looked forward to the day when the hated Roman legions would be driven from their land. Even as we look forward today to the Second Coming of Christ, so did the people of Peter's day look forward to the First Advent.

The ideas that people had about the coming kingdom were often fantastic and farfetched. When the Messiah came the earth would yawn and swallow up the heathen. Jews would live to be a thousand years of age and would beget a thousand children.

When Judas of Galilee revolted against the Romans, Peter was only a small lad. Many of the people hoped that his revolt presaged the coming of the Messiah. Alas, nothing came of it but disaster. The Roman legions crushed the patriots and crucified 2,000 of the youths on crosses. They also carried many of the people away and sold them on the slave market like cattle. But the Galileans hoped on, expecting that in their lifetime they would see the advent of the Messiah. Their hopes were to be realized even sooner than they dared believe.

A prophet was to arise in Israel whose message aroused the attention of the nation. This man was John the Baptist. Elsewhere we have described this prophet's ministry, and in the next chapter we shall take note of some of the disciples he made, which included Peter and his brother Andrew.

Chapter 30

The Appearance of the Forerunner

It was in the fifteenth year of Tiberius Caesar that a rumor went through Galilee that a great prophet had arisen and was even then preaching down at the Jordan. He was a man clad in rough garments, but his voice carried a note of authority. Large numbers of people were coming out of Judea to hear him. His theme was "Repent ye, for the kingdom of heaven is at hand."

The description of the prophet reminded one of the Essenes, who were shocked by the self-indulgence and soft living of the people. They had retired from civilization and had established settlements with vows so strict that a novitiate was required to serve a year as a candidate before he was admitted as a full-fledged member of the sect. It is doubtful that Peter would have made a good Essene.

The Essenes employed bathing in their rituals, and John the Baptist, upon a person's confession of his sins, baptized him in the River Jordan. The fame of the prophet spread abroad and multitudes flocked from the cities to hear him. Peter and his brother Andrew were among those who decided to take a vacation from their fishing and go to the Jordan to hear the prophet. The time must have been winter, since the heat in the valley in the summer is like that of an oven. When Peter and his brother Andrew arrived, he found a vast company of people encamped around the village of Bethabara.

As Peter stood listening to the prophet, there was something about his preaching that witnessed to his spirit. As John pressed for repentance, Peter felt his own conscience awakened. Although he was a believer in the Law of Moses, he realized that he was a sinner. John preached about the One who was to come after him, whose shoelatch he was not worthy to unloose. Peter was uneasy. He had with other Jews looked forward to the coming of the Messiah. But under John's preaching he did not feel that he was ready. He went up to John to ask him what he should do. John told him to confess his sins, and then when he believed that Peter was a true convert he baptized him in the river. The young fisherman felt that something had happened in his life when he was baptized, and ever afterward he emphasized water baptism. On the Day of Pentecost when the multitude asked him, "Men and brethren, what shall we do?" he told them to "Repent, and be baptized every one of you in the name of Jesus."

Peter and Andrew apparently continued with John for some weeks and could be considered as his disciples. John had many things to teach them, and they listened from day to day as the fearless prophet preached repentance to the multitudes that assembled to hear him. There was one part of John's preaching that particularly fascinated him. When John spoke of One who was to come after him, and who would baptize with the Holy Ghost and fire, Peter was extremely interested:

> "I indeed baptize you with water unto repentance: but he that cometh after me is mightier than I, whose shoes I am not worthy to bear: he shall baptize you with the Holy Ghost, and with fire: Whose fan is in his hand, and he will throughly purge his floor, and gather his wheat into the garner; but he will burn up the chaff with unquenchable fire" (Matt. 3:11-12).

Who could this be but the Messiah, the One about whom they had dreamed, the One for whom prayers were made in the meetings in the synagogue for His speedy appearance. John said that this One was already in their midst, but that He had not yet been revealed! (John 1:26).

It was getting near the time when he and his brother must return to Capernaum. Peter had a family to support. But he and Andrew could not tear themselves away. Then one day while Peter was absent, Andrew heard John say, "Behold the Lamb of God." Andrew looked, and there was the Man of whom the Baptist spoke before him! Andrew watched the Man and was fascinated by Him. Surely this was the Messiah! He rushed off to find his brother Peter and said to him, "We have found the Messiah, which is, being interpreted, the Christ" (John 1:41).

From whence was this stranger? Neither Andrew nor Peter knew anything about Him. He had grown up in Nazareth only a few miles away, but they had never heard of Him. Jesus had appeared to John about six weeks before and had been baptized by him. At that time John had seen the Holy Spirit descending on Him like a dove. But the Baptist had no opportunity at the time to introduce Him to his disciples. By the time the service was over Jesus had disappeared.

177

But now Andrew and Peter stood facing the Man. When Jesus saw Peter's face, He said, "Thou art Simon son of Jona: thou shalt be called Cephas, which is by interpretation, a stone" (John 1:42). We are given no further information about the conversation which ensued. Subsequent events show that Peter was as impressed as his brother Andrew had been. When later the call came to Peter to follow Jesus, he was ready.

But Peter had to return to Capernaum. He had been gone longer than he had expected. His wife and family probably were wondering what had happened to him and his brother. His fishing business was suffering. But all the way back strange thoughts were going through Peter's mind. He and his brother Andrew had many things to discuss about their meeting with Jesus.

The One who had been the absorbing topic of their conversation soon came to Capernaum on His way to a wedding at Cana of Galilee. After the wedding He stayed a few days in Capernaum, probably as Peter's guest. Then He left to celebrate the Passover at Jerusalem. Peter remained behind to carry on his fishing. He had lost a lot of time when he was down at the Jordan listening to the Baptist.

One day pilgrims who had visited Jerusalem during the Passover began to return, and they brought back strange reports. This Jesus had made no small stir in the city. The rulers there, however, were by no means enthusiastic about Him. They did not like the way He had gone into the temple and had driven out the animals and the money-changers.

About that time there came startling news that John had been cast into prison by Herod because he had preached against his adulterous marriage with Herodias. Upon hearing this, Jesus came back to Galilee which was in the very heart of Herod's dominion. Later Herod beheaded John. The superstitious king heard of the miracles that Jesus was performing and hastily concluded that He was John the Baptist risen from the dead. For the time being he had no intention of interfering with the ministry of this new preacher.

The Call of Peter and Andrew

"And Jesus, walking by the sea of Galilee, saw two brethren, Simon called Peter, and Andrew his brother, casting a net into the sea: for they were fishers. And he saith unto them, Follow me, and I will make you fishers of men. And they straightway left their nets, and followed him" (Matt. 4:18-20).

178

Early one morning while Peter and Andrew were casting their nets into the sea, they looked up and their hearts leaped with joy. The One who stood before them was none other than the Master, the One whom they believed in their hearts to be the Messiah. At His word they immediately left their nets and their boat and followed Him. Going along the shore a little farther, they came to where their partners, James and John, were mending their nets with Zebedee, their father. The same words were spoken by Jesus to them, and they too joined the party with Peter and Andrew. The call was irresistible.

In a way it was daring act on the part of the four men, for they supposed that the Messiah was to gather men about Him to revolt against Herod. Herod was wary about any new leaders arising, and in fact had beheaded John for alleged conduct that supposedly jeopardized the interests of his kingdom. His superstitious belief that Jesus was John raised from the dead would, however, prevent him for some time from taking any action against the work that Jesus was doing.

What their choice that day would lead to, none of the men who followed Jesus probably had the least idea. Peter, nonetheless, invited the Lord into his house, and thereafter whenever He was in Capernaum He was the honored guest.

Whether the disciples immediately followed Jesus on all His preaching tours throughout Galilee is not certain. Mark 1:39 indicates that He went alone at the beginning. Certainly Peter would have had to do some explaining to his family and to make provision for them before he could pick up and go.

Usually on Sabbath days Jesus remained in Capernaum (Luke 4:31). It was His custom wherever He was, to go to the synagogue. On the first Sabbath He went along with Peter. News of His ministry was just being rumored through the city. Jesus was invited to speak. He accepted the invitation and went up and sat in the rabbi's chair. In the midst of His discourse a demon-possessed man began to cry out. The evil spirit had immediately recognized the identity of the One who was speaking, and it began to cry out saying, "Let us alone; what have we to do with thee, thou Jesus of Nazareth? Art thou come to destroy us? I know thee who thou art, the Holy One of God" (Mark 1:24). Jesus rebuked the demon and it came out of the man much to the amazement of the congregation.

Peter and Andrew walked back to their home with Jesus, their minds awhirl at what had taken place. But another chapter in the drama was about to take place. Peter's mother-in-law apparently had not been feeling well, so she and her daughter had not attended the service. When Peter and his companions reached the door of the house, they were met by Peter's wife who informed them anxiously that her mother had a raging fever. Peter immediately appealed to Jesus, who put His hands on her rebuking the fever. Then with His hand He raised her up. Immediately the fever left and she arose and ministered unto them.

That evening when the Sabbath ended, Jesus had a busy time. We can see Him moving up and down in the crowd laying hands on the sick, casting out the evil spirits that convulsed certain ones, and forbidding the demons to speak. It was truly a night to remember, one which Peter and his wife would never forget. When the last sufferer had been dealt with, Jesus retired, probably to the roof. At dawn He quietly slipped down the outside stairway without disturbing the family below and climbed the hill behind the town to give Himself to prayer. Jesus was not overly pleased with the way things were going. He was willing to minister to the sick, but He also wanted to preach the Word. It was not enough to be known as a wonder-worker.

Peter awoke a little later to find the street full of people again. He went to the roof to awaken Jesus. To his surprise and dismay, Jesus was not there. The crowd, disappointed that the Lord was not available, pressed upon Peter for a promise that their sick ones would be ministered to by Him. Finally, a searching-party went out and they found Him in prayer in a secluded place on the hill. Peter explained that everyone was seeking Him, and Jesus answered that this was just the reason He had left. He had to preach the Word in other towns and villages.

Many weeks passed. Some of the trips Jesus made by Himself. At other times Peter and his brother and James and John went with Him. But the time was at hand when Jesus would give the call to Peter for full-time service. One night he and his brother toiled many hours, but caught nothing. In the morning as he was washing the net, he saw Jesus approaching, followed by a large crowd. Jesus motioned for him to draw his boat close to shore. When Peter did, Jesus got into the ship and began to teach the people. After He had finished, He told Peter to push out into the deep water and let down his net. Peter had great respect for the Lord, but he probably believed that in the matter of fishing he knew more. Half-reluctantly he obeyed the command, but when he did, to his great amazement, he drew up so large a catch that the net began to break.

All during the message Peter's conscience had been pricked by the Lord's forthright preaching. Gently, but forcefully the Lord's words searched the hearts of men. Peter began to realize his own sinfulness. When the miracle of the catch of fishes took place, it was too much. The sense of his own unworthiness overwhelmed him, and with the impetuousness that characterized him he said, "Depart from me; for I am a sinful man, O Lord." But Jesus replied, "Fear not; from henceforth thou shalt catch men" (Luke 5:8, 10). It was Christ's call to Peter for full-time service.

Following this event Jesus called together a band of twelve disciples. Matthew, the tax collector, Philip, Nathanael, Thomas, Judas, one after another, until twelve in all were called. It was a rather oddly assorted group, but their faith and devotion to Jesus bound them together. These men were to be the beginning—the core of the movement.

Previously we have mentioned that Peter's father, Jona, had given him the name of Simon. Jesus surnamed him "Peter" which means "a little rock." Why Jesus used this name is not fully clear. Some think he was so called because he was obstinate as a rock. Peter certainly was not the rock upon which Christ built His church, but He was one of the little rocks of which the apostles with Christ were to form the foundation (Matt. 16:17-18; I Pet. 2:5).

And so Peter and the other eleven left their nets and homes to follow Jesus. Peter himself was later to claim that they "left all" (Mark 10:28). Operating in and out of the city of Capernaum, the disciples had opportunity to return home at intervals, but clearly Peter meant that he had given up his means of earning his living. What arrangements were made for the care of Peter's wife are not recorded. The party appears to have been maintained by the ministry of Christ. Judas was elected to be the treasurer, and he carried the bag.

Chapter 31
The Call of the Other Apostles

Andrew was the brother of Peter. He is scarcely more than a name, being completely overshadowed by his famous brother Peter. He also was a fisherman who shared his brother's house in Capernaum. Peter and James and John became the inner circle of the apostles. Andrew "attained not unto the first three." Yet on occasion he joined himself to them that he might inquire of Jesus concerning things to come (Mark 13:3).

The book of John does give us a closer look at Andrew than the synoptic gospels. Andrew in nearly all instances in which he is mentioned acts as an intermediary. When news reached Capernaum of John the Baptist's preaching, Andrew and his brother Peter, and the two Zebedee sons decided to make a trip to hear the prophet. Arriving at the meeting place, they listened earnestly to the Baptist as he preached repentance and foretold the coming of the Messiah to Israel, as mentioned in the previous chapter. Apparently they were much impressed by the Baptist's preaching, and they lingered on from day to day in the hope that the Messiah would appear.

Then one day Jesus did come and the Baptist proclaimed Him saying, "Behold the Lamb of God, which taketh away the sin of the world." None of the four was present on that occasion. But the next day Andrew and John were on hand. As they stood there beside the great preacher, the Man walked by. John the Baptist cried out, "Behold the Lamb of God!" (John 1:35-36). Andrew and John heard the words and a thrill of excitement went through them. John volunteers no more information, but the two disciples on an impulse began to follow the stranger. The Baptist neither reproaches them nor commends them as they go.

Quickening their pace, they caught up to Jesus. As they did, He turned about and saw them following Him asking, "What seek ye?" The intonation of His voice must have encouraged them. It was not, "Whom seek ye?" but "What seek ye?" Some, for example, sought Jesus for healing and never returned to give God thanks. Others sought Him for the loaves and fishes. A little confused as to what they should say, in a rather embarrassed way they asked, "Rabbi . . . where dwellest thou?" Jesus encouraged them still further and said, "Come and see." What kind of place did they find when they arrived? It could hardly have been more than a bivouac, as it was in the wilderness, far from human habitation. Jesus said later, "The Son of man hath not where to lay his head."

This meeting with Jesus took place at the tenth hour of the day, or about four o'clock in the afternoon. But Andrew not wishing Peter to miss out on what was happening, goes to find his brother Peter, who for some reason was elsewhere. He pursues his quest until he locates him. Then he tells him the great news:

> "One of the two which heard John speak, and followed him, was Andrew, Simon Peter's brother. He first findeth his own brother Simon, and saith unto him, We have found the Messias, which is, being interpreted, the Christ. And he brought him to Jesus. And when Jesus beheld him, he said, Thou art Simon the son of Jona; thou shalt be called Cephas, which is by interpretation, A stone" (John 1:40-42).

Since there is no record of the interview that Andrew and John had with Jesus, we must gauge it by the enthusiastic outburst of Andrew and his brother Peter when he said, "We have found the Messias." Let us for a moment reconstruct the order of events. Apparently the four fishing partners had talked much among themselves about the significance of John the Baptist's preaching. He had told them that the Messiah was present in their midst. He had seen Him and baptized Him. But where was He now? John did not know, but if his disciples would stay with him he would point Him out when He appeared.

This matter must have been the subject of animated conversation between the brethren, and no doubt had been the cause of their protracted stay in Bethabara. On the day when John did point out Jesus, Peter was absent. It was up to Andrew not to lose sight of Him. Peter would have had plenty to say if he had missed out on the experience of meeting the One that John talked about! Although Andrew was not as bold as Peter, he decided that he had to find out where Jesus was staying. Then he would know where to bring Peter when he found him. In the meantime, the conversation that Andrew had with Jesus was enough to convince him that Jesus was indeed the Messiah.

Andrew, thrilled with his discovery, finally located Peter, whose heart had probably already been prepared by John's testimony. It is to the everlasting credit of Andrew and John that they did not allow the golden opportunity to slip through their fingers, but followed it up when they saw Jesus. It was a decision from which both Andrew and his brother Peter, as well as the Zebedee brethren, would reap eternal benefits.

We are to see Andrew again at the time of the feeding of the 5,000. When the question came up about how the vast multitude could be fed, Andrew anticipated the situation and vouchsafed the information that the only one who had brought any food with him was a lad with five barley loaves and two fishes. "One of his disciples, Andrew, Simon Peter's brother, saith unto him, There is a lad here, which hath five barley loaves, and two small fishes: but what are they among so many?" (John 6:8-9).

It turned out to be, to Andrew's surprise, a useful piece of information. Jesus took the five loaves and two fishes, blessed them and broke them, and there was sufficient to feed the whole multitude.

Another brief view of Andrew is found in John 12:21, when certain Greeks desired to see Jesus. Philip brought the word to Andrew and together they went to Him. Then followed the discourse of Jesus on how He must die, but that in His death He would bring forth much fruit. Indeed! His death would result in the salvation of the Gentiles such as these Greeks.

Nathanael and Philip

"Now Philip was of Bethsaida, the city of Andrew and Peter. Philip findeth Nathanael, and saith unto him, We have found him, of whom Moses in the law, and the prophets, did write, Jesus of Nazareth, the son of Joseph. And Nathanael said unto him, Can there any good thing come out of Nazareth? Philip saith unto him, Come and see. Jesus saw Nathanael coming to him, and saith of him, Behold an Israelite indeed, in whom is no guile! Nathanael saith unto him, Whence knowest thou me? Jesus answered and said unto him, Before that Philip called thee, when thou wast under the fig tree, I saw thee. Nathanael answered and saith unto him, Rabbi, thou art the Son of God; thou art the King of Israel. Jesus answered and said unto him, Because I said unto thee, I saw thee under the fig tree, believest thou? thou shalt see greater things than these. And he saith unto him, Verily, verily, I say unto you, Hereafter ye shall see heaven open, and the angels of God ascending and descending upon the Son of man" (John 1:44-51).

The following day after Andrew brought Peter to Christ, Jesus went forth and found Philip, who came from Bethsaida, the same city where Andrew and Peter had been brought up. Hence, it is probable that Peter had known Philip previously. Philip even as Andrew, intuitively believed that Jesus was the Messiah. And as Andrew, he went to find his friend Nathanael and brought him to Jesus. It is puzzling in view of the length of the interview that Jesus had with Nathanael, that he should drop out of the gospel narrative. His name is not seen in any of the lists of the apostles. Yet he does appear again in John 21:2, after the resurrection of Christ, with several of the other apostles. It is conjectured that Nathanael is to be identified with Bartholomew whose name follows immediately after that of Philip on the lists.

When Philip was drawn to Christ, his first act as we have said, was to find his friend Nathanael. He then joyously communicated with him that he and his other friends had found the Messiah of whom Moses in the Law and the prophets had written—Jesus of Nazareth. This latter information somewhat chilled Nathanael, and he replied, "Can there any good thing come out of Nazareth?" Here we see the influence of rivalries between the adjacent towns. Cana was near Nazareth, and neither of the villages had a good opinion of the other. Nathanael was indeed looking for the coming of the Messiah; nevertheless, the idea that He might have come out of Nazareth shocked him.

Philip in his search had found Nathanael under a fig tree, probably in prayer and meditation. Very likely Nathanael had been pondering the words of John the Baptist concerning the coming of the Messiah. How did they relate to the Scriptures which spoke of the Messiah? His meditations were broken by the arrival of Philip who made the bold assertation that he had found the Messiah!

Although Cana is near Nazareth, and Nathanael and Jesus probably knew a number of the same people, it does not appear that Nathanael had met Jesus personally previous to that particular meeting. It is likely, however, that Nathanael and Philip knew Joseph, for Philip spoke of Him as "the son of Joseph." There is no difficulty here, for at this time Jesus was known as the son of Joseph, and the supernatural conception was still a sacred secret known only by a few. But it was not the lineage that troubled Nathanael. It was rather the place of His residence. It does indeed seem that the people of Nazareth were of a mediocre quality. Their rude treatment of Jesus when He sought to minister in His hometown bears this out. Cana was close enough to Nazareth for

Nathanael to have had some first-hand knowledge of the people. In general, the Jews did not expect the Messiah to come out of Galilee (John 7:52).

Philip wisely did not argue the question with Nathanael but merely said, "Come and see." Nathanael's problem was common to the whole Jewish nation. Christ's origin was too humble for them to accept. Their pre-conceived ideas were an effectual barrier that prevented them from recognizing the Messiah when He came. But although Nathanael was perplexed, his mind was not closed on the matter. He quickly accepted Philip's invitation to see Jesus.

When Nathanael approached the Lord, he was met by the strange salutation, "Behold an Israelite indeed, in whom is no guile!" The first Israelite, Jacob, had been full of guile. The Jews of that day were notorious for their guile. The hypocrisies of the Pharisees by which they succeeded in voiding the Word of God through the traditions of men, had become a part of their very nature. They revealed their guile by posing compromising dilemmas before Jesus under the guise of seeking truth, hoping all the while that they might somehow entrap Him.

But Nathanael was free from such deceit and Jesus looked into his heart and knew what was there. Nathanael was startled that Jesus seemed to read his innermost thoughts, and he could only exclaim, "Whence knowest thou me?" Jesus gave him a straightforward answer, "Before that Philip called thee, when thou wast under the fig tree, I saw thee." Since Jesus in His human body was not omniscient, we know that the gift of the Word of Knowledge was operating at this moment. Nathanael realized that Jesus had acquired this knowledge supernaturally. The young man had deliberately sought a place of concealment where he could meditate and pray. He knew he had been followed there by Jesus in Spirit, and this was enough to convince Nathanael that He was more than a man. With forthrightness he made his confession, "Rabbi, thou art the Son of God; thou art the King of Israel."

Some have pointed out the disproportion between the cause and the effect. How apparently inadequate was the simple statement of Christ, to draw out such a spontaneous confession of faith in His Messiahship. But Nathanael had just been in prayer and meditation. His very soul had been penetrated by the searching gaze of the Man who stood before him.

The reply of Jesus to his confession was still more surprising. He told Nathanael that he would see greater things than these. "Hereafter, ye shall see heaven open, and the angels of God ascending and descending upon the Son of man." Jacob's vision formed a background of the statement of the Lord. New truth was brought out. The ladder became a person. Christ is the ladder, the means of communication between earth and heaven. Nothing was mentioned about heaven being opened for Jacob. But it was to be opened for Nathanael and his companions.

"Blessed are the pure in heart: for they shall see God." So the guileless Nathanael was to be able to see heaven open and the harmony restored between God and man.

So one by one Christ added various disciples to His band, until He had altogether twelve, each of a different temperament than the other, but each with one exception fiercely loyal to their Master. The one who would defect was Judas Iscariot, the official treasurer of the group. But that is a story which must be told later.

Chapter 32

Christ Stills the Storm

The mid-Galilean ministry of Jesus was marked by the beginning of His use of the parable, an unusual method of teaching. At this time His fame had so spread abroad that great multitudes were being drawn to hear Him. Men had used the parable before in teaching, but Christ's parables were unique and unparalleled in their scope. Nothing which approached their depth and power, their brevity and manifold application had ever appeared in the entire literature of mankind before or since.

It is not our purpose at the present moment to enter into a detailed exposition of the parables. (These shall be dealt with in a later volume.) We today not only have the parables in written form, but also Christ's explanation of some of them. But it was not so easy for those who heard them spoken for the first time to understand them. Even the disciples failed to catch their significance, and when they were alone with Jesus they sought a fuller explanation.

When the day in which He spoke these first parables of the kingdom had ended, there was a desire on His part for solitude and a time of rest. Thereupon, He called His disciples to prepare the ship that they might go over to the other side.

But before He could get away, an interruption occurred. As anyone who has handled large crowds at a gospel meeting knows, when the service is over there is always a number of people who come forward with special questions or problems, one asking this thing, and another something else. It is not unusual for some to desire to join themselves to the party. It is hardly surprising, therefore, that at the close of this great service by the seashore certain ones should come to Jesus and make request to become members of His band:

> "And a certain scribe came and said unto him, Master, I will follow thee whithersoever thou goest. And Jesus saith unto him, The foxes have holes, and the birds of the air have

nests; but the Son of man hath not where to lay his head. And another of his disciples said unto him, Lord, suffer me first to go and bury my father. But Jesus said unto him, Follow me; and let the dead bury their dead" (Matt. 8:19-22).

The first was a scribe, who said, "Master, I will follow thee whithersoever thou goest." He probably thought that his official rank would make him an acceptable addition to the party. The man had witnessed the surge of popular enthusiasm, and he may have supposed that joining the party of Christ had lucrative possibilities. Jesus quickly disillusioned him on this score, declaring that whereas the foxes had holes and the birds of the air had nests, the Son of Man had nowhere to lay His head.

The second man who approached Him was already a disciple, but he had some matters to which he desired to attend. His father had died. There had to be a period of mourning, and the business of the settlement of the estate had to be taken care of. He would follow Jesus as soon as these things had been resolved. How many since, having received the call of God, have allowed such temporal matters to detain them until the hour of opportunity has passed? Time and tide wait for no man. Jesus, admonishing the man said, "Follow me; and let the dead bury their dead."

The third aspirant had a similar case. He too would follow Jesus, but he had to bid farewell to his friends first. Too often this apparently innocent act has resulted in fatal effects. A young man is convinced that Jesus has called him. But he confides his intentions to someone who is cold to the idea. Plausible arguments could be advanced against his plans. Warnings might be given that the enterprise could fail and come to nothing. The spirit of fear subtly interjects, and the result is that young man's outlook becomes altered. Jesus said, "No man, having put his hand to the plough, and looking back, is fit for the kingdom of God" (Luke 9:62).

Christ Stills The Storm

"And there arose a great storm of wind, and the waves beat into the ship, so that it was now full. And he was in the hinder part of the ship, asleep on a pillow: and they awake him, and say unto him, Master, carest thou not that we perish? And he arose, and rebuked the wind, and said unto the sea, Peace, be still. And the wind ceased, and there was a great calm" (Mark 4:37-39).

With these interruptions over, the disciples lifted anchor and set sail in their ship toward the eastern side of the lake. After they had gotten out a little way, Jesus lay down in the rear of the boat to get some much-needed rest. He could hear the waves as they splashed against the side of the ship and the low murmur of the conversation of the disciples as they discussed the meaning of the strange parables that Jesus had spoken that day to the people. Soon, He was fast asleep.

About the time they had reached the middle of the lake, they became conscious of a brisk wind which was steadily increasing in strength. The Sea of Galilee is especially noted for capricious storms that burst with a sudden fury upon the surface of its waters. Woe to those who are caught in the midst of one of these tempests! With scarcely a moment's notice, the ship began to be buffeted about in a most dangerous way. The disciples let down their sails. Peter availed himself of all his skill at the helm to keep the boat from being swamped. Again and again the ship was half buried amid the foam of the breakers, necessitating the disciples to bail out the water constantly. The spray from the dashing waves must have fallen upon Christ, but apparently He was so fatigued from His long hours of labor that He slept through it all.

But then things took a turn for the worse. The vehemence of the storm produced large billows which broke over into the boat itself, causing it to be so filled with water that it began to sink.

It is a matter of controversy as to just how much control Satan has over the natural elements and to what extent he is responsible for storms of this nature. Certainly the devil does not possess unlimited power, nor can he put the people of God in physical jeopardy at will. Otherwise, he would certainly use those powers without restraint. No doubt there is, confluence, or combination of circumstances, involved. We do know Satan is "the prince of the power of the air" and has a limited power over the natural elements. He was able to send the fire, or lightning, which destroyed Job's flocks (Job 1:12, 16). He also sent the cyclone or windstorm, that destroyed the house where his children were banqueting (Job 1:18-19). Nothing would suit the diabolical purposes of Satan better than for the ship which carried Jesus and the apostolic band to go down with all on board.

It appeared to the disciples that such a fate was highly probable. Despite their desperate efforts, they saw their boat becoming filled with water. Seized with panic, they turned to Christ who was in the rear of the ship still asleep on a pillow, and awoke Him with the cry, "Master, carest thou not that we perish?"

Here was a crisis indeed to test a man's mettle. To be awakened

190

suddenly and find one's self in a ship about to go down is enough to try the courage of any man. The disciples were no weaklings and they knew the ways of the sea. They were hardy fishermen whose courage and know-how could take them through a storm at sea as well as any man, if human skill alone could accomplish it.

But not for a moment was the spirit of the Lord ruffled. Without a single indication of alarm, He arose and took command of the situation. He rebuked the wind. Did His rebuke indicate that there was a diabolical intelligence behind the storm? The majestic Christ stood there only a moment until the pent-up fury of the wind relaxed and the giant waves began to subside. In a matter of minutes the sea became as a mirror and "there was a great calm." For a moment we can assume that the disciples were fully occupied in bailing out the water that had gotten into the ship. Then they turned with faces filled with wonder, exchanging glances with one another and realizing that God was standing before them, clothed in human flesh.

They had in their terror accused Him of indifference. But instead of apologizing for negligence, Jesus said, "Why are ye so fearful? how is it that ye have no faith?" If we take these words literally, we are compelled to come to one conclusion: Christ's philosophy of life envisages a man's putting himself completely into the hands of God, and in that committal he is perfectly safe from all harm. Not that anyone so committed should tempt God. Jesus would not cast Himself down from the pinnacle of the temple to prove the reality of that Divine protection. Men should use all proper precautions in their business of living. Even in the Mosaic Law, those who built a house were commanded to put battlements around the roof to guard against anyone's falling off the edge.

Notwithstanding, when all possible contingencies are anticipated, there is always the danger of the unexpected and that which cannot be foreseen. That is where Divine providence comes in. Jesus was implying that men who put themselves fully under the protection of God need have no fear of the unexpected—they are God's and He will take care of His own.

Therefore, neither men nor devils could harm Christ nor frustrate His mission before His time had come. So why then should His disciples fear the storm or be afraid that the boat would sink? No boat was ever made that could sink if Christ were in it! Those who cry in despair because they think their ship is going down need have no fear. All they have to make sure of is that Christ is in their ship!

The significance of Christ's words appeared to be lost on the disciples. They were saying to each other, "What manner of man is this, that even the winds and the sea obey him?" Nevertheless, these very human disciples made the right choice to obtain the faith that Jesus had. They chose to live where faith was. They walked and talked with Jesus. They saw His miracles; they listened to the words of Him of whom it was said "Never man spake like this man." They saw Him heal the sick, raise the dead, and cast out devils. They learned how He did it, and the day came that they no longer marvelled, but those who saw their works in turn marvelled. When Peter and John healed the lame man at the Beautiful Gate, it was the rulers of the Jews that were amazed; and we are told that they perceived that they had been with Jesus:

> "Now when they saw the boldness of Peter and John, and perceived that they were unlearned and ignorant men, they marvelled; and they took knowledge of them, that they had been with Jesus" (Acts 4:13).

Some would cast doubt on this remarkable intervention of nature and say that what was meant was that Jesus calmed "His terrified companions, and that the hurricane, from natural causes sank as rapidly as it had arisen." Of this, Dean Farrar in his *Life of Christ* declares:

> "I reply, that if this were the only miracle in the life of Christ; if the Gospels were the loose, exaggerated, inaccurate, credulous narratives which such an interpretation would suppose; if there were something antecedently incredible in the supernatural; if there were in the spiritual world no transcendent facts which lie far beyond the comprehension of those who would bid us see nothing in the universe but the action of material laws; if there were no providences of God during these nineteen centuries to attest the work and the Divinity of Christ—then indeed there would be no difficulty in such an interpretation. But if we believe that God rules; if we believe that Christ rose; if we have reason to hold, among the deepest convictions of our being, the certainty that God has not delegated His sovereignty or His providence to the final, unintelligent, pitiless, inevitable working of material forces; if we see on every page of the Evangelists the quiet simplicity of truthful and faithful witnesses; if we see in every year of succeeding history, and in every experience of individual life, a confirmation of the testimony which they delivered—then we shall neither clutch at rationalistic interpretations, nor be much

192

troubled if others adopt them. He who believes, he who knows, the efficacy of prayer, in what other men may regard as the inevitable certainties or blindly-directed accidents of life—he who has felt how the voice of a Saviour, heard across the long generations, can calm wilder storms than ever buffeted into fury the bosom of the inland Lake—he who sees in the person of his Redeemer a fact more stupendous and more majestic than all those observed sequences which men endow with an imaginary omnipotence, and worship under the name of Law —to him, at least, there will be neither difficulty nor hesitation in supposing that Christ, on board that half-wrecked fishing-boat, did utter His mandate, and that the wind and the sea obeyed; that His word was indeed more potent among the cosmic forces than miles of agitated water, or leagues of rushing air."

Chapter 33

The Legion of the Damned

"And they came over unto the other side of the sea, into the country of the Gadarenes. And when he was come out of the ship, immediately there met him out of the tombs a man with an unclean spirit, Who had his dwelling among the tombs; and no man could bind him, no, not with chains; Because that he had been often bound with fetters and chains, and the chains had been plucked asunder by him, and the fetters broken in pieces: neither could any man tame him. And always, night and day, he was in the mountains, and in the tombs, crying, and cutting himself with stones. But when he saw Jesus afar off, he ran and worshipped him, and cried with a loud voice, and said, What have I to do with thee, Jesus, thou Son of the most high God? I adjure thee by God, that thou torment me not" (Mark 5:1-7).

When Christ and His disciples reached the other side of the Sea of Galilee, they did not find the rest that they had anticipated. They were met by a demonstration of diabolic fury that rivalled that which they had encountered on the sea. There in the country of the Gadarenes the mountains rose up sharply from the surface of the water. Near the shore was located an old cemetery where people of the long past lay buried. The hills, too precipitate for ordinary human habitation, were not, however, completely unoccupied. Nearby was a great herd of swine attended by swineherds. In the distance was the city of Gadara.

Two men afflicted with a raging madness inhabited this rocky desolation. They wandered to and fro through the tombs and rocks and came out to meet the group. One of the men appeared to be more dangerous and aggressive. The other kept at a distance and did not take an active part in the unfolding drama. The fiercer of the two began to cry out against Jesus, indicating that he was a lunatic of the most violent kind. Since he was so dangerous to society, many attempts had been made to bind him with strong chains. But when the paroxysms of his mania came upon him, he became possessed of such superhuman force that the chains and the fetters fell away. All attempts to hold him failed, and he had been abandoned to his lunacy. Driven from the haunts of men, wearing no clothes, this raving maniac had been forced to wander in his torment, while night and day he cut himself on the rocks and his voice rang out with wild demented yells. His only companionship was this other demented man who was hovering about some distance away.

When the man possessed with the demons approached Christ, there was a great change in his attitude. The demons recognizing the One who had mastery over them, apparently took an abject attitude, hoping in their desperation that Christ would not send them away into the deep. Here we have one of the few Scriptural examples of a colloquy between a holy person and evil spirits. The man in whom the demons were, fell before Jesus in an attitude of worship and cried with a loud voice:

"What have I to do with thee, Jesus, thou Son of the most high God? I adjure thee by God, that thou torment me not" (Mark 5:7).

It is doubtful that the man himself had any knowledge of what he was saying. The demons had such control over his mind that they completely dominated his personality. Such persons when delivered, rarely have a recollection of events that occurred during the period of their obsession.

Demons know that they are damned spirits beyond the hope and pale of redemption. It is a torment and agony to them to be brought into the presence of a holy being, and thereby be reminded of their irremediable lost condition, the realization of the coming bliss of the righteous, and the awful prospect of their future doom. So what point had they in common with Christ, and why should He come to torment them before their time? (Matt. 8:29).

The fact is that demons have no right to possess a human being made in the image of God. Nevertheless, it is also true that if men through sin break over the barriers, or wander outside the pale of divine protective power, demons are always on the alert to take the advantage allowed them. Indeed Jesus pointed out on another occasion that if the man who was delivered continued to wander outside the realm of divine protection, the exorcised demon would sooner or later return, and seeing the house "swept and garnished," would take unto himself seven other spirits and the last state of the man would be worse than the first:

"When the unclean spirit is gone out of a man, he walketh through dry places, seeking rest; and finding none, he saith, I will return unto my house whence I came out. And when he cometh, he findeth it swept and garnished. Then goeth he, and taketh to him seven other spirits more wicked than himself; and they enter in, and dwell there: and the last state of that man is worse than the first" (Luke 11:24-26).

The demons, therefore, were contesting a point of law as to whether or not they had the right to remain in the man. Jesus overruled their objection and said, "Come out of the man, thou unclean spirit." Having established the fact that the demons would have to come out, He perceived that there was a large number of them present. It is not uncommon after one or more demons are cast out for others to hide away in the victim hoping to escape detection by pretending to have departed. Subsequent events of course show that such persons are not fully delivered. On this occasion Jesus demanded that the demons divulge their name, thus disclosing information concerning their number.

The leader of the demons responded saying, "My name is Legion: for we are many." The name "legion" was adopted from the Romans, whose armies were composed of legions of 6,000 men. This does not necessarily mean that there were exactly 6,000 devils in the man, but it does indicate that there were a great number. Jesus purposed that the whole colony should be ejected from their victim.

This brings up a question that is involved in the study of demonology and the spirit world. The question is, how many demons can inhabit a single human body at the same time? In certain instances, we are told that a person was possessed of as many as seven devils. Mary Magdalene had seven devils cast out of her (Luke 8:2). One thing is clear, spirit and matter can occupy the same space at the same time. No scientific instruments can measure or analyze spirits, but they make their presence known through a human body. Evil spirits can operate through the body of a spiritualist medium. They can speak and carry on intelligent communication, even as the demons were doing through this lunatic. They are the source of all sorts of phenomena, such as causing objects to fly about; they can produce knockings, simulate voices, accomplish levitation, etc. But they must have a physical body to manifest themselves in the physical realm. Demons attach themselves to the nervous system of the body through the auditory nerves, the optical nerves, the nerves of the brain, etc.

The words of Jesus imply that demons crave embodiment in a human body, thus indicating that they are disembodied spirits. When they are cast out, they "walk through dry places, seeking rest; and finding none." They cannot rest until they find and inhabit a human body. Once they enter, they are to a degree able to control it and to share the sensations and appetites of the body. Demons appear willing to share their habitation with other demons, since the increased number apparently give them almost absolute control over their victim (Luke 11:24-26).

Thus can be seen the reason for the demons' apprehension at being cast out. They feared that Jesus for some reason might cast them into the bottomless pit or the abyss:

"And they besought him that he would not command them
to go out into the deep" (Luke 8:31).

We do not have record that Jesus cast any demons into the pit. The devils themselves contended that the time of their punishment had not yet come (Matt. 8:29). This was probably true. Satan and his evil spirits will be incarcerated in the bottomless pit at the end of the age, at which time they will no longer be able to deceive the nations until the thousand years are finished (Rev. 20:1-3).

Notwithstanding, we know that some fallen angels and demon spirits are already in confinement. Jude 6 and Revelation 9:1-3 make this clear. On the other hand, it is certainly true that many demons are free to roam the earth. This gives rise to the question as to whether or not, if demons should disobey the restrictions God has set for them, it might be lawful to take their liberty from them. In other words, the demons seemed to recognize if they did not subject themselves to Christ's authority, He might bind them and cast them into the abyss, a place they feared exceedingly to go.

Actually, the demons wished to remain in the country of the Gadarenes. The people in that region were given to ungodly living and there would be a better chance for them to find further victims whose bodies they might inhabit. So their second plea was that He "would not send them away out of the country" (Mark 5:10).

Not being refused, and there being a large herd of 2,000 swine nearby, all the devils besought Him saying, "Send us into the swine, that we may enter into them" (Mark 5:12). Why did the demons make such a request and hope that it would be granted?

The children of Israel had been given charge by the Mosaic Law not to eat swine flesh. In Jesus' day the time had not yet come when God lifted this ceremonial prohibition (Acts 10:9-16), which would typify the cleansing of the Gentiles (Acts 11:1-18). The people of the Gadarenes were thus deliberately violating the Law of Moses by raising and trafficking in vast numbers of hogs and obviously making swine's flesh available for general consumption.

Since the owners of these swine were disobeying the Law of Moses, could Christ forbid their request and thus actually protect the contraband property of these lawbreakers? Actually, Jesus would not interfere with them for good or ill. Neither would He exercise His power to protect their illicit business. If the devils wished to enter the swine, it was up to them.

Demons when first ejected, like nascent chemicals seem to have unusual power; and upon leaving the man they moved like a gigantic swarm of invisible bats upon the herd of swine. How many of the demons immediately succeeded in entering the swine is not known but the sum result was that the herd became wild and unmanageable, insomuch that they began to stampede. (It has been aptly said that the hogs were different from some people. They couldn't live with the demons.) In their panic, the great herd "ran violently down a steep place into the sea," and perished. It would appear doubtful that the demons had anticipated this result or taken into account what would happen if the swine driven into a frenzy in this precipitous location, panicked.

The narrative at this point ceases to follow the activities of the baffled demons. Disembodied, they probably began the restless search for fresh victims. Some very profound results followed as a result of the incident. The man who a few moments before was a raging maniac suddenly became quiet and calm and was in his right mind. Apparently, he at once realized he was naked. And may we interject? Is not the spirit of nudity and exhibitionism of our day which has affected so many people of careless morals, likewise the spirit of demons? As long as the man was possessed of the devil, he would wear no clothes. Once he was delivered, he wanted his nakedness covered. Perhaps one of the disciples had an extra garment in the boat. At any rate, the man was soon clothed and began conversing in a normal way with Jesus and the disciples.

It can be understood that the event had a startling effect upon the herdsmen. They saw their swine stampeding violently down the mountainside and drowning in the waters below. Far from being able to quiet them, they barely managed to get out of their way in time to escape with their lives. Anything of such a violent and unexpected nature must have had a cause. What was it? They were not long in arriving at the truth. The lunatic who had terrorized the whole countryside with his wild gestures and fierce cries was sitting at the feet of Jesus clothed and carrying on an intelligent conversation.

Realizing that a vast amount of property had been destroyed and that they were accountable to their masters, the keepers fled to the city telling everyone they saw what had happened. Ordinarily such a wondrous miracle would have caused joy and thanksgiving, but in this case men's pocketbooks had been affected. The loss of such a great number of swine, jeopardizing the industry upon which many of the people depended, overruled every other consideration.

The reaction of the Gadarenes who came out to see what had happened was different from that in other places. It is not said that they disbelieved in the deliverance of the lunatic, or said that it was not accomplished by the power of God. But their precious swine had perished, their industry was threatened, and consequently their livelihood imperiled. Jesus might be a great prophet; He might be the Messiah, but they could not afford to accept what would cost them so much. As the demons wanted to be left alone, so did the Gadarenes. Men are always given their free choice of whether or not they will serve Christ. Alas! When the day comes for Christ to be their judge they will not have a choice (Matt. 25).

Jesus turned away. He himself had warned His disciples not to give that which was holy unto dogs, neither to cast their pearls before swine, "Lest they trample them under their feet, and turn again and rend you." These people loved their sins and their swine, preferring them to Christ. Therefore, they entreated Him to leave them alone, and this He sadly agreed to do.

Yet Jesus did not altogether leave the people to their doom. He knew that there were some who did not agree with what the majority had done. There were some precious souls who would have accepted Him if He had remained there. Was the blindness of those who thought only of their swine to deprive all of a chance of salvation? No, Jesus would give those who would an opportunity to reconsider their decision.

Previously in Galilee when a great miracle had been performed, Jesus enjoined silence for reasons mentioned. But in this case there was no need for that prohibition. Jesus would never personally return to the Gadarenes.

The people had prayed that Jesus would depart and He complied with their request. But the man who had been healed "prayed him that he might be with him" (Mark 5:18). Jesus suffered him not. He had a task for him to perform instead:

"Howbeit Jesus suffered him not, but saith unto him, Go home to thy friends and tell them how great things the Lord hath done for thee, and hath had compassion on thee" (Mark 5:19).

Much disappointed that he could not go with Jesus, the man once possessed of devils, nevertheless, faithfully obeyed the Lord's request. He returned to the people and began to publish in all the cities of Decapolis what great things that Christ had done for him. Those of that region had hoped that Jesus would go away and let them forget. But with this man who once had been demented, whom no prison chains could hold nor man could tame, going up and down the country telling people of the great things that God had done for him, how could they forget?

There is one last word that we might say concerning the people of Gadara. The day was to come (A.D. 67) when Vespasian and Titus would enter that region, massacring the inhabitants and burning to the ground the city of Gadara (Josephus B. J. III 7, 1). And so it was as Jesus said of Jerusalem, "Thou knewest not the time of thy visitation." The man in whom the legion of the damned dwelt became a great missionary for Christ, but the people of that region who turned Christ away lived to join the damned.

Chapter 34

The Raising of Jairus' Daughter and Other Miracles

So Jesus and His disciples retraced their journey back across the Sea of Galilee. What marvelous events had transpired in the short space of just twenty-four hours! But other remarkable miracles were to take place that day before the sun would set. The return to Capernaum was without incident; but when the sail of their ship was observed in the distance, crowds at once began gathering on the shore. Some who had witnessed the curing of the lunatic had hurried back to carry the news of what had happened. At any rate, when Jesus reached the shore there was a vast multitude waiting to meet Him.

The Paralytic Healed After Being Let Down From the Roof

"And it came to pass on a certain day, as he was teaching, that there were Pharisees and doctors of the law sitting by, which were come out of every town of Galilee, and Judea, and Jerusalem: and the power of the Lord was present to heal them. And, behold, men brought in a bed a man which was taken with a palsy: and they sought means to bring him in, and to lay him before him. And when they could not find by what way they might bring him in because of the multitude, they went upon the housetop, and let him down through the tiling with his couch into the midst before Jesus. And when he saw their faith, he said unto him, Man, thy sins are forgiven thee" (Luke 5:17-20).

Jesus went directly to a house—perhaps Peter's, or it might have been one loaned to Him, and began to teach. He probably sat near the doorway while the crowd pressed as close as possible to Him from every side. After He had taught for a while, He began to minister to some of the people for healing, for we are told that the "power of the Lord was present to heal them." There is such a thing as an atmosphere of faith that makes it easy for people to get

201

healed. The very opposite condition had prevailed during His second visit to Nazareth. He could do no mighty work there because of their unbelief (Mark 6:5).

When a man on a cot was brought into the courtyard, the place was so thronged that there was no way for those who brought him to get near. The sick man was in a desperate condition, paralyzed with the palsy. The four who sought to get him to Jesus could find no way of doing so directly. They were determined men, however, and they made their way up onto the roof of the outer stairway (Luke 5:19). Then making an opening by removing a few tiles, they lowered the man on his cot to a place near where Jesus sat. The palsied man had nothing to say, probably embarrassed by the manner in which his friends had brought him into the presence of Jesus.

But the Lord, looking around, appeared to be pleased by their faith, instead of rebuking them for tearing up the roof of the house:

> "And when he saw their faith, he said unto him, Man,
> thy sins are forgiven thee" (Luke 5:20).

The fact that the words, "their faith" is used is highly significant. The poor paralytic probably was so shaken up by being brought into the building in such an unorthodox fashion that he manifested no active faith in his healing. But Jesus showed that it is possible for others to supply the needed faith when the sick person is unable to exercise it for himself. So He said to the paralytic, "Man, thy sins are forgiven thee."

The Lord knew there were Pharisees and doctors of the law present, some of them emissaries from Jerusalem, and He realized that His word about forgiving the man's sins had made an unfavorable impression upon them. He observed the exchange of glances and looks of disapproval on their countenances as they whispered among themselves, "Who can forgive sins, but God alone?"

> "But when Jesus perceived their thoughts, he answering said unto them, What reason ye in your hearts? Whether is easier to say, Thy sins be forgiven thee; or to say, Rise up and walk? But that ye may know that the Son of man hath power upon earth to forgive sins, (he said unto the sick of the palsy,) I say unto thee, Arise, and take up thy couch, and go into thine house" (Luke 5:22-24).

Anyone can say, "Thy sins be forgiven thee," and who can say whether he is telling the truth? But when one says to a paralytic,

"Arise and walk," and he walks, the person who speaks obviously must have authority. If God gave Him power to do the first, was not that evidence that He had given Him power to do the other? But obstinacy is a peculiar trait and subsequent events were to show that the Pharisees would not accept the explanation. As the old saying goes, "He that is persuaded against his will is of the same opinion still."

Nonetheless, although the doctors of the Law opposed the work of Jesus in healing the paralytic, the rest of His audience when they saw what was happening began praising and glorifying God. Strength surged into the paralyzed limbs, and at the same time peace came to the man's soul. He arose and lifted his cot upon which he had been lying, and carried it triumphantly out through the doorway while the people made way for him. As he disappeared, he was still shouting praises to God. The people who witnessed this extraordinary miracle gave way to exclamations of astonishment not unmixed with awe, and said, "We have seen strange things today." They had never seen it in this fashion.

The Call of Matthew (Matt. 9:9)

The gospel narrative as most Bible readers know does not by any means give a complete record of all things that Jesus did, nor does it always present them necessarily in the order in which they took place (John 21:25). We do know, however, that it was about this time that Jesus gave the call to Matthew, whom He saw sitting at the receipt of customs. Apparently the Lord after healing the man of the palsy, had gone back to the seashore where He could more conveniently minister to the people. Matthew's office of custom was located nearby, and when Jesus passed that way He said to Matthew, "Follow me." At once the man arose and followed Him. Years afterward, Matthew would write the Gospel that bears his name.

A little later that day, Jesus went to the home of Matthew who had prepared a feast for Jesus and had invited many of his own personal friends. We shall not linger over this event, save to say that certain of the scribes and Pharisees were closely observing those who attended the feast. Christ's cordiality to the sinners present caused them no little misgivings. But as for the people, they were more and more convinced that Jesus was that great prophet who should come into the world. Unfortunately, they, as well as Christ's own disciples, shared the illusion that the Messiah would begin at once after a brief period of preaching to set up a visible earthly kingdom.

The Healing of the Woman With
The Issue of Blood

"And it came to pass, that, when Jesus was returned, the people gladly received him: for they were all waiting for him. And, behold, there came a man named Jairus, and he was a ruler of the synagogue: and he fell down at Jesus' feet, and besought him that he would come into his house: For he had only one daughter, about twelve years of age, and she lay a dying. But as he went, the people thronged him. And a woman having an issue of blood twelve years, which had spent all her living upon physicians, neither could be healed of any, Came behind him, and touched the border of his garment: and immediately her issue of blood stanched" (Luke 8:40-44).

The feast at Matthew's house had scarcely come to a conclusion when one of the most prominent men of the city came to Jesus with a most urgent personal request. It was none other than the ruler of the synagogue, and the one who probably invited Jesus to speak on the day He healed the demoniac. Moreover, it is very likely that he was among the deputation who came to Jesus to plead the case of the centurion for the healing of his servant. If this be true, it would explain his faith in Jesus who he believed could save the life of his daughter that lay dying.

Falling at the feet of Christ, his speech rendered almost incoherent by bursts of grief, he informed Jesus that his young daughter—his only daughter—lay at the point of death. If Jesus would but come and lay His hand upon her, she would live. It is possible that Jesus had seen the little girl when she came with her father to the synagogue on one of the days He had preached there. At any rate, Jesus touched by the appeal, arose at once and went with him, with a large crowd following.

But there was a woman in the multitude who had stood about Matthew's door while the feast had been going on. Not invited to the banquet, but daring to hope that when Jesus passed by the opportunity she had been looking for would come, she patiently waited. When the throng started for Jairus' house, she joined it by mingling with them. For she was indeed in a pitiful condition, having been afflicted with an issue of blood for no less than twelve years. It was a most distressing case. She had done everything possible to be cured, but having spent all her living on the physicians she got no better—only worse.

One day news had reached her of people who had been healed of incurable diseases by the Great Physician. Probably from modesty, she hesitated to reveal to Jesus the particular kind of affliction of which she had been suffering. It occurred to her that if she could only get near Him and touch the hem of His garment, she would be made whole. Therefore, when Jesus came out of the door with His disciples, she slipped in behind them, and while the multitude thronged about Jesus, she put out her trembling hand and touched the hem of His robe. And then, wonder of wonders, even as she drew her hand back, she felt the power of God go through her disease-wracked body, making her completely whole!

She now shrank back; her act was quite unnoticed by the crowd, but not by Jesus. He perceived immediately that virtue had flowed out from Him. He turned quickly and said, "Who touched me?" Jesus could have discovered the woman, but He preferred for her to come forward and make herself known. One by one all denied that they were responsible. Indeed, Peter came forward and said rather impatiently, "Master, the multitude throng thee and press thee, and sayest thou, Who touched me?" Peter was not a complex man, and he thought it absurd that the Lord would ask such a question, with the crowd pressing in all around Him.

But Jesus was insistent, and His eyes wandered from face to face, looking at the people to distinguish between those who were curiosity-seekers and the one who had the touch of faith. Then His glance fell upon the poor woman, who saw she could not hide; she came forward to fall at His feet and tell Him the truth. Perhaps she feared His anger, for the Law declared that anyone who was touched by a person so afflicted was made ceremoniously unclean until evening (Lev. 15:19).

It is sad to note the pitiful attempts of some who try to explain the operation of the gifts of the Spirit from a purely psychological basis. As Jesus said to the Sadducees, "Ye do err not knowing the scriptures, nor the power of God." We who have witnessed the gifts of the Spirit in operation have observed similar manifestations of the Word of Knowledge and Discerning of Spirits many times. When those given to unbelief and ignorance have finally wrecked their lives upon the shoals of unbelief, we shall see that the Word of God has stood the test and those whose faith is in its veracity shall never come to shame.

If the poor woman who had been healed had any apprehension of the Lord's displeasure, those fears were quickly dispelled. Her touch could not pollute Him, but rather it cleansed her. Far from being indignant, the Lord's gracious words spoke peace to her troubled life. He said, "Daughter, be of good comfort: thy faith hath made thee whole; go in peace" (Luke 8:48).

That healing virtue is a tangible thing which can be transmitted through pieces of cloth such as aprons and handkerchiefs, is no mere fancy, as seen in the case of Paul. After cloths had touched his body, he sent them out to the sick and they were healed; even evil spirits went out of those possessed by them:

> "And God wrought special miracles by the hands of Paul: So that from his body were brought unto the sick handkerchiefs or aprons, and the diseases departed from them, and the evil spirits went out of them" (Acts 19:11-12).

Tradition declares that the woman's name was Veronica. At one time a house in the city of Caesarea Philippi was pointed out as hers, and at the gates of the house was a sculptor's work of a woman kneeling with outstretched hands before a man extending a hand to her. It was said that she erected the monument in memory of her healing. It is not unlikely that the woman was a Gentile, for had she been a Jewess she would not have dared to go abroad in her uncleanness.

The Raising of Jairus' Daughter

> "While he yet spake, there cometh one from the ruler of the synagogue's house, saying to him, Thy daughter is dead; trouble not the Master. But when Jesus heard it, he answered him, saying, Fear not: believe only, and she shall be made whole. And when he came into the house, he suffered no man to go in, save Peter, and James, and John, and the father and the mother of the maiden. And all wept, and bewailed her: but he said, Weep not; she is not dead, but sleepeth. And they laughed him to scorn, knowing that she was dead. And he put them all out, and took her by the hand, and called, saying, Maid, arise. And her spirit came again, and she arose straightway: and he commanded to give her meat. And her parents were astonished: but he charged them that they should tell no man what was done" (Luke 8:49-56).

The incident that had just occurred had occasioned a brief delay, and though it must have profoundly impressed the people who were following Jesus, to Jairus who knew his daughter was gasping her last breaths, it must have caused deep anguish. It was only a few minutes' interruption, but it seemed like hours to the father. And then, as the company started on its way again a messenger reached Jairus saying, "Thy daughter is dead; trouble not the Master." It was too late after all! How those words must have stung the father's heart. If Jesus had only gotten there a little

206

sooner his child would have lived. But it was too late. Although the message was not addressed to Jesus, He overheard it, and knowing the anguish of the father, He said, "Fear not; believe only, and she shall be made whole." At such a time, faith grasps at the impossible and the words of Jesus must have been reassuring.

As the company drew near the house, they could hear the hired mourners and minstrels as they beat their breasts and set up their wailing chants. When Jesus arrived He sought to still them by saying, "Weep not: she is not dead, but sleepeth." The professional mourners thought this was a poor joke, and they ceased their mercenary wails only long enough to give Him a derisive laugh. Jesus did not prolong the unprofitable conversation, but ordered them put out of the house and commanded that none other should enter save Peter, James, John, and the parents.

There was a reason for this. The kind of spiritual atmosphere produced by a mixed crowd—if it is one of unbelief—has much to do with the effectiveness of the working of the Gifts of Healing and Miracles. A gaping curiosity-seeking audience is far from a help when ministering to serious cases.

Having put the crowd out, Jesus took the hand of the little girl. He spoke two words, "Talitha cumi" which means, "Maid, arise." Then suddenly, out of eternity the spirit of the girl returned, and she arose and walked before them. An amazement took hold of the parents so that they scarcely knew what to say. Who can describe the wild emotions of joy that thrilled them when they saw what had happened! But Jesus calmly told them to give their daughter some nourishment. Therein is a simple lesson for those who teach Divine healing. Rest, proper food, and care of the body is important if one is to maintain health after receiving healing. Had the girl not been fed and proper nourishment given her, she might have had a relapse. On the other hand, the person who receives healing is not to be treated as an invalid. It is good for those who have been healed to arise from their bed and walk. Faith is an act; faith and works must function as one.

While we are discussing the subject of the raising of the dead, we may note that those Jesus raised were comparatively young persons with most of their lives before them. It is ordinarily the will of God for people to live out their days in this world—for as has been said, "Earth is a school to prepare us for glory." Divine providence so designed earth for that purpose. Nevertheless, there is nothing immortal about the temple of clay that we live in. The human body in its physical state, with its frailties and weaknesses, is not designed for immortality. There comes a time when we must put off this tabernacle that we might receive a glorified body like unto that of Christ's.

Jesus cautioned the ruler of the synagogue to say nothing to the crowd outside. Concealment of the fact of the miracle of course would be impossible, for neighbors would soon learn about it. But it seemed to be a consistent policy with Jesus that He never sought to prove His power to unbelief. He had performed more than enough miracles to attest His Divinity, and it was important that men should hear and heed His mission before He gave them more. It is a terrible thing for a person to get hardened to an acceptance of miracles before he has been moved to repentance. For there is little left to move him.

The Healing of the Two Blind Men

As Jesus slipped out of the house, He gave no word to the wondering crowd who stood about the door waiting to hear what was happening inside. They would have to get their information from others. The Lord now hastened homeward. But as He went, two blind men posted themselves in His path. Realizing that He could not allow a healing line to be formed outside the house of Jairus, which might continue through the night, He hurried on.

The blind men, nonetheless, were persistent. They followed Him, probably guided by some friend, crying in a loud voice, "Thou son of David, have mercy on us" (Matt. 9:27). "Son of David" was a Messianic title, but Christ never accepted it, except in the sense of His mother's lineage (Matt. 22:41-46). Although Jesus went on without pausing, the blind men managed to follow Him to His house. They were at His door importuning Him for admittance, and He could not turn them away.

Nevertheless, before the Lord healed them, He paused to give them certain instructions. One of the mistakes of some who minister healing is that they often fail to give their listeners proper instructions. Consequently, many who receive deliverance lose it (Luke 11:24-26). Jesus, however, in His perfect understanding of the human heart, always went directly to the seat of the trouble. Perhaps in this case He would say something to draw out their faith. It is one thing to be desperate for healing; it is another thing to have faith. The two circumstances are not exactly the same, although there is such a thing as the desperation of faith.

The two blind men were desperate enough. They were so determined to get their healing that they had overcome all obstacles and had pressed their way until they were in His presence. Was it just a hope on their part, or did they really believe He was able to give them their sight? That was the question Jesus wanted to know. Sometimes when people are asked this question, the note of hesitancy is apparent in their voice. They are relying altogether on the other person's faith. In such case, their request for healing is premature. They need to listen to teaching until faith springs up in their hearts. "Faith cometh by hearing, and hearing by the word of God" (Romans 10:17).

The desperation of the blind men evidently begat faith. And in a chorus they answered, "Yea, Lord." Then Jesus touched their eyes saying, "According to your faith be it done unto you." Thus did Jesus show that men's faith was an essential element of healing—that He was not just a miracle man wandering around performing wonders, but that people receive healing, according to the faith they exercise. So when Jesus had spoken the words their eyes came open. Then as they looked, wonder of wonders, the first thing they saw was the kind compassionate eyes of the One who had healed them.

Jesus foresaw what would happen if word of this miracle went abroad. Popular excitement was steadily rising. News of the girl who had been raised from the dead would soon get around. Therefore, He strictly charged the blind men to say nothing about receiving their sight. Nevertheless they paid no heed to His command. They did not pause to consider that obedience is better than sacrifice, and to hearken than the fat of rams. There is such a thing as service which instead of honoring Christ, only hinders His purpose and results in harm instead of good. So they went out from the presence of Jesus to tell the story far and wide, with the very result that Christ anticipated.

Chapter 35

The Disciples Are
Commanded to Heal the Sick

"And Jesus went about all the cities and villages, teaching
in their synagogues, and preaching the gospel of the kingdom,
and healing every sickness and every disease among the people. But when he saw the multitudes, he was moved with
compassion on them, because they fainted, and were scattered abroad, as sheep having no shepherd" (Matt. 9:35,36).

So great were the multitudes that came to hear the preaching of
Jesus, that He saw that the time had come for Him to make a
change. Hitherto the Twelve had followed Him on all occasions.
But it was time that they were to launch out on their own. There
were two reasons for this. One was that the day was not far off
when the Lord would be taken from them. The other was that by
dividing up the work, more could be accomplished. As Jesus looked
out on the fields and saw the multitudes without a shepherd, He
turned to the disciples and said, "Pray ye therefore the Lord of the
harvest, that he will send forth laborers into his harvest." He not
only saw the people of the regions where He had been ministering,
but He saw the field as the whole world. Soon He would be saying
to His followers, "Go ye into all the world, and preach the gospel
to every creature."

The men around Him came from humble stations in life, but
they were the ones to whom would be given the work of the
Christian Church. They were to be great, but their greatness was
to come from Christ alone. It was the magnitude of His character
that made them fit for the gigantic task. In the beginning they were
rude and carnal, but Christ patiently taught them, ridding them of
their earthly illusions concerning the coming kingdom. He had
made their training His most constant work. They saw all He did
and heard all He said. Often He took them aside to give them some
special teaching. Gradually, He stamped His own image upon them.

210

The time had come for them to be sent forth on their first preaching mission, and He called them unto Himself:

"And when he called unto him his twelve disciples, he gave them power against unclean spirits, to cast them out, and to heal all manner of sickness and all manner of disease" (Matt. 10:1).

It was an ordination service, in which He would give them final instructions before sending them out two by two. Although it is not explicitly stated, the order of the apostles as they were sent out was probably as is listed in Matthew 10:2:

1. Peter and Andrew
2. James and John
3. Philip and Bartholomew (Nathanael)
4. Thomas and Matthew
5. James and Lebbaeus (Thaddaeus)
   (James is also called Cleopas, Lebbaeus was also called Judas)
6. Simon and Judas Iscariot

The Instructions Given the Twelve

1. They were to limit their ministry to Israel. They were not to go to Samaria nor to any city of the Gentiles (Verses 5-6).

2. They were to go forth in the ministry of deliverance, the same ministry that Jesus had demonstrated:

"And as ye go, preach, saying, The kingdom of heaven is at hand. Heal the sick, cleanse the lepers, raise the dead, cast out devils: freely ye have received, freely give" (Matt. 10:7-8).

This remarkable commission to minister to the sick was given at the head of the list of His instructions, and shows the importance of this ministry.

3. They were to take nothing with them; neither money in their purses nor scrip to buy food. Nor were they to take two coats, nor an extra pair of shoes. "For the workman is worthy of his meat."

There were several reasons why Jesus gave these instructions. First, when God calls a man for the ministry, He wants him to learn to depend entirely upon Him. Second, the disciples were on an urgent errand; He did not want them to waste time in making

211

unnecessary preparations. Jesus had spent many months preparing them spiritually, but He did not wish them to encumber themselves on their preaching tour with unnecessary baggage. Third, Jesus pointed out that the "workman was worthy of his meat." They were going to bless the people, heal them, give them the good news of the kingdom. They were worthy to receive in return those things which were necessary.

They were not beggars in any sense of the word; those who entertained them would receive a rich reward (Matt. 10:40-42). When, therefore, they arrived in a city, they were to inquire who was worthy, and then abide at that place. They were not to move from house to house. In other words, they were not to waste their time in social visits. While under a man's roof they were to bear themselves graciously and considerately, finding no fault with the food or accommodations.

They were to bless the house in which they were guests, saying, "Peace be unto you." Sometimes they would be ill-received and their message would be rejected. They were then to take their departure, after first solemnly protesting against that city, and shaking off the dust of their feet as a witness against it:

"And whosoever shall not receive you, nor hear your words, when ye depart out of that house or city, shake off the dust of your feet" (Matt. 10:14).

We should note in passing that Christ at the end of His ministry changed His instructions in the matter of not taking a purse. At the present time He wished to show His disciples that regardless of what circumstances they might meet, God would always take care of His own when they were on His business. Nevertheless, the Lord did not want people to get the idea that His plan for the ministry was that it should be supported in strange and mysterious ways. Nor did He wish to deprive the people of the blessing that comes from giving and supporting the ministry. Later, when the disciples returned, the apostolic party had a common purse. And still later He reminded them that although He had told them they were to take no purse, they were now to carry one (Luke 22:36).

Next, Jesus gave them a warning: "Behold, I send you forth as sheep in the midst of wolves: be ye therefore wise as serpents, and harmless as doves" (Matt. 10:16). They were warned against recklessness. Certainly the minister needs wisdom in facing the forces of evil that seek to entrap him. Wisdom was to be the first gift of the Spirit (I Cor. 12:8). Indeed God has promised this to all who ask for it (James 1:5-6). Alas, many, because they have lacked that wisdom, have had their ministry end in calamity.

The disciples were not to invite danger openly. If it seemed as if physical force were about to be used on them, they were to leave at once and go to the next city. Nevertheless, in their lifetime, some would be taken before magistrates and even governors or kings. If and when that happened, they were not to depend upon their human wisdom, but on the wisdom given by the Holy Ghost:

> "But when they deliver you up, take no thought how or what ye shall speak: for it shall be given you in that same hour what ye shall speak. For it is not ye that speak, but the Spirit of your Father which speaketh in you" (Matt. 10:19-20).

It is obvious that the instructions that Jesus was giving to the apostles went beyond their immediate mission. Prophetically, it was projected into the years and centuries ahead, when many of their successors would give their lives as martyrs. Especially did it refer to the age of persecution of the second and third centuries, when believers were "hated of all men for my name's sake" (Verse 22).

The 23rd Verse is of singular importance, for Christ leaps ahead in time to the very end of the age, when the messengers of the Kingdom would complete the work of the apostles. The preaching of the Gospel would practically cease in Israel after about 66 A.D., when the Jewish-Roman wars would begin. The dispersion of Israel would follow and last for many centuries. Then as the age would draw to an end, God would gather His people again into their land—yet in unbelief. Then would come the task of carrying the Messianic message to them. The workers would have to finish the task in a hurry, for the work would scarcely be completed before the coming of the Son of man:

> "But when they persecute you in this city, flee ye into another; for verily I say unto you, Ye shall not have gone over the cities of Israel, till the Son of man be come" (Matt. 10:23).

Truly, the evangelization of Israel is one of the most urgent tasks which confronts the church today.

When the Lord had finished giving His instructions, He sent them out two by two, and then He went His way, also to preach and teach in the cities of Galilee. That He did not continue long in Galilee is probable, for about this time John informs us that Jesus made a visit to Jerusalem to attend a feast, and He went alone. As Dean Farrar brings out in his *Excursus VIII,* this feast probably was the Feast of Purim, one that occurred about a month before the Feast of the Passover. It was not a Passover Feast, since John always mentions those feasts by name (John 2:13; 6:4; 11:55). Moreover, if this were a Passover Feast, then John omitted a whole year of Christ's ministry (John 6:4). There are several things that we need not discuss here which indicate that this was the Feast of Purim.

The Feast of Purim was a saturnalia of Judaism, one without divine authority, and one which had its roots in the vindictive and provincial feelings of the nation, and was unconnected with religious service. Why Jesus departed for Jerusalem at this time is not explained, but nothing is said that He went merely to attend the feast. He may have gone up to Jerusalem to be present at the later Passover Feast. He would leave early in order to avoid the publicity and the dangerous excitement involved in joining the caravans that travelled at that time. The opportunity obviously presented itself at the time when His disciples were engaged in their missionary work.

Nevertheless, Jesus did not remain for the Feast of the Passover, and the events of the next chapter reveal the reason why He did not.

Chapter 36
The Pool of Bethesda

"After this there was a feast of the Jews; and Jesus went up to Jerusalem. Now there is at Jerusalem by the sheep market a pool, which is called in the Hebrew tongue Bethesda, having five porches. In these lay a great multitude of impotent folk, of blind, halt, withered, waiting for the moving of the water. For an angel went down at a certain season into the pool, and troubled the water: whosoever then first after the troubling of the water stepped in was made whole of whatsoever disease he had. And a certain man was there, which had an infirmity thirty and eight years. When Jesus saw him lie, and knew that he had been now a long time in that case, he saith unto him, Wilt thou be made whole? The impotent man answered him, Sir, I have no man, when the water is troubled, to put me into the pool: but while I am coming, another steppeth down before me. Jesus saith unto him, Rise, take up thy bed, and walk. And immediately the man was made whole, and took up his bed, and walked: and on the same day was the sabbath" (John 5:1-9).

Over one year of the ministry of Christ had been completed, and the time of the Passover came around again. As we have seen, Jesus probably had been in Jerusalem for some weeks. During His visit He was kept under close surveillance. The emissaries of the Sanhedrin had brought back a report of His doings in Galilee, and it was a heavy indictment. He had consorted with sinners, they said; He claimed power to forgive sins, and showed laxity in the matter of keeping the Sabbath. Moreover, in their opinion He had been guilty of blasphemy. They were soon to find occasion against Him in Jerusalem.

In Jerusalem near the sheep-gate there was a pool known by the name of Bethesda, which it was claimed had remarkable properties. Around a pentagonal masonry, a multitude of sick folk gathered— sufferers from blindness, deafness, lameness, and from every manner of disease. It was said that at certain times an angel went down into the water and troubled it. Whoever then went down first after the troubling of the water "was made whole of whatsoever disease he had."

Many scholars believe that the evidence against the genuineness of this passage is strong, since it is omitted in so many manuscripts. Of this, Dean Farrar in his *Life of Christ* makes the following remarks which may be of interest to the reader:

> "The weight of evidence both external and internal against the genuineness of John 5:3, 4 is overwhelming. It is omitted by not a few of the weightiest MSS, and versions (B. D. the Cureton Syriac). In others in which it does occur it is obelisked as dubious. This abounds in various readings, showing that there is something suspicious about it. It contains in the short compass of a few lines no less than seven words not found with a different sense. It relates a most startling fact, one wholly unlike anything else in Scripture, one not alluded to by a single other writer, Jewish or heathen, and one which, had there been the slightest ground for believing in its truth, would certainly not have been passed over in silence by Josephus. Its insertion (to explain the word in Verse 7) is easily accounted for; its omission, had it been in the original text, is quite inconceivable. Accordingly, it is rejected from the text by the best editors as a spurious gloss, and indeed there is no earlier trace of its existence than an allusion to it in Tertullian (De Bapt. 5). (Ob. circ. A. D. 220)."

While it is possible that the verse could have been interjected and, therefore, spurious, we do not believe the proof is absolute. We leave it to the reader to draw his own conclusions.

Among the sufferers lying some distance from the water was one in an especially pitiful condition, who had been a paralytic for thirty-eight years. He had come to the pool either by crawling there, or by whatever means he found available. Being left there unaided, and as the motion of the water occurred at irregular intervals, others less feeble than himself were always able to get into the water before him.

Jesus looked on the man with deep pity. It is obvious that his whole life had been one of frustration and despair. He was a beaten man—a soul for whom no man cared. Still notwithstanding all that, he held a slender hope. Who knows—some day someone could take pity on him, and when the water was troubled might assist him into the pool first.

216

To attract the man's attention, Jesus said, "Wilt thou be made whole?" So long had been the hopelessness of his lot, that the words scarcely stirred him. Nevertheless, thinking perhaps that this stranger might be kind enough to help him get into the water when the moving again took place, he explained the sad story of his long frustration.

It is notable that Jesus had nothing to say, either for or against the efficacy of the pool. Jesus' ministry was not negative, but positive. He spoke a word of command, "Rise, take up thy bed, and walk." His voice carried such a weight of authority that the man involuntarily made an effort to rise. And as he did, to his unspeakable joy, he found the atrophied muscles responding! After thirty-eight years of lying on a cot, he suddenly found that he could walk. It is a strange commentary on the multitude of sufferers, that the man was able to do so without attracting their attention. But they had their gaze so transfixed on the pool as they watched for the moving of the water, that even the commotion caused by the man taking up his cot failed to get their attention. Surely they represent many today whose gaze is upon physical remedies. We would not speak against these things, nor the physicians who serve to alleviate the suffering of mankind. Jesus never spoke against them. Nonetheless, the average physician will be as ready as anyone to admit that there are many diseases that medical science cannot cure. Some poor people go from one operation to another, and they are so intent in trying to find a cure that they miss the Great Physician altogether.

The people at the pool evidently failed to notice the man's healing or they would have clamoured for Jesus to heal them. Nevertheless, the ecclesiastics took quick note of the situation. Not that they noticed he had been healed, for these hireling shepherds did not recognize the man as the erstwhile paralytic. They apparently cared little about the sick and broken of their flock. But the matter that angered them was that the man was carrying his cot on the Sabbath day. This they considered a flagrant violation of the Sabbath. The man answered saying, "He that made me whole, the same said unto me, Take up thy bed, and walk" (Verse 11).

As the inner life of a professor of religion becomes dead, even the more does he become attached to formalism and the observance of petty rules. The Sabbath was made for man, but the Jews had changed it around until it seemed that man was made for the Sabbath. The observance of the Sabbath had practically become a fetish, a custom hedged with innumerable frivolous and senseless restrictions. The great provisions of the Mosaic Law of mercy and judgment were passed by.

These heresy-hunters already half-suspecting that this Jesus who had come from Galilee was the source of the miracle, began to question the man as to who it was that told him to take up his bed and walk. It is to be observed that they didn't ask him who had healed him. They purposely ignored this fact, but pressed their interrogation as to who told him to take up his bed. The imagined breach of their law was their sole concern.

They believed that they had a clear-cut precedent of the violation of the Law. Had not a man during the days of the children of Israel's wandering in the wilderness, been stoned for gathering sticks on the Sabbath days? And did not Jeremiah say, "Take heed to yourselves, and bear no burden on the Sabbath?" (Jer. 17:21).

But the reason for these injunctions was the one of mercy intended to protect the oppressed from a life of incessant toil. Had it not been for the institution of the seventh day as a day of rest, the greed of employers would have exacted from the working man labor without cessation. Now when a man who had been healed wished to carry home his pallet, why should the commandment be interpreted to force the man to leave behind his bed, probably the only thing that he possessed? "Where is that fellow who told you to carry your cot?" Their voices rose in indignation. But the man could not tell, for Jesus had conveyed Himself away.

After a while the man went to the temple. This would seem to be in his favor. It would appear that he had gone there to give God thanks. While in the temple, Jesus saw him and gave him a word of warning, "Behold, thou art made whole: sin no more, lest a worse thing come unto thee" (John 5:14). In the hearing of the crowd, Jesus said nothing to embarrass him, but He sought him out and brought to his remembrance his sin—a sin that might have been the cause of his affliction. He had to forsake it.

There are those who would tell us that if a man is truly healed by God, the affliction cannot come back on him. Such statements are in total variance with the Scriptures. Not only may the affliction return, if a man fails to go on with God or lapses back into sin, but an even worse thing may come unto him. Surely some are in sore need of Biblical teaching if they are to understand God's way of healing.

It is at this point that we are confronted with a rather peculiar circumstance. The man went and told the Jewish authorities that Jesus had healed him, with the result that the Jews sought to kill Jesus. Dean Farrar makes some interesting remarks on this in his *Life of Christ*:

> "Perhaps the warning had been given because Christ read the worthless nature of the man; at any rate, there is something at first sight peculiarly revolting in the 15th verse. The man went and told the Jewish authorities that it was Jesus who had made him whole. It is barely possible, though most unlikely, that he may have meant to magnify the name of One who had wrought such a mighty work; but as he must have been well aware of the angry feelings of the Jews—as we hear no word of his gratitude, no word of glorifying God—as too, it must have been clear to him that Jesus in working the miracle had been touched by compassion only, and had been anxious to shun publicity—it must be confessed that the prima facie view of the man's conduct is that it was an act of contemptible delation—a piece of pitiful self-protection at the expense of his benefactor—an almost inconceivable compound of feeble sycophancy and base ingratitude. Apparently the warning of Jesus had been deeply necessary, as, if we judge the man aright, it was wholly unavailing.
>
> For the consequences were disastrous. They changed, in fact, the entire tenor of Christ's remaining life. Untouched by the evidence of tender compassion, unmoved by the display of miraculous power, the Jewish inquisitors were up in arms to defend their favourite piece of legalism. 'They began to *persecute Jesus because He did such things on the Sabbath day.*' "

We must say that if the man did this deliberately, he was a monster of ingratitude, one who would betray his benefactor in order to clear himself from the charge of Sabbath-breaking. Nevertheless, it is more likely that he testified of a miracle of mercy in gladness of heart supposing it would evoke their wonder and admiration. Then too, his presence in the temple would indicate that he had gone there as a penitent to give thanks to God and to vow to lead a new life. Moreover, it is unlikely that the man, having been in the condition he was, had any knowledge of the Jews' hatred of Christ. What he did, therefore, would seem to be in all simplicity and good faith.

At any rate, the result of the miracle was that the Jews came to Jesus, angrily charging Him with violation of the Sabbath day.

In answer to their charge, Jesus delivered the wonderful discourse recorded in the fifth chapter of John. He said, "My Father worketh hitherto, and I work" (Verse 17). God had worked through the creative week and rested on the seventh day (Gen. 2:1-2). Alas, man's disobedience disturbed the Sabbath paradise, and forced God to resume His work in the redeeming of a race that had fallen into sin.

Just where the discourse took place, we are not told. Whether it was delivered in the temple, before the Sanhedrin, or before some committee of the Jews cannot be determined, except that some of the chief rabbis and priests were present. They were ready to instruct Him and set Him right on the Sabbath day. But it was He who did the instructing. For when they mentioned the Sabbath He declared He was emulating His Father, thus "making himself equal with God." They were horror-stricken. In their eyes, He was not only guilty of Sabbath-breaking, but also of blasphemy. This crime was worthy of death. But Christ, instead of backing down, only amplified His claim. As Son of God, He stood in a unique relation to the Father.

This discourse is one of the most remarkable of the Gospels. We cannot go into it in detail, but we give a brief synopsis of its important truths:

1. There is a distinction of persons in the Godhead. "The Son can do nothing of himself, but what he seeth the Father do ... For the Father judgeth no man, but hath committed all judgment unto the Son" (John 5:19, 22). Although a distinction of persons is made, one does not act independently of the other. There is a perfect unity of action, even as there is a perfect unity of nature.

2. Christ reveals man's duty. "That all men should honor the Son, even as they honour the Father. He that honoureth not the Son honoureth not the Father which hath sent him" (Verse 23). Jesus went further than making known His Messiahship, for the Jews generally did not expect a Divine Messiah. He revealed His Divinity.

3. Christ attests His deity with a four-fold witness:
  (a) By John who bare witness of Him (John 5:33-35).
  (b) By His miracles (Verse 36).
  (c) By the Father (Verses 37-38). This was a witness that John the Baptist saw, but not the Jews.
  (d) By the Scriptures (Verses 39-47).

220

Through these witnesses, God had provided the means by which all men might know the true Messiah, the Son of God in whom is life eternal.

But Jesus charged that their great error was in failing to believe the witness of the Word of God. True, the Jews gave the Scriptures superstitious reverence. They counted the very letters in them. Why then could they not believe them? What was standing in their way?

Surely, this was an important question. We today witness the amazing manner in which the prophets foretold all things about the Messiah. Of His birth in Bethlehem, of His humanity and divinity, of His mission and ministry, all were told beforehand. That His coming would be in humility and condescension, the 53rd Chapter of Isaiah plainly showed. The prophet Daniel even gave the time that the Messiah would appear—sixty nine weeks of years after the commandment went forth to rebuild Jerusalem (Dan. 9:24-27).

Why then could they not believe? They were intelligent men in temporal matters; why were they so grossly blind in spiritual things?

Jesus gives the answer: It was because of their pride. "How can ye believe, which receive honour one of another, and seek not the honour that cometh from God only?" (John 5:44). Their pride made them see a different kind of Messiah, one who would throw off the yoke of the Romans and make Jewry a world power, one who would bring great prosperity. They wanted a Messiah who would defeat Israel's enemies and usher in a golden age. This pride made it constitutionally impossible for the Jews to accept such a Messiah as Jesus, who came in meekness and lowliness of heart.

Hence, they rejected Him who came in His Father's Name and instead became ready victims of every false Messiah that appeared on the scene. A century later, they would accept Bar-Cachebas, whose fanaticism resulted in the final destruction of the Jewish nation. In all, some sixty false Messiahs have appeared—each in his own name. Alas, the most wicked and deceptive of them all will appear just before the days of the Great Tribulation. Jesus referred to him when he said, "I am come in my Father's name, and ye receive me not: if another shall come in his own name, him ye will receive" (John 5:43).

The Resurrection of the Dead

Jesus at the same time gave another revelation—the truth of the resurrection of the dead. The Old Testament hints at it, makes allusions to it, but Christ was the One who brought to light the glorious truth of immortality and of life beyond the grave. He did not speak of the Christians' future existence as that of disembodied spirits—but that their bodies should be raised from the graves and glorified:

> "Marvel not at this: for the hour is coming, in the which all that are in the graves shall hear his voice, And shall come forth; they that have done good, unto the resurrection of life; and they that have done evil, unto the resurrection of damnation" (John 5:28-29).

Jesus by no means was a universalist. Not all would share the resurrection of life. There was also a resurrection of judgment. Those who did evil would have their part in the resurrection of damnation.

How could a man have a part in the resurrection of life? He could by hearing the voice of the Son of Man. All were spiritually dead, but if they listened to His voice in this world, they would pass from death unto life:

> "Verily, verily, I say unto you, He that heareth my word, and believeth on him that sent me, hath everlasting life, and shall not come into condemnation; but is passed from death unto life. Verily, Verily, I say unto you, The hour is coming, and now is, when the dead shall hear the voice of the Son of God: and they that hear shall live" (John 5:24-25).

What a sermon it was! In Galilee, Jesus had suppressed the revelation concerning Himself, that the truth might come gradually to those who heard His words. But at Jerusalem where the decisions of the nation were made, where His appearances would be briefer and His mighty works fewer in number, He revealed His identity and mission in its fulness. But, alas! it was to be rejected. Yet at the moment the Jews could do nothing. They could only gnash their teeth in impotent rage, and wait for an opportunity to pass the sentence of death. Under these circumstances, it was useless for Jesus to remain in Jerusalem. He returned to Galilee with a clear vision of what the end would be. He would continue His work, but He was racing against time, when the conspirators would come, take Him and condemn Him to death.

Chapter 37

The Feeding of the
Five Thousand

."And the apostles gathered themselves together unto Jesus, and told him all things, both what they had done, and what they had taught. And he said unto them, Come ye yourselves apart into a desert place, and rest a while: for there were many coming and going, and they had no leisure so much as to eat" (Mark 6:30-31).

When Jesus returned to Galilee, the apostles "gathered themselves together unto Jesus," to give a report of all that had taken place in their preaching mission. It must have been an exciting story, although the details are not preserved to us. However, we are told later about the Seventy who were sent out, and afterwards returned with joy saying that even the devils were subject to the name of Christ. The Twelve who were closer to the Lord must have had a glowing report of their victories, though it was tempered with the sad news of the untimely death of John the Baptist, an event that had just occurred.

Jesus considered the time opportune to take a few days' rest before they continued their activities. Folk were coming and going steadily; the sick were being brought for healing; others were asking questions. We are told that the little band had no opportunity even to eat. So at Jesus' direction, they took a boat over the sea to a desert place near the city of Bethsaida-Julia. In noting these words of Jesus, we are made aware of the importance of regular times of rest. If Jesus and His apostles required seasons of relaxation, certainly all Christian workers need such periods of rest. Many have developed neurotic symptoms simply because they neglect the obvious requirements of the physical body.

Having arrived at the eastern shore near Bethsaida-Julia (named in honor of Julia, the beautiful but infamous daughter of Emperor Augustus), Jesus and His disciples found a fertile and well-watered plain which was situated on the farther side of the town. Since it

223

was springtime, just before the Passover (John 6:4), the grass formed a soft green carpet. Here they hoped to find a quiet retreat where they could rest a few days.

But Christ was unable to hide Himself from the people. His departure had been observed, and a vast crowd had set out from Capernaum and had walked around the edge of the lake to join Him on the other side. After some time, for it took a considerable while to detour around the lake, the disciples spied a great company making their way toward them. Jesus would fain have departed at once and out-distanced the people, but He would not disappoint them. Some had come from a great distance, bringing their sick for healing. He could not leave them.

Jesus forewent all plans for taking a rest that day, giving the people a kindly welcome. After healing their sick, He began to teach them many things (Mark 6:34). The multitude listened with breathless interest, forgetting that there was such a thing as mealtime. But as the day was beginning to wane, the disciples came to Jesus and said, "This is a desert place, and now the time is far passed: send them away, that they may go into the country round about, and into the villages, and buy themselves bread: for they have nothing to eat" (Mark 6:35-36).

It is a commentary on the eagerness of the people to hear the Master, that they had taken off so suddenly that they had not paused to purchase or prepare any food to take along. Some had actually outrun the boat and arrived in the area before Jesus and His little company! But with darkness approaching, the disciples became apprehensive that there might be trouble with the people's fainting from hunger, since they were a long way from shelter or supplies of any kind.

Jesus turned to Philip, one of His disciples, and said to him, "Whence shall we buy bread, that these may eat?" (John 6:5). Philip was a man who thought for himself. He had accepted Christ as the Messiah because he had studied the prophecies and saw that they were fulfilled in Him (John 1:45). Philip was computing what it would take to feed the multitude and when Jesus asked him the question, he had a ready answer. He said, "Two hundred pennyworth of bread is not sufficient for them, that every one of them may take a little" (John 6:7). A penny, or denarius, was approximately a shilling, equivalent to a fair day's wage. A denarius would have fed approximately 25 people, but would have provided each person of the multitude but a mouthful.

Andrew, always trying to be helpful, came up with a suggestion, though he was apologetic in making it: "There is a lad here, which hath five barley loaves, and two small fishes; but what are they among so many?" (Verse 9). Somewhere in the crowd he had found a little boy that wanted to see and hear Jesus so much that he had come along with the adults. But he had more foresight than they. He had remembered to take a lunch with him. And though he might have quite properly eaten it himself, he offered to share it with Andrew, and in so doing he immortalized himself in the Bible narrative.

Jesus did not turn down the lad's contribution. Some think that the church could make great missionary gains if only the rich could be induced to give large sums. But it is a truth that the money which blesses the Kingdom of God must be that given out of sacrifice and devotion to God. He can bless the little and multiply it in His own mysterious way.

The Lord now proposed, much to the amazement of the disciples, to feed the people. But first He gave some instructions. The disciples were to make the multitude to sit down on the grass in companies of fifties and hundreds. This was a sensible arrangement which prevented confusion and at the same time assured them that no one would be overlooked. Jesus then blessed the food, and breaking it, gave it to the disciples for distribution to the people. And lo, as He continued to break it, the few loaves and fishes became an inexhaustible supply.

One thing the disciples did carry with them apparently were baskets. These were retrieved from the boat and used to distribute the food. To show that it is not God's will to waste anything, Jesus commanded the disciples to gather up the fragments when the meal was concluded. And when this was done, there were twelve basketsful. Each apostle came back with his basket loaded!

There are some things about this incident that need to be especially noted. Christ did not ordinarily use His supernatural powers to produce that type of miracle. He fed the multitude because He had compassion on it (Matt. 15:32). But events that followed indicate that He had a further purpose in the miracle. The news that His cousin, John the Baptist, had just given His life for the cause, reminded Him of His own approaching death. He had taken His disciples to the desert that He might have some time to instruct them and give them a true conception of the purpose of His coming into the world. But the multitude had descended upon Him and interfered with His plans.

But as the people came and stood about Him, He had formed His decision to perform this miracle. The Passover, we are told, was nigh at hand (John 6:4). This was the sacred feast in which the children of Israel ate unleavened bread. As Paul has stated in his writings, He, Christ, was the world's Passover (I Cor. 5:7).

A year later, after the miracle of the loaves, Jesus would become that Passover, and on its eve, He would break bread with the disciples. He would take the bread, bless it, break it, and give it to the disciples saying, "Take, eat: this is my body" (Mark 14:22). This did Jesus also when He blessed the bread, broke it and fed the multitude. There was, therefore, a greater purpose behind the miracle of the loaves than just satisfying the physical hunger of the people. Actually, Jesus was preparing the multitude for the Bread-of-Life discourse He would deliver to them on the morrow in Capernaum, when He would say:

> "I am that bread of life ... I am the living bread which came down from heaven: if any man eat of this bread, he shall live for ever: and the bread that I will give is my flesh, which I will give for the life of the world" (John 6:48, 51).

In witnessing the miracle of the loaves and the fishes, the hearts of the people would be prepared for the truth that Christ was the Bread of Life, which if any man eat would give him eternal life. The miracle at Bethsaida was, therefore, actually a prophecy of the sacrament of the communion.

The remarkable event produced a profound impression on the multitude. It was exactly in accordance with what they had in mind. They were convinced that Jesus was the prophet that Moses had foretold (Deut. 18:15-18).

> "Then those men, when they had seen the miracle that Jesus did, said, This is of a truth that prophet that should come into the world" (John 6:14).

The moment seemed ripe to the leaders of the people. The Passover was at hand. Why should they not take Jesus to Jerusalem and in a triumphant procession there proclaim Him king? He would be hailed everywhere as the Messiah, for whom the nation had hoped for fifteen hundred long years. Jesus saw them whispering among themselves. He perceived their undisguised admiration. Yet if they took Him by force and proclaimed Him king, it would have upset the entire purpose for which He came into the world. His own disciples seemed to share in the excitement. The situation called for instant action. Jesus immediately commanded His disciples to get into their ship and go before Him to Capernaum (Matt. 14:22). Then, ere the leaders could further pursue their purpose to make Him king, He dispersed the multitude, perhaps reminding them that they had to leave quickly or be caught in the darkness of nightfall. He then departed into the mountain to pray.

Chapter 38

The Miracle of Christ's Walking on the Water

"And when he had sent the multitudes away, he went up into a mountain apart to pray: and when the evening was come, he was there alone. But the ship was now in the midst of the sea, tossed with waves: for the wind was contrary. And in the fourth watch of the night Jesus went unto them, walking on the sea. And when the disciples saw him walking on the sea, they were troubled, saying, It is a spirit; and they cried out for fear. But straightway Jesus spake unto them, saying, Be of good cheer; it is I; be not afraid. And Peter answered him and said, Lord, if it be thou, bid me come unto thee on the water. And he said, Come. And when Peter was come down out of the ship, he walked on the water, to go to Jesus. But when he saw the wind boisterous, he was afraid; and beginning to sink, he cried, saying, Lord, save me. And immediately Jesus stretched forth his hand, and caught him, and said unto him, O thou of little faith, wherefore didst thou doubt? And when they were come into the ship, the wind ceased. Then they that were in the ship came and worshipped him, saying, Of a truth thou art the Son of God" (Matt. 14:23-33).

After the miracle of feeding the multitude, Jesus went up into the mountain. Realizing that there was a very real possibility of things taking a wrong turn, the Lord spent hours in prayer that night. The recent murder of John the Baptist, His forerunner, brought home to Him the possibility of His own early death. The false popularity that had resulted from His miracles was His most immediate danger, and it could not be allowed to develop further.

As Jesus prayed alone on the mountain, a violent wind arose and swept down through the barren hills. This gave Him a new cause for solicitude. Satan knows how to strike one blow after another and to confuse the person who is trying to do the will of God. Jesus knew what the wind meant: it meant that His disciples who had started across the sea at His command would run into real trouble.

When the first light of dawn appeared, Jesus looked out and saw the disciples' ship in the midst of the sea, tossing heavily in the waves. The disciples had not gotten started on their trip as soon as they should have, hoping that Jesus would come to them. When at last darkness fell, Jesus had not come to them, and they belatedly started out. But they had not gone far when the contrary wind arose, and they had to take the sail down and use the oars. As anyone familiar with the sea knows, a ship can make little headway against a strong wind. So it was that at the fourth watch of the night, they were still in the midst of the sea and making no progress.

There is a parallel here that we should note. Satan had presented Jesus with three temptations in the wilderness. These same three courses of action arose again, but the circumstances were altered. In the wilderness the devil had suggested to Jesus that He make bread to satisfy His hunger. But Jesus refused to use His miraculous power for the gratification of His own personal needs. Nevertheless, when the eager multitude which had forgotten to take any bread with them needed food, He made sufficient food to satisfy five thousand and had twelve basketsful over.

Second, Satan had suggested giving Christ the kingdoms of this world and the glory of them, if He would but fall down and worship him. Jesus spurned the offer. In this case, the people, after they had been fed the loaves and fishes, wanted to make Him king (John 6:15). But it was not the time nor the place. This offer did not come from the heavenly Father, and Jesus would have none of it. He would indeed become Israel's king in due time— not of a temporal kingdom, but of one whose subjects would have life eternal. On the very morrow, Jesus would present His claims as the Bread of Heaven, which if any man would eat, would cause him to live forever (John 6:58).

Satan in his third temptation had proposed that Jesus cast Himself down from the pinnacle of the temple (Luke 4:9-12). He had also refused this proposition. He would not startle the people with prodigies and wonders. But when His disciples were in the midst of the lake in mortal jeopardy, He would perform a greater miracle. He would overrule the law of gravity and walk out on the waters to come to the assistance of His faithful band that had risked their lives to obey His command. Why did He do it? Because it was He that had commanded the disciples to make the trip. We may meet grave dangers in obeying Christ, but if we do not throw away our confidence, God will move heaven and earth, if need be, to come to our aid.

As Jesus drew near the disciples, the waves were still high, and it was just getting light. The disciples did not see Him approaching until He was almost upon them. According to Mark, He "would have passed by them." But as they looked up, they saw a Figure with a fluttering robe, treading upon the ridges of the waves. In the semi-light they could not see clearly, and thinking they beheld a ghost, they cried out in fear. But the voice reassured them. He said, "Be of good cheer; it is I; be not afraid" (Matt. 14:27). The familiar voice of the Master who meant so much to them made them lose their fear. Impetuous Peter recovered from his momentary fright, and since he always had something to say, he asked, "Lord, if it be thou, bid me to come unto thee on the water (Matt. 14:28). Once he had said, "Depart from me" (Luke 5:8), but now he just could not wait for the Lord's approach. When Jesus said, "Come," Peter was over the side of the ship into the troubled waters while the other disciples, content to be observers, looked on and watched his rashness with undisguised amazement. Nevertheless, as long as Peter kept his eyes on Jesus, he was safe. Most sermons dealing with this event emphasize Peter's sinking, but the fact is that as long as his gaze was on Jesus, Peter walked on the water.

But alas! when his attention was diverted to the waves, and when he felt the boisterous wind, fear came into his heart. Why had he attempted to walk on the water? Why had he been so reckless as to try to do what only Jesus could do? And as Peter let fear possess him, he began to sink.

Herein is an important truth for all who seek deliverance. As long as they keep their eyes upon Christ and His promise, they will have victory. But if, like Peter, they look at the water and the waves, if they look at the symptoms, the feelings, they too will go down. Let us resolve, therefore, not to look at conditions, but rather at the promise that Christ has given. It can never fail.

There are those who would tell us that if God really performs a miracle, it can never be lost. They point to some poor soul that has lost his healing, and declare that this is proof that he was never healed in the first place, else he would not have become sick again. What men may think, and what is fact, are often a long way apart. The truth is that we receive by faith, and we walk by faith. Doubts can well cause us to lose what God has already done for us. When

Peter walked on the water, it was a miracle. Yet when he took his eyes off of Christ, and looked at the waves and the tempest, he began to sink.

One thing Peter did do, and he did it in the nick of time. When he ran out of his own faith, he depended upon the faith of Christ. Jesus once said to the apostles, "Have the faith of God." When natural faith fails, we may depend upon the supernatural faith of Christ. Here we see the difference between natural faith and supernatural faith. Peter started walking on the water on the strength of his own natural faith, and it was not sufficient. In this moment of peril, he cried out, "Lord save me." So Jesus stretched out His hand and drew him up, and together they made their way back to the boat.

Herein is a picture of the two phases of a Christian life. The first phase is that of the Christian who has been redeemed, but who walks to a considerable extent in the flesh. He still has confidence in his natural abilities and would seek to accomplish spiritual things in his own strength. But as he continues to walk in his Christian faith, sooner or later he will meet a crisis which is beyond his own ability to solve. When his own faith fails, he at last in desperation will cry out as Peter did, "Lord, save me." The Lord in His mercy will then reach down a hand and lift him up. Together the two can walk through life victoriously over the threatened waves. The trust must be in Christ instead of one's own natural abilities.

Supernatural Transportation

When Jesus and Peter got into the ship, we are told that the wind ceased. But that was not all. There was still one more miracle that morning. John says, "And immediately the ship was at the land whither they went" (John 6:21). The 19th Verse informs us that when the Lord met the disciples, they had rowed 25 or 30 furlongs, which is a distance of three or four miles—just half-way across the lake. Since the Sea of Galilee is seven or eight miles wide, the disciples were, at the time Jesus entered the ship, in the very midst of the sea (see Matthew 14:24). Yet the ship was immediately at land! When the waves subsided, and they looked toward land, they saw the familiar shoreline where they had so often drawn up their boats. The implication is clear that the miracle of transportation had taken place. Here we see faith not only overruling the law of gravity, but superseding laws inherent in physical matter, making possible instantaneous transportation. The events of this night involved both the gift of faith and the working of miracles.

Will such occurrences as this (or that of the transportation of Philip—Acts 8:26-40— when he was supernaturally taken to Azotus forty or fifty miles away) take place again in these last days? No doubt they will. However, such happenings were rare even in Bible days, and no doubt they will never be common. Jesus could have been transported from place to place by the Spirit, had He so chosen. Yet until after the resurrection, we have record of such a miracle's happening only once or twice in His ministry. On this occasion His disciples, exhausted from battling the wind and waves through the long hours of the night, needed to reach shore so that they could get rest and sleep.

It is amusing, if it were not so tragic, to note the pathetic attempts to explain what happened on this occasion on purely natural grounds. It is alleged by some that under the stress of the storm the boat had gotten close to land so that what the disciples really saw was Jesus, not walking on the water, but on the shore! This attempt to dismiss the miracle in this fashion borders on the ridiculous. The whole ministry of Christ was a series of supernatural occurrences, and no one can do away with His miracles without doing away with Christ. But man would have to reach up and take the stars out of the heavens before he could do this.

Chapter 39

The Discourse on the Bread of Life

We are told that not all of the people who had followed Jesus to the place where the miracle of the loaves and fishes had taken place returned home that evening. Despite the fact that the Lord had dismissed them, they lingered on in the little plain of Bethsaida-Julia, that they might follow the movements of Christ and share in the triumphs that they thought were to take place. Evidently they laid down on the grassy green and slept through the night. When morning came, they awaited Him to come down the hill where He had gone to pray. When they saw that He did not appear, they finally decided to return to the other side in the boats that came over from Tiberias.

When they arrived in Capernaum, they were mystified to discover that Jesus had already arrived. How did He get there? This was a mystery they could not fathom, and they asked, "Rabbi, when comest thou hither?" But Jesus did not explain about the miracle of walking on the water. It did not concern them, and He did not wish to claim their allegiance on the basis of these miracles.

The truth was that these people were already convinced of Jesus' Messiahship. The miracle that had taken place the day before had fully strengthened their conviction. But their conception was that of a different kind of Messiah than Jesus really was. It was a current expectation that the Messiah when He came would feed them manna as did Moses in the wilderness (John 6:30-31). The miracle of the loaves and the fishes had seemed to prove to them that their anticipations had been correct. Why then did Jesus elude them and go away into the mountain when they were ready to acclaim Him king? The people wanted an answer to that.

It so happened that on that day, there was a service in the synagogue (John 6:59). Jairus, whose daughter He had raised from the dead, had charge of the synagogue and would have given Jesus full freedom to preach in it. Therefore, the Lord led the people

233

there where He could teach and preach to them. And as was the custom in the synagogue, they could ask Him questions. Alas, this was to be one of the saddest days of His life; for He had to disabuse the people's expectations that He had come at this time as an earthly king to set up a temporal kingdom. He had to remove from their minds the false ideal of His mission, on which their enthusiasm was based.

> "Jesus answered them and said, Verily, Verily, I say unto you, Ye seek me, not because ye saw the miracles, but because ye did eat of the loaves, and were filled. Labour not for the meat which perisheth, but for that meat which endureth unto everlasting life, which the Son of man shall give unto you: for him hath God the father sealed" (John 6:26-27).

Jesus went to the heart of the matter. The people wanted Him to be their king, because He had fed them with loaves and fishes. This has been a fateful error of others besides the Jews. People become totally absorbed in the physical needs of the present, to the total disregard of the future. They dedicated their lives to the amassing of wealth with never a thought for eternity. Therefore, He told them not to labor for that which perisheth, but to labor for that which would endure unto everlasting life, which He, the Son of Man, would give to them.

The people were touched and a little abashed. The Lord had read their hearts correctly. So they queried, "What are we to do that we may work the works of God?" Jesus then answered that the work of God was to believe on Him whom God hath sent. This statement is the foundation-truth of Christianity. Salvation is through faith in Christ. The work of redemption from man's standpoint is accomplished by simple faith in Christ's finished work.

His hearers were not satisfied. They were not to be sidetracked from what was to be the most important matter of interest. Moses had given them bread from heaven. Christ also had the power to feed them supernaturally, as He had proved on the day before. Their question they believed was based on Scriptural grounds. The pot of manna and the grape-clusters, incidentally, had been carved on the lintels of the very synagogue they were in at that moment. Plenty of bread seemed to the Jews the most important thing in life.

They were willing to go along with Christ's mystical interpretation that He was the true manna, but was there not something more? If He were the real Messiah according to all traditions of the nation, He would enrich them, banquet them on the delicacies of heaven, besides giving them the regular manna, even as Moses did. They questioned, "What sign shewest thou then, that we may see, and believe thee? What dost thou work? Our fathers did eat manna in the desert; as it is written, He gave them bread from heaven to eat" (John 6:30-31).

The people had quoted Nehemiah 9:15. But if they had only read a little further, they would have seen how little spiritual good this great gift of earthly manna had done the children of Israel. The context records that the people of that day dealt proudly, refused to obey, hardened their hearts, made a molten image, wrought great provocations, and slew the prophets (Nehemiah 9:16-26). For that reason God had to deliver them over to their enemies. And because not only their fathers, but the generations that had come and gone since, had done the same thing (Nehemiah 9:28) that was the reason that the children of Israel were at that time under the yoke of the Romans. But alas, like many others that read the Scriptures, they took the promise and overlooked the conditions.

Thus Jesus would show them that faith must rest on a deeper foundation than signs and wonders. They had to have other bread than the manna in the wilderness. They had to have the bread of life that the Father sent from heaven. They responded by saying, "Lord evermore give us this bread,'" but their minds were still fixed on material things. They were asking for this bread as the woman of Samaria sought for the water that quenched all thirst. But Jesus answered, "I am the bread of life: he that cometh to me shall never hunger; and he that believeth on me shall never thirst" (John 6:35).

This brought an angry response, not from the multitude, but from his opponents who were always lurking in the crowd to catch Him in some way. They began to exchange questions, directed not at Him personally, but to those close by: "Why was Jesus saying He came down from heaven?" "Why does He call Himself the Bread of Life?" "Do we not know Joseph His father, and His mother Mary, and was not this man a mere carpenter?" (Mark 6:3; John 6:41-42).

Jesus did not answer these questioners by explaining His supernatural birth. He did not argue the fact of His divinity. He merely pointed out that it was not given to a heart of unbelief to come to Him (Verse 44). But "All that the Father giveth me shall come to me; and him that cometh to me I will in no wise cast out" (John 6:37). He repeated what He had said before. Moses gave the children of Israel bread in the wilderness, but they all died. He was the true bread, and if any man ate of that bread, he would live forever.

> "I am the living bread which came down from heaven: if any man eat of this bread, he shall live for ever: and the bread that I will give is my flesh, which I will give for the life of the world" (John 6:51).

This was the stumbling block. How could Jesus give His own flesh to them? So carnal-minded were they that instead of seeking the true significance of the metaphor, they began to wrangle on the question, "How can this man give us His flesh to eat?"

Some of these things were hard to understand. But they had seen enough to trust Him. The miracle of yesterday was enough to show them that this was the true Messiah. Moreover, they had to agree that all those who ate manna in the wilderness died. Therefore, something more than manna was needed. Nevertheless, it was just too difficult to understand. Slowly the people began dispersing. The excitement of the day before was gone. Several of His disciples said, "This is a hard saying; who can hear it?"

When most of the multitude had gone along with many of His followers, Jesus turned to the Twelve and said, "Will ye also go away?" His own disciples looked sad. The great enthusiasm which had existed only twenty-four hours ago was gone. Some of the disciples had departed also. But even though the Twelve did not understand all that was said, they did understand what He meant by eternal life. And Peter speaking out impetuously for the rest, told Him what was in their hearts:

> "Then Simon Peter answered him, Lord, to whom shall we go? thou hast the words of eternal life. And we believe and are sure that thou art that Christ, the Son of the living God" (John 6:68-69).

It was a rather faltering confession. For even the disciples had supposed as had the multitude that Jesus was soon to set up an outward kingdom of splendor. But understand it or not, the disciples still believed in Jesus and that He had the words of eternal life.

There was one exception. The events of the day must have been a bitter disappointment to Judas. How thrilled he was the day before with the way the tide was moving. When the leaders of the multitude informed Jesus of their plans to make Him king, it seemed as if all his hopes and anticipations were to come true. He was shocked by the turn of events. He wanted time to think it over. Was this Jesus of Nazareth the Messiah after all—a man who did not know how to seize an opportunity when it was dropped in His lap? The seeds of doubt were there, but they were not yet fully germinated. Judas little realized how fearfully dangerous such seeds were. He probably understood no more than the other disciples what Jesus meant when He said:

> "Have not I chosen you twelve, and one of you is a devil? He spake of Judas Iscariot the son of Simon: for he it was that should betray him, being one of the twelve" (John 6:70-71).

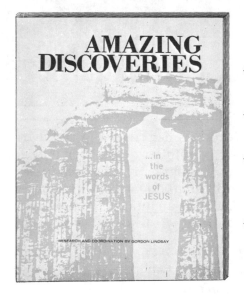

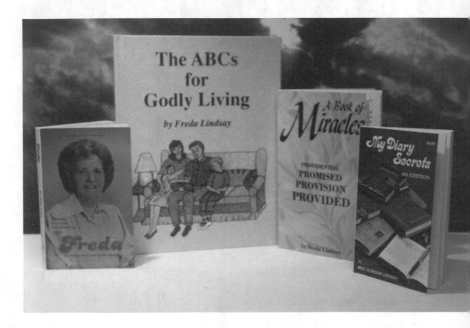